The Apocryphal Acts of the Apostles

The Apocryphal Acts
of the Apostles

An Introduction

Hans-Josef Klauck

Translated by Brian McNeil

BAYLOR UNIVERSITY PRESS

English Translation © 2008 by Baylor University Press
Waco, Texas 76798

Translated from *Apokryphe Apostelakten. Eine Einführung.* Stuttgart: Katholisches Bibelwerk. Hans-Josef Klauck © 2005 with revisions and additions for the English edition. Translated by Brian McNeil.

Cover Design: Pamela Poll
Cover Image: Christ and the Twelve Apostles. Byzantine ivory relief, 6th c. Musee des Beaux-Arts, Dijon, France. *Photo Credit:* Bridgman-Giraudon/ Art Resource, NY. Used by permission.

Library of Congress Cataloging-in-Publication Data

Klauck, Hans-Josef.
  [Apokryphe Apostelakten. English]
  The apocryphal acts of the apostles : an introduction / Hans-Josef Klauck ; translated by Brian McNeil.
    p. cm.
  Includes bibliographical references (p.   ) and indexes.
  ISBN 978-1-60258-159-3 (pbk. : alk. paper)
  1. Apocryphal Acts of the Apostles--Criticism, interpretation, etc. I. Title.

  BS2871.K57313 2008
  229'.925--dc22

                              2008010621

Printed in the United States of America on acid-free paper with a minimum of 30% pcw recycled content.

Contents

Translator's Note

Biblical texts are taken from the New Revised Standard Version. New York and Oxford: Oxford University Press, 1989.

Texts from Nag Hammadi and BG are taken from James M. Robinson, ed. *The Nag Hammadi Library*. Leiden: Brill, 1977.

Except where otherwise stated, apocryphal texts are taken from J. K. Elliott, ed. *The Apocryphal New Testament*. Oxford: Clarendon, 1993.

Preface

Besides this, we find a wealth of miraculous paraphernalia, with visions, apparitions of angels, voices from heaven, speaking animals, and demons who admit with shame that they are powerless; we see the radiance of a light never found on earth, mysterious signs gleam from heaven, earthquakes, thunder, and lightning terrify the godless; fire, earth, wind, and water put themselves at the service of the pious; serpents, lions, leopards, tigers, and bears are tamed by a word from the apostle and direct their rage against the persecutors; the dying martyrs are surrounded by radiant crowns, roses, lilies, and a marvelous perfume, while the abyss opens up to swallow their foes. The devil too, who appears in the form of a black Ethiopian, and demons in the most various disguises play an important role in these stories. But the greatest attention is given to the elaboration of the visionary element. Christ appears to his believers now as a handsome boy, now as a sailor or a shepherd, or in the form of an apostle; the saints who were tortured return to life after their death and show themselves now to their disciples, now to their persecutors; dreams and visions tell the apostles of the fates that await them and announce to pagans who seek salvation that their wishes will soon be fulfilled.

—R. A. Lipsius, *Die apokryphen Apostelgeschichten* I (1883) 7f.

This colorful description is taken from the monumental introduction to the apocryphal Acts of the Apostles that Richard Adalbert Lipsius of Jena published in four volumes between 1883 and 1890. His work remains unsurpassed even today. The present, much slimmer volume cannot compete with Lipsius nor does it seek to do so; but it seemed to me that a new brief introduction to this field was needed. More than one hundred years have passed since the work of Lipsius, and a great deal has happened in recent decades in the study of the apocryphal early Christian literature. New editions, monographs, and essays on specific topics have been published. This means that a reader who is looking for a first general introduction will welcome what we might call a "stocktaking" of scholarly research.

This introduction was first published in German in 2005 under the title *Apokryphe Apostelakten: Eine Einführung* (Stuttgart). The bibliography in every chapter of the English edition has been expanded; some of the new entries are from the year 2007. In some passages, the argumentation has been altered slightly, taking account of new insights.

I am particularly grateful to my translator, Brian McNeil (Munich), who has translated the German text with his customary mastery and accuracy, producing an English text that reads well. I am also very grateful to Carey C. Newman of Baylor University Press, who immediately agreed to include my book in the program of his publishing house. Speaking as an author, I look back with great pleasure on my collaboration with my translator and my publisher.

Hans-Josef Klauck
The University of Chicago
Divinity School
October 2007

List of Abbreviations

AAAp	Acta Apostolorum Apocrypha
AJSL	*American Journal of Semitic Languages and Literature*
AnBoll	*Analecta Bollandiana*
ANCL	Ante-Nicene Christian Library
ANF	Ante-Nicene Fathers
AnGr	Analecta Gregoriana
ANRW	*Aufstieg und Niedergang der römischen Welt: Geschicte und Kultur Roms im Spiegel der neueren Forschung.* Edited by H. Temporini and W. Haase. Berlin 1972–
APF	*Archiv für Papyrusforschung*
ATANT	Abhundlungen zur Theologie des Alten und Neuen Testaments
ATLA	American Theological Library Association
Aug	*Augustinianum*
BBB	Bonner biblische Berträge
BCNH	Biblithèque Copte de Nag Hammadi
BETL	Bibliotheca ephemeridum theologicarum lovaniensium

BG	Berolinensis Gnosticus
BHG	*Bibliotheca hagiographica Graece*. Brussels, 1977
BIS	Biblical Interpretation Series
BJRL	*Bulletin of the John Rylands University Library of Manchester*
BZNW	Beihefte zur Zeitschrift für die neutestamentliche Wissenschaft
CChrSA	Corpus Christianorum Series Apocryphorum
CChrSL	Corpus Christianorum Series Latinum
COr	Cahiers d'orientalism
CQ	*Classical Quarterly*
CRB	Caliers de la Revue biblique
CRThPh	Cahiers de la Revue de théologie et de philosophie
CSEL	Corpus scriptorium ecclesiasticorum latinorum
EHPhR	Études d'histoire et de philosophie religieuses
EPRO	Etudes préliminaires aux religions orientales dans l'empire romain
EssBib	Essais bibliques
EstBib	Estudios biblicos
FGH	*Die Fragmente der griechischen Historiker*. Edited by F. Jacoby. Leiden, 1954–1964
FKDG	Forschungen zur Kirkhen- und Dogmenpealichte
FRLANT	Forschungen zur Religion und Literatur des Alten und Neuen Testaments
GCS	Die griechischen christlichen Schriftsteller der ersten [drei] Jahrhunderte

GLB	de Gruyter Lehrbuch
GRBS	*Greek, Roman, and Byzantine Studies*
GSAI	*Giornale della Società Asiatica Italiana*
HDR	Harvard Dissertations in Religion
HNTA	Handbuch zu den neutestamentlichen Apokryphen. Tübingen, 1904
HoRe	Homo religiosus
HTR	*Harvard Theological Review*
JAC	Jahrbuch für Antike und Christentum
JECS	*Journal of Early Christian Studies*
JR	*Journal of Religion*
JRS	*Journal of Roman Studies*
JSNTSup	Journal for the Study of the New Testament: Supplement Series
JSPESup	Journal for the Study of the Pseudepigrapha: Supplement Series
JTS	*Journal of Theological Studies*
KGA	Kirchengeschichtliche Abhandlungen
KP	Der kleine Pauly
KT	Kaiser-Tractate
LD	Lectio divina
LTK	*Lexicon für Theologie und Kirche*
Mn.S	Mnemosyne: Supplements
NAWG	Nachrichten (von) der Akademie der Wissenschaften in Göttingen
NHC	Nag Hammadi Codices
NHMS	Nag Hammadi and Manichean Studies

NHS	Nag Hammadi Studies
NovT	Novum Testamentum
NovTSup	Novum Testamentum Supplements
NTAbh	Neutestamentliche Abhandlungen
NTAbh.NF	Neutestamentliche Abhandlungen: Neue Folge
NTApo	New Testament Apocrypha/Neutestamentliche Apokryphen
NTS	*New Testament Studies*
OCP	*Orientalia christiana periodica*
OrChr	*Oriens christianus*
PaP	*Past and Present*
PETSE	Papers of the Estonian Theological Society in Exile
PFTUG	Publications de la Faculté de Théologie de l'Université de Genève
PG	Patrologia graeca [= Patrologiae cursus completus: Series graeca]. Edited by J.-P. Migne. 162 vols. Paris, 1857/1886
Phil	*Philologus*
PW	*Paulys Realencyclopedie der classichen Altertumwissenschaft*
PSB	*Princeton Seminary Bulletin*
PVTG	Pseudepigraphica Veteris Testamenti Graece
RAC	*Reallexikon für Antike und Cristentum.* Edited by T. Klauser et al. Stuttgart, 1950–
RB	*Revue biblique*
RHE	*Revue d'histoire ecclésiastique*
RMP	*Rheinisches Museum für Philologie*

RHPR	*Revue d'historie et de philosophie religieuses*
RHR	*Revue de l'historie des religions*
RQ	*Römische Quartalschrift für christliche Altertumskunde und Kirchegeschichte*
RSLR	*Rivista di storia e letteratura religiosa*
RSR	*Recherches de science religieuse*
RTCHP	Recueil de travaux. Conférence d'Histoire et de Philologie
RTL	*Revue théologique de Louvain*
RTP	*Revue de théologie et de philosophie*
SBLCA	Society of Biblical Literature Texts and Translations: Christian apocrypha
SBLDS	Society of Biblical Literature Dissertation Series
SBLSP	*Society of Biblical Literature Seminar Papers*
SBLsymS	Society of Biblical Literature Symposium Series
SBLTT	Society of Biblical Literature Texts and Translations
SBS	Stuttgarter Bibelstudien
ScR	*Sciences religieuses*
SecCent	*Second Century*
SGRR	Studies in Greek and Roman Religion
SHAW	Sitzungsberichte der Heidelberger Akaemie der Wissenschaften
SHG	Subsidia hapiographica
StPatr	*Studia Patristica*
ST	Studia theologica

SWR   Studies in Women and Religion

TANZ   Texte und Arbeiten zum neutestamentlichen
             Zeitalter

TS   Texts and Studies

TRE   *Theologische Realenzyklopädie*

TThSt   Trierer theologische Studien

TU   Texte und Untersuchungen

TzF   Texte aur Forschung

UUA   Uppsala Universitetsårskrift

VF   *Verkündigung und Forschung*

VC   *Vigiliae christianae*

WSt   *Wiener Studien*

WUNT   Wissenschaftliche Untersuchungen zum Neuen
             Testament

ZDMG   *Zeitschrift der deutschen morgenländischen*
             Gesellschaft

ZKG   *Zeitschrift für Kirchengeschichte*

ZKT   *Zeitschrift für katholische Theologie*

ZNW   *Zeitschrift für die neutestamentliche Wissenschaft*
             und die Kunde der älteren Kirche

ZPE   *Zeitschrift für Papyrologie und Epigraphik*

Bibliography

Abbreviations follow S. Schwertner, *Internationales Abkürzungsverzeichnis für Theologie und Grenzgebiete*, 2nd edn. Berlin: 1992 (this is the list of abbreviations in the *TRE*). In the bibliographies to the individual sections, the works mentioned here are cited only with the author's name and a short title.

A. Sources and Translations

Bovon, F., and P. Geoltrain. *Écrits apocryphes chrétiens* I (Bibliotheque de la Pléïade 442). Paris: 1997. 875–1551. (The leading edition in French.)

Budge, E. A. W. *The Contendings of the Apostles.* Vols. 1–2. London: 1899–1901. Repr. Amsterdam: 1976. (Ethiopic text with English translation.)

Elliott, J. K. *Apocryphal New Testament: A Collection of Apocryphal Christian Literature in an English Translation.* Oxford: 1993. 227–533. (The most recent edition of a standard work in English.)

Erbetta, M. *Gli apocrifi del nuovo testamento.* Vol. 2: *Atti e legende.* Turin: 1966. Repr. 1983.

Leloir, L. *Écrits apocryphes sur les apôtres: Traduction de l'édition arménienne de Venise.* Vol 1: *Pierre, Paul, André, Jacques, Jean* (CChrSA). Turnhout: 1986; Vol. 2: *Philippe, Barthélémy, Thomas, Matthieu, Jacques frère du Seigneur, Thaddée, Simon, listes d'apôtres* (CChrSA 4), Turnhout: 1992.

Lewis, A. Smith. *Acta Mythologica Apostolorum (Horae Semiticae 3)/The Mythological Acts of the Apostles (Horae Semiticae 4).* London: 1904. (Arabic and Syriac texts with English translation.)

Lipsius, R. A., and M. Bonnet, ed. *Acta Apostolorum Apocrypha.* Vols. 1–2: 1.2. Leipzig: 1891–1903. Repr. Hildesheim: 1972. (This remains the indispensable edition of the Greek text, which has only been replaced in part by new editions in the series CChrSA.)

Michaelis, W. *Die apokryphen Schriften zum Neuen Testament* (Sammlung Dieterich 129). 3rd edn. Bremen: 1962. 216–438.

Moraldi, L. *Apocrifi del Nuovo Testamento.* Vol. 2: *Atti degli Apostoli.* 1994. 2nd edn. Casale Monferrato: 2000.

Schneemelcher, W. *New Testament Apocrypha: Writings Relating to the Apostles, Apocalypses and Other Subjects.* Engish translation edited by R. McL. Wilson. Rev. edn. London: 1992.

Wright, W. *Apocryphal Acts of the Apostles: Edited from Syriac Manuscripts in the British Museum and other Libraries.* Vols. 1–2. London 1871. Repr. Amsterdam: 1968. (Syriac texts with English translation.)

B. Bibliographies

Geerard, M. *Clavis Apocryphorum Novi Testamenti* (CChrSA). Brepols: 1992.

Charlesworth, J. H. *The New Testament Apocrypha and Pseudepigrapha: A Guide to Publications, with Excursuses on Apocalypses* (ATLA Bibliography Series 17). Metuchen, NJ: 1987.

DiTommaso, L. *A Bibliography of Pseudepigrapha Research 1850–1899* (JSPESup 39). Sheffield: 2001.

C. Secondary Literature on the Apocryphal Acts of the Apostles

Achtemeier, P. J. "Jesus and the Disciples as Miracle Workers in the Apocryphal New Testament." Pages 149–86 in *Aspects of Religious Propaganda in Judaism and Early Christianity.* Edited by E. Schüssler-Fiorenza. Notre Dame: 1976.

Bauckham, R. "Imaginative Literature." Pages 791–812 in *The Early Christian World.* Vol. 2. Edited by P. F. Esler. London: 2000.

Blumenthal, M. *Formen und Motive in den apokryphen Apostelgeschichten* (TU 48.1). Leipzig: 1933.

Bovon, F. et al. *Les Actes apocryphes des Apôtres: Christianisme et monde païen* (PFTUG 4). Geneva: 1981.

Bovon, F. "Miracles, magie et guérison dans les Actes apocryphes des apôtres." *JECS* 3 (1995): 245–59. Also pages 253–66 in idem, *Studies in Early Christianity* (WUNT 161). Tübingen: 2003.

Bremmer, J. N. "The Five Major Apocryphal Acts: Authors, Place, Time and Readership." Pages 149–70 in *The Apocryphal Acts of Thomas* (Studies on the Apocryphal Acts of the Apostles 6). Edited by idem. Louvain: 2001.

Burrus, V. *Chastity as Autonomy: Women in the Stories of Apocryphal Acts* (SWR 23). Lewiston: 1987.

Cangh, J. M. van. "Les origines de l'Eucharistie. Le cas des Actes des Apôtres." Pages 393–414 in *L'Évangile exploré* (Festschrift for S. Legasse) (LD 166). Paris: 1996.

Cerro, G. del. "Los Hechos apócrifos de los apóstoles. Su género literario." *EstBib* 51 (1993): 207–32.

———. *Las mujeres en los hechos apócrifos de los apóstoles* (Supplementa Mediterranea 5). Madrid: 2003. (I have not been able to consult this book.)

Czachesz, I. *Commission Narratives: A Comparative Study of the Canonical and Apocryphal Acts* (Studies on Early Christian Apocrypha 8). Louvain: 2005.

Davies, S. L. *The Revolt of the Widows: The Social World of the Apocryphal Acts*. Carbondale, Ill.: 1980.

Findlay, A. F. *Byways in Early Christian Literature: Studies in the Uncanonical Gospels and Acts*. Edinburgh: 1923.

Gallagher, E. V. "Conversion and Salvation in the Apocryphal Acts of the Apostles." *SecCen* 8 (1991): 13–29.

Guidi, I. "Gli atti apocrifi degli Apostoli nei testi copti, arabi ed etiopici." *GSAI* 2 (1988): 1–66.

Gutschmid, A. von. "Die Königsnamen in den apokryphen Apostelgeschichten. Ein Beitrag zur Kenntnis des geschichtlichen Romans." *RMP* 19 (1864): 161–83, 380–401. Also pages 332–94 in idem, *Kleine Schriften*. Vol. 2. Edited by F. Rühl. Leipzig: 1890.

Haines-Eitzen, K. "The Apocryphal Acts of the Apostles on Papyrus: Revisiting the Question of Readership and Audience." Pages 293–304 in *New Testament Manuscripts: Their Texts and Their World* (Texts and Editions for New Testament Study 2). Edited by Thomas J. Kraus and Tobias Nicklas. Leiden: 2006.

Hamann, A. "*Sitz im Leben* des actes apocryphes du Nouveau Testament." *StPatr* 8 (1966): 62–69.

Hernandez, J. A. A. *Estudios sobre la lengua de los Hechos apócrifos de Pedro y Pable*. Vols. 1–2. Theological diss. Murcia: 1994. (I have not been able to consult this work.)

Hertling, L. "Literarisches zu den apokryphen Apostelakten." *ZKT* 49 (1925): 219–43.

Hills, J. V. "Tradition, Redaction, and Intertextuality: Miracle Lists in the Apocryphal Acts as a Test Case." *SBLSP* (1990): 375–90.

Hock, R., B. Chance, and J. Perkins, eds. *Ancient Fiction and Early Christian Narrative* (SBLsymS 6). Atlanta: 1998.

Houghton, H. "The Discourse on Prayer in the Major Apocryphal Acts of the Apostles." *Apocrypha* 15 (2004): 171–200.

Jacobs, A. S. "A Family Affair: Marriage, Class, and Ethics in the Apocryphal Acts of the Apostles." *JECS* 7 (1999): 105–38.

Jones, F. S. "Principal Orientations on the Relations between the Apocryphal Acts." *SBLSP* 32 (1993): 495–505.

Junod, E. "Créations romanesques et traditions ecclésiastiques dans les Actes apocryphes des Apôtres. L'alternative fiction romanesque—vérité historique: une impasse." *Aug* 23 (1983): 271–85.

Kaestli, J.-D. and D. Marguerat, eds. *Le mystère apocryphe. Introduction à une littérature méconnue* (EssBib 26). Geneva: 1995.

Kampen, L. van. *Apostelverhalen. Doel en compositie van de oudste apokriefe Handelingen der apostelen*. Diss. Utrecht: 1990. (I have not been able to consult this work.)

Klauck, H.-J. *Die apokryphe Bibel: Ein anderer Zugang zum frühen Christentum*. Tübingen: 2008.

Konstan, D. "Acts of Love: A Narrative Pattern in the Apocryphal Acts." *JECS* 6 (1998): 15–36.

Lapham, F. *An Introduction to the New Testament Apocrypha.* London: 2003.

Leloir, J. "Utilité ou inutilité de l'étude des apocryphes." *RTL* 19 (1988): 38–70. (Mainly about the Apocryphal Acts.)

Levine, A.-J., with M. M. Robbins (eds). *A Feminist Companion to the New Testament Apocrypha.* London: 2006. (Twelve articles, mainly on the Apocryphal Acts.)

Liechtenhahn, R. "Die pseudepigraphe Litteratur der Gnostiker III: Offenbarungen der Apostel." *ZNW* 3 (1902): 286–99.

Lipsius, R. A. *Die apokryphen Apostelgeschichten und Apostellegenden: Ein Beitrag zur altchristlichen Literaturgeschichte und zu einer zusammenfassenden Darstellung der neutestamentlichen Apokryphen.* Vols. I–II: 1.2 and Supplement. Braunschweig: 1883–1890. Repr. Amsterdam: 1976. (A fundamental work with a comprehensiveness that remains unequalled.)

Liungvik, H. *Studien zur Sprache der apokryphen Apostelgeschichten* (UUA 8). Uppsala: 1926.

MacDonald, D. R., ed. *The Apocryphal Acts of Apostles* (Semeia 38). Chico, Calif.: 1986.

McGowan, A. *Ascetic Eucharists: Food and Drink in Early Christian Ritual Meals* (Oxford Early Christian Studies). Oxford: 1999. 183–94.

Matthews, C. R. "Articulate Animals: A Multivalent Motif in the Apocryphal Acts of the Apostles." Pages 205–32 in *The Apocryphal Acts of the Apostles.* Edited by F. Bovon et al.

Nagel, P. "Die apokryphen Apostelakten des 2. und 3. Jahrhunderts in der manichäischen Literatur." Pages 149–82 in *Gnosis und Neues Testament. Studien aus Religionswissenschaft und Theologie.* Gütersloh: 1973. Edited by K.-W. Tröger.

Onuki, T. "Asketische Strömungen im antiken Christentum: Gnosis, Apokryphe Apostelakten und Frühes Mönchtum." Pages 271–330 in Idem, *Heil und Erlösung: Studien zum Neuen Testament und zur Gnosis* (WUNT 165). Tübingen: 2004.

Petracca, V. *Gott oder das Geld: Die Besitzethik des Lukas* (TANZ 39). Tübingen: 2003. 361–73.

Pick, B. *The Apocryphal Acts of Paul, Peter, John, Andrew, and Thomas.* London: 1909.

Piontek, F. *Die katholische Kirche und die häretischen Apostelgeschichten bis zum Ausgange des 6. Jahrhunderts. Ein Beitrag zur Literaturgeschichte* (KGA 6). Breslau: 1908.

Plümacher, E."Apokryphe Apostelakten." *PW* Suppl. 15 (1978) 11–70.

———. *Geschichte und Geschichten: Aufsätze zur Apostelgeschichte und zu den Johannesakten* (WUNT 170). Tübingen: 2004.

Prieur, J. M. "L'eucharistie dans les Actes apocryphes." Pages 252–69 in *Les Repas de Dieu/Das Mahl Gottes* (WUNT 169). Edited by C. Grappe. Tübingen: 2004.

Pupon, G. "L'accusation de magie dans les Actes apocryphes." Pages 71–93 in *Les Actes apocryphes des Apôtres*. Edited by F. Bovon et al.

Rebell, W. *Neutestamentliche Apokryphen und Apostolische Väter.* Munich: 1992. 137–80.

Rhee, H. *Early Christian Literature: Christ and Culture in the Second and Third Centuries* (Routledge Early Christian Monographs). London: 2005.

Schmidt, K. L. *Kanonische und apokryphe Evangelien und Apostelgeschichten* (ATANT 5). Basle: 1944.

Söder, R. *Die apokryphen Apostelgeschichten und die romanhafte Literatur der Antike* (Würzburger Studien zur Altertumswissenschaft 3). Stuttgart: 1932.

Spittler, Janet E. *Wild Kingdom: Animals in the Apocryphal Acts.* Ph.D. thesis. University of Chicago, 2007. (To be published in WUNT II).

Stoops, R. F., Jr., ed. *The Apocryphal Acts of the Apostles in Intertextual Perspectives* (Semeia 80). Atlanta: 1997.

Szpessy, T. "Les actes d'apôtres apocryphes et le roman antique." *Acta Antiqua (Budapest)* 36 (1995): 133–161. (I have not been able to consult this work.)

Uytfanghe, M. van. "Encratisme en verdrongen erotiek in de apocriefe 'apostelromans'. Omtrent de christelijke problematisering van de sexualiteit." *Handelingen der Koninklijke Zuidnederlandse Maatschappij voor Taal- en Letterkunde en Geschiedenis* 45 (1991): 175–91.

Zelzer, K., and P. L. Schmidt. "Acta Apostolorum apocrypha." Pages 391–405 in *Die Literatur des Umbruchs: Von der römischen zur christlichen Literatur 117–283 n.Chr.* (Handbuch der lateinischen Literatur der Antike 4). Edited by K. Sallmann. Munich: 1997.

Zimmermann, R. *Geschlechtermetaphorik und Gottesverhältnis: Traditionsgeschichte und Theologie eines Bildfelds im Urchristentum und antiker Umwelt* (WUNT II/122). Tübingen: 2000. 521–61.

D. Other Relevant Works, Cited in Abbreviated Form

Allberry, C. R. C. *A Manichaean Psalm-Book* (Manichaean Manuscripts in the Chester Beatty Collections 2). Stuttgart: 1938.

Blond, G. "L'hérésie encratite vers la fin du quatrième siècle." *ScR* 32 (1944): 157–210.

Cooper, K. *The Virgin and the Bride: Idealized Womanhood in Late Antiquity.* Cambridge, Mass.: 1996.

Döpp, S., and W. Geerlings. *Lexikon der antiken christlichen Literatur.* 3d edn. Freiburg: 2002. (Brief, informative articles on almost all the texts discussed in the present book.)

Egger, B. "Zu den Frauenrollen im griechischen Roman. Die Frau als Heldin und Leserin." Pages 33–66 in *Groningen Colloquia on the Novel.* Vol. 1. Edited by H. Hofmann. Groningen: 1988.

Elm, S. *Virgins of God: The Making of Asceticism in Late Antiquity* (Oxford Classical Monographs). Oxford: 1994.

Francis, J. A. *Subversive Virtue: Asceticism and Authority in the Second-Century Pagan World.* University Park, Pa.: 1995.

Gaca, K. L. *The Making of Fornication: Eros, Ethics, and Political Reform in Greek Philosophy and Early Christianity* (Hellenistic Culture and Society 40). Berkeley: 2003.

Johne, R. "Women in the Ancient Novel." Pages 151–207 in *The Novel in the Ancient World* (Mn.S 159). Edited by G. Schmeling. Leiden: 1996.

Perkins, J. *The Suffering Self: Pain and Narrative Representation in the Early Christian Era.* London: 1995.

Perry, B. E. *The Ancient Romances: A Literary-Historical Account of Their Origins* (Sather Classical Lectures 37). Berkeley: 1967.

Petersen-Szemerédy, G. *Zwischen Weltstadt und Wüste: Römische Asketinnen in der Spätantike. Eine Studie zu Motivation und Gestaltung der Askese christlicher Frauen Roms auf dem Hintergrund ihrer Zeit* (FKDG 4). Göttingen: 1993.

Sfameni Gasparro, G. "Gli Atti apocrifi degli Apostoli e la tradizione dell'enkrateia." *Aug* 23 (1983): 287–307.

———. *Enkrateia e antropologia. Le motivazioni protologiche della continenza e della verginità nel cristianesimo dei primi secoli e nello gnosticismo*. Rome: 1984.

Stark, I. "Religiöse Elemente im antiken Roman." Pages 135–49 in *Der antike Roman: Untersuchungen zur literarischen Kommunikation und Gattungsgeschichte* (Veröffentlichungen des Zentralinstituts für Alte Geschichte und Archäologie der Akademie der Wissenschaften der DDR 19). Edited by H. Kuch et al. Berlin: 1989.

Vielhauer, P. *Geschichte der urchristlichen Literatur. Einleitung in das Neue Testament, die Apokryphen und die Apostolischen Väter* (GLB). Berlin: 1975.

Williams, M. A. *Rethinking Gnosticism: An Argument for Dismantling a Dubious Category*. Princeton: 1996.

Introduction

A. The Texts

Bibliography: **C. R. C. Allberry**, *A Manichaean Psalm-Book*. – **F. Bovon**, "The Synoptic Gospels and the Non-canonical Acts of the Apostles." *HTR* 81 (1988): 19–26; also in idem, *Studies in Early Christianity*. 209–25. – Idem, "Canonical and Apocryphal Acts of Apostles." *JECS* 11 (2003): 165–94. – **R. Gounelle**, "Actes apocryphes des apôtres et Actes des apôtres canoniques. État de la recherche et perspectives nouvelles." *RHPR* 84 (2004): 3–30, 419–41. – Idem, "Les Actes apocryphes des Apôtres témoignent-ils de la réception des Actes des Apôtres canoniques?" Pages 177–211 in *Les Actes des Apôtres. Histoire, récit, théologie* (LD). Edited by Michel Berder. Paris: 2005. – **J.-D. Kaestli**, "L'utilisation des Actes apocryphes des apôtres dans le manichéisme." Pages 107–16 in *Gnosis and Gnosticism* (NHS 8). Edited by M. Krause. Leiden: 1977. – **P. Nagel**, *Die apokryphen Apostelakten*. – **R. I. Pervo**, *Profit with Delight. The Literary Genre of the Acts of the Apostles*. Philadelphia: 1987. – **C. K. Rothschild**, *Luke-Acts and the Rhetoric of History. An Investigation of Early Christian Historiography* (WUNT II: 175). Tübingen: 2004.

The fifth text in the canon of the New Testament writings, after the four gospels, is a work titled "Acts of the Apostles" (in Greek *Praxeis Apostolôn*, in Latin *Acta Apostolorum*). Its introduction—"In the first book, Theophilus, I wrote about all that Jesus did and taught" (Acts 1:1)—presents it as a continuation of the Gospel of Luke, as the second part of the so-called Lukan double work. The title, more literally translated as *Deeds of the Apostles*, may have been bestowed only at a secondary stage when the book was separated in the canon by the Gospel of John from its first part, the

Gospel of Luke. As is well known, the title is not particularly suit-able, because this work does not in the least describe what hap-pened to the twelve apostles. The first chapters are dominated by the figure of Peter, and from the midpoint onward, it is Paul who takes over the leading position: It would therefore be more appro-priate to speak of the "Acts of Peter and of Paul." In terms of genre, most scholars accept the designation "historical mono-graph" in the tradition of tragic-pathetic (as distinct from more pragmatic) historiography. Some detect the influence of novels (cf. Pervo), but this assuredly does not play a leading role in Luke's Acts of the Apostles.

The same cannot be said of another group of early Christian writings, which are classified under the heading of "Apocryphal Acts of the Apostles." This title itself implies both some form of relationship to the canonical Acts of the Apostles—or, more pre-cisely, to Luke's Acts of the Apostles, which subsequently became canonical—and a comparison with this book. The individual points of this relationship are a matter of great controversy, and different evaluations have been made of the various Apocryphal Acts. The spectrum of scholarly positions runs from the thesis that the Apocryphal Acts were written in complete ignorance and inde-pendence of the canonical Acts to the supposition that they were attempting to imitate, supplement, or even suppress it. It is also worth keeping the Gospel of Luke in view here, because the struc-ture of the Apocryphal Acts is more similar to the gospels than to the canonical Acts of the Apostles, since the apocryphal texts con-centrate on one central figure who, like Jesus, wanders around, preaches, performs miracles, and (in most cases) finally suffers martyrdom (cf. Bovon).

In the present book, we must discuss in each individual instance the relationship of the Apocryphal Acts to the canonical Acts of the Apostles, but we may anticipate some points here. In the case of the Acts of John, for example, it is certainly possible that their author is writing polemically against the canonical Acts and wishes to replace these by giving the central position to another apostolic figure, namely John, instead of to Peter and Paul. It is not by chance that in this book it is John, not Paul, who conducts successful missionary work in Ephesus.

The most prominent representatives of this genre are the five ancient Acts of the Apostles, which form a group on their own; to these we can add the Pseudo-Clementines, which could also be classified as Acts of Peter. Unfortunately, with the exception of the Acts of Thomas (and of the Pseudo-Clementines), only fragments of these works have survived. This makes it very difficult to determine their chronological sequence and their interrelationships. In the nature of things, absolute certainty is unattainable. In our discussion of the individual texts, we shall present the arguments that support the following proposed order:

1. The Acts of John (ca. 150–160 CE)
2. The Acts of Paul (ca. 170–180 CE)
3. The Acts of Peter (ca. 190–200 CE)
4. The Acts of Andrew (ca. 200–210 CE)
5. The Acts of Thomas (ca. 220-240 CE)

These five writings formed a collection that was known and popular among the Manichaeans no later than the fourth century. We have evidence of the reception of these Acts among the Manichaeans in an impressive passage from the "Pilgrim Psalms" of the Manichaean Psalter (Allberry, 142.17–143.9):

> All the Apostles that endured their pains:
> Peter, the apostle, who was crucified upside down,
> how many tortures did he suffer . . . with this purity.
> Andrew the Apostle,—they set fire to the house beneath him,
> he and his disciples—all hail to them, they were crucified.
> The two sons of Zebedee were made to drink the cup of the . . .
> John the Virgin, he also was made to drink the cup,
> fourteen days imprisoned that he might die of hunger.
> And James also, he was stoned and killed.
> They all threw their stones at him that he might die beneath the
>   storm.
> The same things also did Thomas endure in his cross.
> Four soldiers at once pierced him with the point of the lance.
> They surrounded him on four sides and made his blood flow . . .
> Paul, the Apostle,—they went against him that they might kill him.
> How great then is their wrath. He expired; he did not escape.
> I too therefore have endured the things which he suffered before
>   today.
> He was thrown into a basket and hung outside the wall.
> All these things he suffered, he did weary, he did not flinch.
> He left the open court of the Lord, knowing that . . .

> Thecla, the lover of God, who was made to go up on the fire.
> She received the sign of the cross, she walked into the fire rejoicing.
> Yet was she not ashamed, naked in the midst of the crowd.
> She was thrown to the bears, the lions were let loose to her.
> She was bound on the bulls, the seals were let loose to her.
> All these things that she suffered, she did not flinch . . .

Three other women from the Apocryphal Acts are mentioned—Drusiana, Maximilla, and Aristobula—until the text reaches a preliminary goal in the words: "All the godly that there have been, male, female, all have suffered, down to the Glorious One, the Apostle Mani. Our Lord Mani himself also was made to drink the cup" (143.15–17). Another text in the Manichaean Psalter, an exposition of the parable of the ten virgins (Matt 25:1–12) in a Psalm of Heraclides, shows that in addition to the apostles, women also play a special role in the Apocryphal Acts. We must examine this role more closely below (Allberry, 192.25–193.3; cf. Nagel):

> A despiser of the body is Thecla, the lover of God.
> A shamer of the serpent is Maximilla the faithful.
> A receiver of good news is Iphidama her sister also,
> Imprisoned in the prisons.
> A champion in the fight is Aristobula the enduring one.
> A giver of light (to others?) is Eubula the noble woman, drawing
>   the heart of the prefect.
> A [woman] that loves [her] master is Drusiana, the lover of God,
>   shut up for fourteen days, questioning her Apostle.
> . . . who was found is Mygdonia in the land of India.

Here too, the list concludes with Mani himself: "A north wind blowing upon us is our Lord Mani, that we may put out with him and sail to the Land of Light" (193.4f).

Our discussions in this book will concentrate on the five ancient Apocryphal Acts, which are echoed in the texts just quoted, as well as on the often neglected Pseudo-Clementines; wherever possible, other (mostly less ancient) texts will be examined in the context of the older works. For example, it is meaningful to follow the study of the ancient Acts of John by looking at the more recent Acts of John by Pseudo-Prochorus, the Virtutes Johannis, and the Acts of John in Rome. The Acts of Paul find an obvious continuation in other legends about Thecla and Titus.

And indeed, when we discuss the Acts of Peter, we are obliged to look also at the Act of Peter from BG 4. A separate chapter is devoted to the only directly relevant example from the Nag Hammadi corpus, entitled *The Acts of Peter and the Twelve Apostles.* A concluding chapter offers a summary discussion of the remaining shorter texts (e.g., the Acts of Bartholomew, of Matthew, of the two Jameses, of Mark and Luke, of Xanthippe and Polyxena, and so forth). We shall pay special attention to the extensive Acts of Philip, which are extremely interesting both as narrative and as theology.

B. The Testimony of Photius

Bibliography: R. Henry, *Photius: Bibliothèque*, Vol. 2: *"Codices" 84–185* (Collection Byzantine). Paris: 1960. – **E. Junod**, "Actes apocryphes et hérésie: le jugement de Photius." Pages 11–24 in *Les Actes apocryphes des Apôtres.* Edited by F. Bovon et al. – **R. A. Lipsius**, *Die apokryphen Apostelgeschichten.* – **M. A. Williams**, *Rethinking Gnosticism.*

As late as the ninth century CE, the learned patriarch Photius in Byzantium read the five ancient Acts of the Apostles, which he regarded as a collective work (Cod. 114), in addition to the Pseudo-Clementines, which he discusses in Cod. 112–13 (English translation by J. H. Freese, London: HJ 1920): "I read a book entitled *Circuits of the Apostles*, comprising the Acts of Peter, John, Andrew, Thomas, and Paul, the author being one Lucius Charinus, as the work itself shows." The name of the alleged author, Lucius Charinus, was probably linked originally to the Acts of John and was then extended in Manichaean circles to all five of the ancient Acts. The patriarch finds nothing good to say about this book. He begins by criticizing its style, which does not in any way resemble the language of the gospels and the apostolic Epistles, and then turns to the doctrine. It is worth reading this lengthy passage *in extenso*, because we shall in fact meet most of the phenomena he describes here in our examination of the texts below. This poses with all desirable clarity the question of how they are to be categorized in terms of the history of ideas and of theology:

The style is altogether uneven and strange; the words and construc-
tions, if sometimes free from carelessness, are for the most part common and hackneyed; there is no trace of the smooth and spontaneous
expression, which is the essential characteristic of the language of the
Gospels and Apostles, or of the consequent natural grace. The contents also are very silly and self-contradictory. The author asserts
that the God of the Jews, whom he calls evil, whose servant Simon
Magus was, is one God, and Christ, whom he calls good, another.
Mingling and confounding all together, he calls the same both
Father and Son.

He asserts that he never really was made man, but only in
appearance; that he appeared at different times in different form to
his disciples, now as a young, now as an old man, and then again as
a boy, now taller, now shorter, now very tall, so that his head reached
nearly to heaven.

He also invents much idle and absurd nonsense about the cross,
saying that Christ was not crucified, but someone in his stead, and
that therefore he could laugh at those who imagined they had crucified him. He declares lawful marriages to be illegal and all procreation of children is evil and the work of the evil one. He talks
foolishly about the creator of demons. He tells monstrous tales of
silly and childish resurrections of dead men and oxen and cattle. In
the Acts of St. John he seems to support the opponents of images in
attacking their use. In a word, the book contains a vast amount of
childish, incredible, ill-devised, lying, silly, self-contradictory, impious, and ungodly statements, so that one would not be far wrong in
calling it the source and mother of all heresy.

The patriarch mentions here a number of phenomena that
must be regarded from his perspective as heretical. We meet inter
alia the "heresiarch" Simon Magus and (implicitly) Marcion with
their distinction between the evil god of the Old Testament and
the good God of Jesus Christ. Photius' polemic also attacks a
modalism that does not distinguish between the divine Persons; a
docetism which attributes only the appearance of a body to Christ
and wants to spare him from crucifixion; the mutability of his form
(also known as the "polymorphy of the Redeemer"); and finally an
ascetical rigorism that rejects even marriage. The texts also display
a delight in crude miracle stories involving speaking animals.

Much of what is mentioned here is commonly summarized
under the heading of gnosis, a phenomenon of the first Christian
centuries that includes a devaluation of the creation and of the creator God, a strict division between spirit and matter, and the rejec-

tion of marriage and procreation. Richard Adalbert Lipsius, the great pioneer of research into the apocryphal Acts of the Apostles, regarded the five ancient Acts without exception as originally gnostic works that had later been subjected to a catholicizing revision. In recent decades, we have learned to be much more cautious here. Scholars of gnosticism find that the object of their studies becomes ever more imprecise; it dissolves into a plurality of differentiated trajectories of development, so much so that some have even proposed that we should simply eliminate the concept of gnosis (cf. Williams). Another reason for qualifying Lipsius' judgment is that a more precise analysis of the individual Apocryphal Acts shows that they take different positions with regard to what is commonly called gnosis. This applies even to individual parts within one and the same work, as the example of the Acts of John shows. And no one disputes that the Apocryphal Acts of the Apostles offer us an invaluable insight into the history of piety and theology in the second and third centuries.

C. The Question of Genre

1. The Ancient Novel

Texts: B. Kytzler, ed. *Im Reiche des Eros. Sämtliche Liebes- und Abenteuerromane der Antike*, Vols. 1–2. Munich: 1983. – **B. P. Reardon**, ed. *Collected Ancient Greek Novels*. Berkeley: 1989. – **S. A. Stephens and J. J. Winkler**, *Ancient Greek Novels: The Fragments*. Princeton: 1995. – **H. van Thiel**. *Leben und Taten Alexanders von Makedonien. Der griechische Alexanderroman nach der Handschrift L* (TzF 13). Darmstadt: 1974. – **C. Burchard**, *Joseph und Asenath, kritisch herausgegeben* (PVTG 5). Leiden: 2003.

Bibliography: K. Haynes, *Fashioning the Feminine in the Greek Novel*. London: 2003. – **N. Holzberg**, *Der antike Roman. Eine Einführung*. Düsseldorf: 2006. (Bibliography) – **K. Kerényi**, *Die griechisch-orientalische Romanliteratur in religionsgeschichtlicher Beleuchtung*. 1927. 2nd ed. Darmstadt: 1962. – **D. Konstan**, *Sexual Symmetry: Love in the Ancient Novel and Related Genres*. Princeton: 1994. – **F. Letoublon**, *Les lieux communs du roman. Stéréotypes grecs d'aventure et d'amour* (Mn.S 123). Leiden: 1993. – **R. Merkelbach**, *Roman und Mysterium in der Antike*. Munich: 1962. – **B. E. Perry**, *The Ancient Romances*. – **E. Rohde**, *Der griechische*

Roman und seine Vorläufer. 1876. 2nd edn. Leipzig: 1900. – **I. Stark,**
Religiöse Elemente. – **J. M. Wills,** *The Jewish Novel in the Ancient World.*
Ithaca: 1995.

The word *novel* has already been used above, and we must now say
something about the Hellenistic novel of the imperial period. The
term *novel* (*Roman* in German) is not ancient; it was coined in the
modern period as a designation for narrative texts in the vernacu-
lar "Romanisch" (which means Romanic languages, especially
French) but can also be applied to longer fictional prose narratives
from classical antiquity. Its origins probably go back to the first
century BCE, although the relevant texts have survived only in
fragmentary form. The golden age of this genre lasted from the
first to the fourth centuries CE. There has been much speculation
about the genesis of this genre; most likely, a number of factors
were at work, leading ultimately to a hybrid mixed form. The epic
travel narrative modeled on the *Odyssey* was one contributing factor; the dramatic developments, the dialogues and monologues,
and the pathos were taken over from tragedy, and the psychologi-
cal characterization of the protagonists was borrowed from the
new comedy. Historiography also played a role: Many novels consciously employ historical personages and events, thereby creating
the appearance of a historical narrative. In the case of the
Apocryphal Acts, we must also take a look at the biographies of
rulers (cf. Xenophon's *Cyropaedia*) and philosophers (cf. the *Life of
Apollonius of Tyana* by Flavius Philostratus or Iamblichus' *Life of
Pythagoras*), which likewise contain novelistic elements. (Holzberg
speaks here of "fringe novels," i.e., marginal phenomena; on the
vitae of the philosophers, cf. also R. Goulet, "Les Vies de
philosophes et leur portée mystérique," pages 161–208 in *Les Actes
apocryphes des Apôtres*, edited by F. Bovon et al.) Sociological factors
were also involved, including the simultaneous processes of a
wider perception of the world and a stronger individualization;
specific evaluations of marriage and changes in the definitions of
gender roles; and the contact with the political power of Rome,
which was partly experienced as foreign domination. (Cf.
Holzberg, 60: "Novels of the type of the *Ephesiaka* are not relating
a myth of salvation, but the myth of the self-assertion of Greek
culture—supported by a great cultural past—in a hostile world";
cf. also the explanation of the role of the women, who are often

stronger than their male partners, in Haynes, 161: ". . . at least in part conditioned by the need to assert an almost provocative sense of Hellenic superiority. The heroines resist violation, and so the borders of Greek cultural integrity remain uncontested.")

The classic form of the Greek novel was the love novel (which Holzberg calls the "idealizing novel"). A young man and a young woman, both exceedingly beautiful and clearly meant for each other, are parted by a cruel fate and are happily reunited at the close only after many adventures and journeys, both voluntary and involuntary. Despite all sexual temptations, they preserve their chastity and thus remain faithful to each other (although there are occasional "falls from grace" in this area). Of this genre, there are five representatives that have attained what might be called a canonical status. Their probable chronological sequence is as follows:

1. Chariton, *Callirhoë*
2. Xenophon of Ephesus, *Ephesiaka* (surviving only in an epitome)
3. Achilleus Tatius, *Leucippe and Cleitophon*
4. Longus, *Daphnis and Chloe* (with a bucolic character)
5. Heliodorus, *Aethiopica*

It is significant that the Christian legend of Achilleus Tatius and Heliodorus tells us that when they were older they turned their backs on the follies of their youth—which included their novels—and became Christian bishops. We may suspect that such inventions were intended to allow Christian readers to enjoy the moral right to an "edifying" reading of this kind of literature. This may have been made easier by the fact that the novels include not only the proven spice of "sex and crime," but also a generous helping of "religion" (cf. Stark)—the mysterious kind of religion associated with the mystery cults, served up not in the form of coded knowledge for initiates (as Merkelbach argues), but as an attractively cooked half-knowledge for the general readership.

In the Latin sphere, two works achieved a comparably dominant position: the *Satyricon* of Petronius and the *Metamorphoses* of Apuleius. They retain the motifs of love, but these appear in the form of a parody; one might almost call them "picaresque" (Holzberg calls them "comic-realistic novels"), but the fact that Apuleius draws on an earlier Greek text (the novel *The Ass*, which may ultimately be a work of Lucian), and the existence of Greek fragments with a similar tendency, warn us against a too clear-cut categorization of these types as belonging respectively to the Greek and the Roman spheres.

Other works also belong to this genre. We know *The Wonders beyond Thule* only from a lengthy account by Photius and three papyrus fragments; this novel has an enormously complicated structure and includes utopian elements. The anonymous family novel *Apollonius, King of Tyre* was particularly popular in the Middle Ages, and was therefore Christianized to some extent in the manuscripts; we shall return to it in our discussion of the Pseudo-Clementines. Finally, we must mention the *Alexander Romance*, which takes as its theme the historical figure of the man who conquered the world. This gives the novel a historiographical varnish, which is strengthened by the use of apparently documentary materials such as letters and speeches; in fact, however, it is descriptions of imaginary journeys and marvelous experiences that predominate. The *Alexander Romance* is found in a variety of versions in the manuscripts. These must be edited separately by modern scholars, since they cannot be pieced together to form one unified work. This makes it very clear that works of this kind could be subject to constant mutations and that their appearance could alter from one oral or written "performance" to the next. We must bear this possibility in mind when we examine the Apocryphal Acts.

In evaluating the possibility of a Christian reception of this genre, it is significant that we know at least one Jewish example of such an adaptation, namely, the conversion novel *Joseph and Aseneth*, which was probably written no later than the early second century CE in the Hellenistic diaspora Judaism of Egypt. On the basis of Genesis 41:45-50 (cf. 46:20), it describes the love story of the two protagonists. Here, as was so often the case, Hellenistic Judaism may have functioned as a bridge between the pagan world and Christianity; we should also bear in mind the novelistic traits in the books of Esther, Judith, and Tobit (cf. Wills).

2. Christian Adaptation

Bibliography: E. von Dobschütz, "Der Roman in der altchristlichen Literatur." *Deutsche Rundschau* 111 (1902): 87–106. – **O. Ehlen**, *Leitbilder und romanhafte Züge in apokryphen Evangelientexten. Untersuchungen zur Motivik und Erzählstruktur* (Altertumswissenschaftliches Kolloquium 9). Stuttgart: 2004. (Examines the Protevangelium of James and the Acts of

Pilate, Greek B.) – **R. I. Pervo**, "Early Christian Fiction." Pages 239–54 in *Greek Fiction. The Greek Novel in Context*. Edited by J. R. Morgan and R. Stoneman. London: 1994. – Idem, "The Ancient Novel Becomes Christian." Pages 685–711 in *The Novel in the Ancient World* (Mn.S 159). Edited by G. Schmeling. Leiden: 1996. – **I. Ramelli**, *I romanzi antichi e il Cristianesimo: contesti e contatti* (Graeco-Romanae Religionis Electa Collectio 6). Madrid: 2001. (With extensive bibliography.) – **R. Söder**, *Die apokryphen Apostelgeschichten*.

On the basis of Erwin Rohde's pioneering work, Ernst von Dobschütz was probably the first to look for novels in early Christian literature. In 1902, he discovered them in the Apocryphal Acts of the Apostles. After further groundwork by Friedrich Pfister (in the second edition of NTApo in German of 1924, on pp. 163–69), Rosa Söder presented a comprehensive examination of this subject in the dissertation she wrote under Professors Martin and Pfister in Würzburg. She begins by identifying five elements "that constitute the essence of the novel in Greek literature: (1) the element of wandering; (2) the aretalogical element; (3) the element of the marvelous; (4) the tendentious element—religious, philosophical, political, and ethical; (5) the erotic element, which however reaches its full elaboration only in the sophistic novel" (3f.). She then investigates the presence of these motifs in the Apocryphal Acts of the Apostles (although she does not sufficiently differentiate between the individual Acts). Some of these apostles are in fact constantly traveling, and their journeys include sea crossings with storms and shipwrecks (motif 1). The aretalogical element (motif 2) is exemplified above all in the miracles performed by the apostles, their omniscience, their gift of predicting the future, and their rescue from dangerous situations. Precisely this element is not very much developed in the novels, as she admits on page 185: "The aretalogical element is almost completely lacking in the novel." This leads Söder to appeal to the somewhat vague categories of "the deeds of famous men" and "vitae and aretalogies of the philosophers" (74f.). She finds the element of the marvelous ("teratology," motif 3) in the description of fabulous peoples, cannibals, wonderful plants, speaking animals, and natural phenomena. The closest parallels are found in the *Alexander Romance*. A tendentious element (motif 4) in the novels would be, for example, the propagation of monogamous marriage as the basic societal structure, realized in the stereotypical "happy ending." In the Apocryphal Acts, the corresponding tendentious element is the Christian missionary preaching and the spreading of the faith in a general sense; more specifically, we also have the exhortation to practice asceticism, which leads into the fifth motif, namely, eroticism (5). One may be surprised that the erotic element, which plays a central role in the novels, should feature at all in the Apocryphal Acts, but it appears there in an inverted (and sometimes also perverted) form. It is inverted when marriages are forcefully prevented and sabotaged by the requirement to live in chastity, while instead of an erotic relationship there is a close spiritual relationship between the apostle and some particular women, a relationship that finds expression in the gestures and the language of love. As for the perversions, it suffices here to mention the attempted necrophilia in the Acts of John and the treatment of the bulls in the Acts of Thecla (see below).

Söder mentions other individual motifs: the selling of slaves, persecution, the crowd, and help in the moment of supreme peril, as well as oracles, dreams, and divine commands (for a critical examination and a partial reconfiguration of Söder's catalog of motifs, cf. Ehlen, 81–90). On the basis of her observations, however, she draws a surprising conclusion: One can indeed call these Acts of the Apostles novelistic narratives, but their model is *not* the Greek/Roman novel. Instead, she defines the Apocryphal Acts as "the literary *witnesses*, given a fixed form in a Christian spirit, of *ancient narratives* of the adventures, marvelous deeds, and love affairs of great men, which were alive in popular memory" (187; emphasis in original). Although she does not say this explicitly, we are no doubt intended to assume that this material also found its way into the novels, and that this is the explanation of the similarities between the Acts and this non-Christian literature. Söder thus agrees with her teacher, Pfister, in transposing the question one decisive step backward—although she has not actually demonstrated the necessity of doing so.

3. Conclusions

Bibliography: G. Bowersock, *Fiction as History: Nero to Julian* (Sather Classical Lectures 58). Berkeley: 1994. – **J. N. Bremmer**, "The Five Major Apocryphal Acts." – **B. Egger**, "Zu den Frauenrollen." – **R.**

Johne, "Women." – **H.-J. Klauck**, "Religionsgeschichte wider den Strich—ein Perspektivenwechsel?" Pages 117–40 in *Paradigmen auf dem Prüfstand: Exegese wider den Strich* (Festschrift for K. Müller) (NTAbh.NF 47). Edited by M. Ebner and B. Heiniger. Münster: 2004. – **E. Plümacher**, "Apokryphe Apostelakten." – **R. M. Price**, "Implied Reader Response and the Evolution of Genres: Transitional Stages Between the Ancient Novels and the Apocryphal Acts." *Hervormde Teologiese Studies* 53 (1997): 909–38. – **P. Vielhauer**, *Geschichte*.

On this point, subsequent scholarship has rightly gone beyond Söder and formulated judgments such as the following: "In terms of the history of literature, the Apocryphal Acts of the Apostles belong beyond doubt to the context of the *classical novel*" (Vielhauer, 715; emphasis in original). All the observations by Söder and other researchers bring "the Apocryphal Acts so close to the genre of the Hellenistic love novel that it is virtually impossible to understand them as anything other than Christian variants of precisely this genre" (Plümacher, 63). "In fact, the intertextuality of the AAA[p] with the novel cannot be doubted, if we look at the cumulation of similar motifs, as collected by Söder: shipwreck, brigands, sale into slavery, putting girls in brothels, unruly crowds, travel around the empire, thinking of suicide, sending messages, corrupting a servant, trials, locking up in tombs, endless journeys and loving couples (Platonic or not)" (Bremmer, 164). We should also mention the facts that novels too could appear with a historiographical varnish and that the text of some novels was fluid, so that their transmission could take the form of very independent variants.

No serious chronological problems are involved when the relationship between the novels and the Apocryphal Acts is defined in this way. For example, the latest date for the fragments of the Ninos romance is the early first century CE, or perhaps even the last century BCE; a similar dating has been suggested for Chariton's *Callirhoë*. This means that the Apocryphal Acts were composed at a period when a number of novels had already found a wide readership, which included many women (cf. Egger, Johne).

There is therefore no reason to reject the idea that at least one or another author of the Apocryphal Acts of the Apostles (and the Pseudo-Clementines) knew one or more novels and found inspiration there for the motifs and the narrative structure in his own

work—thereby in turn becoming a model for successors and imi-
tators. (For a critical discussion of the proposal to reverse the relationship of dependence and to postulate an influence from the
Apocryphal Acts on the novels—a position to which Bowersock
and Price incline—see Klauck, with the bibliography cited there.)
One need not deny that this adaptation entailed the creation of
something new; continuity and renewal often go hand in hand in
the history of a literary genre and are indeed quite normal. Other
factors involved in the composition of the Apocryphal Acts are the
data available in the Christian communities, for example, the traditions about Jesus in the gospels, possibly already Luke's Acts of
the Apostles (later to become canonical), individual traditions
about the apostles and persons such as Thecla, as well as other
community traditions such as hymns and prayers.

I have consistently treated the five ancient Acts here as a
group. It is in fact difficult to avoid doing so, but one should not
forget that each work has its own literary and theological profile.
One important goal in the relatively detailed discussion of the
individual works in this book is to balance the general treatment
by paying greater attention to their specific characteristics.

Chapter 1

The Acts of John

Editions: M. Bonnet, AAAp II: 1. 151–216. – **E. Junod and D. Kaestli**, *Acta Iohannis*, Vols. 1–2 (CChrSA 1–2). Turnhout: 1983. (With French translation) – **T. Zahn**, *Acta Ioannis unter Benutzung von C. Tischendorf's Nachlass bearbeitet*. Erlangen: 1880. Repr. Hildesheim: 1975. (On the later Acts of John by Pseudo-Prochorus.)

Translations: K. Schäferdiek, NTApo II, 6th ed. 138–93. – **J. K. Elliott**, *Apocryphal NT.* 303–49. – **E. Junod and J.-D. Kaestli**, Pages 973–1037 in *Écrits apocryphes chrétiens*, Vol. 1. Edited by F. Bovon and P. Geoltrain.

Secondary literature: J. N. Bremmer, ed. *The Apocryphal Acts of John* (Studies on the Apocryphal Acts of the Apostles 1). Kampen: 1995. – **I. Czachesz**, "Eroticism and Epistemology in the Apocryphal Acts of John." *Nederlands Theologisch Tijdschrift* 60 (2006): 59–72. – **R. A. Culpepper**, *John the Son of Zebedee: The Life of a Legend* (Studies on Personalities of the New Testament). Edinburgh: 2000. – **A. Jakab**, "Actes de Jean: État de la recherche (1982–1999)." *RSLR* 36 (2000): 299–334. – **E. Junod and J.-D. Kaestli**, *L'histoire des Actes apocryphes des apôtres du IIIe au IXe siècle: le cas des Actes de Jean* (CRThPh 7). Geneva: 1982. – **P. J. Lallemann**, *The Acts of John: A Two Stage Initiation into Johannine Gnosticism* (Studies on the Apocryphal Acts of the Apostles 4). Louvain: 1998. – **R. A. Lipsius**, *Die apokryphen Apostelgeschichten*, Vol. 1: 348–542. – **K. Schäferdiek**, "Johannes-Akten." *RAC* 18 (1998): 564–95. – **G. Sirker-Wicklaus**, *Untersuchungen zu den Johannes-Akten. Untersuchungen zur Struktur, zur theologischen Tendenz und zum kirchengeschichtlichen Hintergrund der Acta Johannis* (Beiträge zur Religionsgeschichte 2). Witterschlick: 1988.

A. Context

The earliest certain testimonies to the existence of the Acts of John (ActJoh) are the use made of them in the Manichaean Psalter toward the end of the third century and their inclusion by Eusebius, together with other Acts of Apostles, among the heretical writings (*Hist. eccl.* 3.25.6). Possible links to other, older texts and authors (the Apocryphon of John, Clement of Alexandria, the other Apocryphal Acts) remain a matter of dispute. In the West, Augustine quotes some lines from the dance hymn in ActJoh 94–96 in a letter (*Ep.* 237.5–9). A decisive turning point comes with the Second Council of Nicaea in 787, in the context of the iconoclastic controversy. The Council gives a literal quotation from §§27f., 93–95, and 97f., in order to demonstrate the heretical character of these passages and to condemn them to the flames.

Doubts about the orthodoxy of the Acts of John are probably the principal reason why this work did not survive completely. The Greek text or the translation into a modern language that we find in our editions is a composite that was assembled from several sources and that displays some gaps. The connected frame consists of §§18–36, 37–55, 58–86, and 106–15 (a lacuna must be posited between §36 and §37). These passages were included in some manuscripts together with the later Acts of John by Pseudo-Prochorus (see below); but the concluding passage, ActJoh 106–15, with the farewell discourse and the death of the apostle, was also handed on independently, since it could be used as a reading on feasts of Saint John; it was also translated into several oriental languages. Two episodes from other recensions of the Acts of John by Pseudo-Prochorus are counted as §§56–57 (see below). The section numbered §§87–105 is preserved in only one manuscript, C (written in 1319). This is a first-person account by John in which he looks back on the period before Easter and the passion of Jesus. In terms of genre, it could be regarded as a "gospel" or a "proclamation of the gospel." Scholars dispute whether it is correctly placed between §86 and §106 of the basic frame, or whether the gap between §36 and §37 would be a more appropriate place, but there can be no doubt that it belongs originally to the Acts of John, since excerpts from this passage were quoted at the Second Council of Nicaea (see above).

In view of this textual question, we may ask how much of the original Acts survives and how much has been lost. According to the so-called *Stichometry* of Nicephorus, it ran to 2,500 *stichoi*. A *stichos* corresponds roughly to the length of one hexameter line. The surviving text amounts to about 1,700 *stichoi*. Accordingly, if Nicephorus is correct, we can assume that two-thirds of the text has survived (see Junod and Kaestli, 71). We shall look in greater detail at the reconstruction of the narrative sequence and the gaps when we present the text.

We shall return to the section ActJoh 87–105, which is marked off from the rest of the work not only by an isolated transmission and the characteristics of a different genre but also by two passages—the dance hymn in §§94–96 and the revelation of the cross of light in §§97–102—with a theology that must be judged gnostic. This verdict does not apply to the rest of the narrative (with the exception of §109, which ought perhaps to come after §102). Junod and Kaestli maintain that §§94–102 and 109 are an interpolation by a later author, a foreign body inserted into an already complete text of the Acts. An alternative model (cf. Schäferdiek, Lallemann) would envisage one and the same author who knew traditions of varying provenance, including the parts with a gnostic coloring, and who combined these to form a work with a unified message. We will keep this question in mind and return to it at the close of the chapter.

Sections 87–105 show clearly that the author knew the synoptic gospels (or at least one of them) and the Gospel of John. For example, §88 contains an obvious allusion to the story of the calling of the disciples (Mark 1:16-20 par.), and §90 presupposes the synoptic tradition of the transfiguration of Jesus. In §§94–102, the author not only employs numerous Johannine images, metaphors, and concepts but also undertakes a direct correction of the Johannine passion narrative, as we shall see. This also shows that the fact that the synoptics and John's gospel were known does not in the least mean that these were received as canonical, or that they were regarded as authoritative; indeed, the opposite is the case.

When this is recognized, one will be more inclined to admit the possibility that the author also drew on Luke's Acts of the Apostles. One argument in favor of this is the surprising transition from the authorial third-person narrative to the first-person plural ("we") in the narrative account outside of direct speech (cf.

§§18f., 56, 60f., 72f., 110f.). The only parallel to this is in Luke's work (Lallemann, 74–98).

We have no external data to help determine the provenance and age of the Acts of John; we depend entirely on internal data. On the basis of a number of considerations and indications, Junod and Kaestli suggest that the main narrative (without the gnostic part) was composed in Egypt; but as so often in such cases, these indications cannot be considered probative. (In particular, the argument based on the occurrence of the rare Greek expression *dikrossion*, "undergarment," in §§71, 74, 80, and 111 is not convincing.) One argument in favor of Syria (Schäferdiek) is the use of the word *aroubaton* for the day of the crucifixion in §97, since this is not attested in Greek as the name of a weekday but is borrowed from Syriac. Ephesus is excluded, because the author displays no familiarity with the local conditions and makes egregious errors. (H. Engelmann has presented counterarguments in *ZPE* 103 [1994]: 297–302, but he is not completely convincing.) However, this need not mean that Asia Minor is impossible in principle. The author's conscious clash with the ecclesiastical Johannine tradition, which centered on Ephesus, could certainly point to a provenance somewhere in Asia Minor (Lallemann, 265, suggests Smyrna, the perennial rival of Ephesus; cf. ActJoh 37, 55, and so forth).

The Ephesian Johannine tradition is already attested to in its broad outlines by Irenaeus of Lyons ca. 180, and its formation may well go back two or three decades before that date without conflicting with the differentiated data in Papias and Polycrates. The christology of the Acts of John displays elements that make the impression of great age, such as the polymorphy of the Redeemer and a remarkable one-nature doctrine (see below). Although there are points of contact between the section with a gnostic coloring and the Eastern version of Valentinianism, it also seems to predate the elaboration of the great gnostic systems. There is little sign of a developed church structure or liturgy. The Lord's Supper is usually celebrated with bread alone, and we find a laying-on of hands, but baptism is never mentioned (with the exception of a later interpolation in §57). I believe that the best dating for the ActJoh in the form in which this text has come down to us is ca. 150–160.

B. Contents

The continuous text of ActJoh begins with §18. In his edition of the Greek text, which was long the standard work, Bonnet—who is also responsible for the division into paragraphs—placed two texts from other contexts of transmission before what remained of the ancient ActJoh: In §§1–14, he printed two recensions of a passage from later Acts of John, which is set in Rome (see below); and in §§14 [sic]–17, he placed an intermezzo found in manuscripts containing the more recent Acts of John by Pseudo-Prochorus, where it forms a transition between John's period on Patmos to the death scene of the apostle, which is borrowed from ActJoh.

The genuine beginning of ActJoh is lost, and we can only speculate about what preceded the journey from Miletus to Ephesus—perhaps a self-presentation by the author (Leucius), or events from the apostle's early years on which ActJoh 113 looks back, especially the thwarting of his marriage plans; or the division of the missionary territories among the apostles in Jerusalem and the start of their travels, which in John's case (as scholars have suggested) included a shipwreck; or simply the end of his exile on Patmos (Lallemann, 16)? We do not know the answer. But the missing passage was probably not very lengthy (although the §§1–17 supplied by Bonnet naturally give us no relevant indications), and it must at any rate have introduced the characters who accompany the apostle in §18: Demonicus, Aristobulus, Cleobius, and the wife of Marcellus.

1. The First Period in Ephesus (ActJoh 18–55)

The surviving text of ActJoh begins in §18 with the journey of the apostle and his companions from Miletus to Ephesus, prompted by a vision. After they have "covered about four miles, a voice from heaven was heard" while *we* (!) all listened: "John, you are to procure for your Lord at Ephesus the glory which you know." This happens immediately afterward through a double miracle, which oscillates in a strange way between the healing of a life-threatening illness and a raising from the dead.

Cleopatra and Lycomedes

"When we came near the city" (§19), Lycomedes, the *stratêgos* (i.e., a high dignitary) of Ephesus, comes to meet the travelers. His wife, Cleopatra, has lain close to death for seven days, almost without breathing. But an unidentified "man" has promised him that John will come to rescue her and "raise her up" or "restore her to health" (the motif of a double vision is hinted at, as in Acts 10). Lycomedes utters a rhetorically impressive lamentation, in which he expresses thoughts of committing suicide (20), before—after reproaches by the apostle—he himself apparently collapses and dies (21).

John sees the two corpses as the work of the adversary (21: "Woe to the new craft of him who devises cunnings against me!") and addresses an urgent prayer to Christ as the physician "who heals freely" (cf. Acts 3:20). "For you have said yourself, O Christ, 'Ask and it shall be given you'" (22; cf. Matt 7:7 par.). He then turns at once to Cleopatra and commands her in the name of the Lord, "Rise and become not a pretext for many who will not believe, and an affliction for souls who hope and could be saved" (23).

When she has returned to life, Cleopatra's first question is about her husband; her faith is immediately put to the test when the apostle brings her into her bedroom and she sees her dead husband. Although she loses her voice, weeps, and closes her eyes, her entire attention is directed to the apostle, who bids her speak with a loud voice to her husband: "Arise, and glorify God's name, because he gives the dead to the dead!" (22; cf. Matt 8:22 par.). In this way, Cleopatra herself raises her husband from the dead. Through their insistent entreaties, they persuade the apostle to remain in their house so that he may deepen their hope in God (25). This request, taken together with the large number of speeches in this long miracle story, indicates that the double raising of the dead is also meant to be read symbolically as a sign of inner repentance to a new life, that is, as a spiritual event that can touch other people even without a direct intervention by the apostle.

The Apostle and His Portrait

Lycomedes persuades a friend who is a painter to make a portrait of the apostle while he is preaching to a great crowd, without the apostle himself noticing this (26). John does, however, notice that

Lycomedes often withdraws into his bedroom alone and decides to investigate this conduct. He finds "the crowned picture of an old man, and candlesticks and an altar before it," and he takes this to be a painting of a pagan god (27). Lycomedes defends himself with an argument that reflects an important component of the societal structure in classical antiquity, the cult of benefactors: "If one is permitted next to God to call those gods who are our benefactors, then it is you, father, who are painted in the picture, whom I crown, love, and worship . . ." (27).

On this occasion, the apostle sees his own reflection in a mirror for the very first time and is obliged to admit the similarity to his portrait. But at once he dismisses the painting because it captures only his fleshly appearance (28), "the dead picture of what is dead" (29). What matters is a suitable picture of the soul, painted with colors supplied by Jesus, "who paints us all for himself." Such colors are for example "belief in God, knowledge, fear of God, love, fellowship, meekness . . ." (29). In its substance, this story is strikingly similar to an episode in the *vita* of the Neo-Platonist philosopher Plotinus (in Porphyry, *Life of Plotinus*, 1).

The Old Women

Section 30 begins to set the scene carefully for another mass healing that is a work of love. Verus, one of the serving brothers ("deacons"), is told to gather together the elderly women aged sixty and above from all Ephesus. When they come to the theater, only four are found to be healthy; all the others suffer from various illnesses. Many spectators assemble, including the proconsul and another office-bearer, a "first *stratêgos*" of the city named Andronicus, who takes the role of the doubter: The apostle is to "come to the theater naked, without holding anything in his hands; let him not pronounce that magic name which I heard him name!" (31).

The scene is theatrical (in the literal sense of the word) and corresponds to a general "theatricalization" of public life at that historical period. The apostle takes the opportunity to deliver a great address. He has come to Ephesus in order to proclaim Jesus Christ—and it is obvious that this has never happened before in the city (33). His preaching includes social criticism (the poor and the rich, 34) and moral criticism (adultery, avarice, anger, and drunkenness, 35). It concludes with a veritable catalog of vices (36).

Unfortunately, the text breaks off at this point. The healing itself is mentioned only summarily in one brief sentence, which does its best to fill the gap. The lost passage must have related the conversion of Andronicus, as well as of his wife Drusiana, of whom we will hear more.

The Destruction of the Temple of Artemis

After this gap, we continue with §37 (although we bear in mind that the proclamation of the gospel in §§87–105, which we discuss below, originally may have preceded §37). John makes his next major appearance on the birthday of Artemis, the goddess of the city, but now he consciously risks his life. As the only one dressed in black in the midst of a crowd in festal (white) garments, he mounts a podium in the temple precincts and challenges those present to a duel in prayer: They are to pray to Artemis that he may die, and he will call on his God and kill all of them because of their unbelief (39). The crowd is by now familiar with his power and implores him not to carry out his threat. He accepts their plea and limits his threat to the goddess herself and her cult. At his prayer, the altar is shattered, all the votive gifts fall to the ground, and half of the temple collapses, killing a priest of Artemis. This leads the crowd to exclaim: "There is only one God, that of John" (42). The apostle asks, almost in scorn: "Where is the power of the deity? Where are the sacrifices? Where the birthday? Where the festivals? Where the garlands? Where the great enchantment and the poison allied to it?" (43).

The people pull down with their own hands those parts of the temple that are still standing and declare themselves ready to convert (44). In order to "wean them from the milk of the nurse and set them upon a firm rock" (45; cf. 1 Cor 3:2-10f.), the apostle remains with them for a time, postponing his planned journey to Smyrna and other cities (which may have been the seven cities from Revelation 2–3).

As a kind of counterfoil to the cult of Artemis, which is now obsolete, John celebrates a service in the house of Andronicus (see above). This consists of a sermon, prayer, thanksgiving (Eucharist), and the laying-on of hands (46). A relative of the dead priest of Artemis is also present; earlier he had laid the corpse before the door, and the apostle, who is inspired by the Spirit, knows this. He charges the young man to raise up the dead man with the words, "The servant of God, John, says to you, 'Arise!'" This takes place, but it is only a first step: the apostle explains that the man who has been raised does not yet live truly, since he has not yet attained the true life (47). The former priest of Artemis understands the adjuration, converts, and joins the apostle.

We should note that this whole episode borrows motifs from 1 Kings 18 (Elijah and the priests of Baal) and Daniel 14:1-22 (Daniel and the priests of Bel). It presupposes only a general knowledge of the forms of temple worship and does not reveal any specific local knowledge of Ephesus.

Fornication with Dramatic Consequences

Bibliography: E. Plümacher. "Apostolische Missionsreise und statthalterische Assisetour—Eine Interpretation von Acta Johannis c.37.45 und 55." Pages 207–28 in idem,, *Geschichte und Geschichten.* – Idem,, "Der θεὸς ἄφθονος in Acta Johannis 55 und sein historischer Kontext." Pages 229–73 in idem,, *Geschichte und Geschichten.*

After receiving instructions in a dream, the apostle goes on the following day to the scene of a crime outside the city. A farmer had an adulterous relationship with the wife of one of his colleagues. When his aged father reproached him for this, he kicked him so violently that he died (in the text of §48, we read only "he left him speechless"; but cf. Chariton, *Callirhoë* I: 4.12–5.1). The young man realizes that he has ruined his own life and runs away, armed with a sickle. When the apostle stops him and calls him to account, he tells John what he planned to do: He wanted to kill the woman, then her husband, and finally himself, "For I could not bear her husband seeing me being executed" (49; this reaction lies within the parameters of "honor, disgrace, and shame"). But he promises not to carry out his plan if John restores his father to life.

This time, it is John himself who raises the father from the dead. Initially, this man is not at all pleased at this. The young man castrates himself with the sickle, runs to the woman's house, and throws down his genitals before her—the cause of all this distress (53). But the apostle does not at all approve of this drastic action: rather, like the murder, it is inspired by the devil. What counts is not the instruments or organs, but the inner disposition, the "hidden sources" (54) within the human person. This guards against the misunderstanding of Matthew 19:12—which may have been in vogue among groups of radical Christian ascetics—as an exhortation to a literal self-castration.

The young man displays complete penitence and seeks the company of the apostle. In §55, emissaries from Smyrna bring John a reproachful message, appealing to "the unenvious God" (cf. Plümacher, "ActJoh 55"), and this reminds him that it is now time to start out on the journey he had planned. (On the rivalry between Ephesus and Smyrna, which we glimpse here, and for a comparison between the apostolic wanderings and the journeys of a proconsul for judicial assizes, see Plümacher, "Missionsreise").

2. Intermezzos (ActJoh 56–61)

After §55, we must once again assume a large gap in the text that has come down to us, because the apostle sets out on his return journey to Ephesus already in §§58–59; according to some manuscripts, he leaves from Laodicea (cf. Rev 3:14-22). Among the traveling companions mentioned in §59, we have not yet heard anything of Aristobula, who has lost her husband Tertullus; Aristippus; Xenophon; and the "chaste prostitute." They were presumably introduced to the reader in that part of the travel narrative that is now lost. We can only speculate about the crises in relationships and the conversion experiences that lie in the background, with the possible exception of Aristobula. The Manichaean Psalter tells us that she fought for her purity (Allberry, 143.13f.), probably by refusing to have intercourse with her husband.

A Partridge or the Sons of Antipatros?

The editions present two short narratives as §§56–57 (both are printed in Elliott, 326f.). Bonnet, 178f., and NTApo 4th ed. II: 164f., following him, inserted here the episode of the partridge from a manuscript of Pseudo-Prochorus. John takes pleasure in a partridge that flies past him and plays in the dust. A priest rebukes him, but the apostle tells him that this harmless enjoyment is far preferable to the disgraceful and wicked acts of the priest. He interprets the partridge as the soul of the priest. This episode seems to have circulated independently; in his *Conlationes*, the monastic writer John Cassian reports it slightly differently (24.21): John caresses a partridge, and a hunter who comes by mocks him for spending his time in this way. John explains to him that he himself would not carry around his bow fully strung all the time, because it would lose its tension. In the same way, the spirit needs "relaxation" from time to time.

Junod and Kaestli (238–43) and NTApo 5th/6th ed. II: 176f. prefer to insert here the "healing of the sons of Antipatros," which is found in two other manuscripts from Athos and Sinai. This episode is located in Smyrna. Antipatros, one of the dignitaries of the city, promises to give the apostle ten thousand pieces of gold if John can expel from his sons, twins now aged thirty-four years, the terrible demons that torment them. The apostle proves to be a successful physician but, like his master, refuses to accept any payment in silver. Instead, he asks for the souls of those whom he has healed; Antipatros is to give the money to the needy. This is doubtless meant as a polemic against money-hungry doctors and expensive cults of healing.

The Obedient Bugs

Bibliography: E. Buck, "Das Paraklausithyron: Die Entwicklungsgeschichte eines Motivs der antiken Liebesdichtung." Pages 244–56 in idem, *Vom Menschenbild in der römischen Literatur: Ausgewählte Schriften.* Heidelberg: 1966. – **F. O. Copley**, *Exclusus Amator: A Study in Latin Love Poetry* (Philological Monographs 17). Madison, Wisc.: 1956. – **E. Plümacher**, "Paignion und Biberfabel: Zum literarischen und popularphilosophischen Hintergrund von Acta Johannis 60f.48–54." *Apocrypha* 3 (1992): 69–109; also pages 171–206 in idem, *Geschichte und Geschichten.* – **J. E. Spittler**, *Wild Kingdom.*

With §§60–61, we return to the main textual witnesses to large sections of ActJoh and encounter an episode which is much more enigmatic than it at first sight appears. It is introduced as a *paignion*, that is, "a comic piece, a playful game, a little joke, a light intermezzo," and is written in the first person plural (and once indeed in the first person singular) throughout. At a lonely inn, John's companions generously give him the only bed, and sleep on the floor. But the bed teems with innumerable bugs. At midnight, when the bugs annoy the apostle too much, he commands them to leave their home and to stay far away from "the servants of God."

In the morning, the narrator and the other brethren see a huge number of bugs waiting patiently at the door of the room. When the apostle wakes up and sees them waiting there, he permits them to return to their former place, and the bugs rush to do so as soon as the apostle has gotten out of the bed. The apostle then formulates the lesson to be drawn from this story: "This creature heard the voice of a man and kept quiet and was obedient. We, however, hear God's voice, and yet irresponsibly transgress his commandments. And how long will this go on?"

Is this the entire moral of the story? Perhaps there is more to come. To begin with, it is worth noting that similar stories about animals circulated in non-Christian traditions too—we hear of crickets and frogs that allow the exhausted hero to take his rest and therefore fall silent, or of flies that depart from human dwellings during the period of the Olympic Games or a feast of Apollo. And the legend tells us that animals obeyed the commands of Pythagoras (for individual references, cf. Junod and Kaestli, 535–38). Besides this, there may be a play on words in the text, lending the episode a slight erotic touch: the Greek word for "bug" (*kôris*) is very similar to the word for "girl" (*kôrê*). Accordingly, when the apostle addresses the bugs (whom he actually calls *kôrai*, "girls," according to manuscript M), he would be signaling that female beings must stay far away from his bed. And classical literature has a minor genre called *paraklausithyron*, the lament of a scorned lover before the closed door (cf. Burck, Copley). Finally, the "keeping quiet" of the bugs has a special meaning: In other contexts, the same verb is used to describe a temperate ascetic Christian lifestyle (cf. the conclusion to §54).

3. The Second Period in Ephesus (ActJoh 62–86)

The story of John's second period in Ephesus is almost completely dominated by the events concerning Drusiana. The description has a partly suppressed erotic potential that is fully equal to the explicit scenes in the novels of the imperial age. We learn only in a flashback in §63 that Drusiana has separated from her husband Andronicus, that is, that she no longer has intercourse (here characterized in an aside as "the repugnant act") with him. Andronicus had reacted by shutting her up in a tomb and demanding that she choose either to fulfill her obligations as a wife or to die. Shortly afterward, however, he must have changed his mind, because now he is called "godly" and accepts his wife's refusal to sleep with him (cf. the flashback in §82).

The Death of Drusiana

At this point in the narrative, a man falls in love with Drusiana. We learn his name, Callimachus, only later on (in §73), but the narrative loses no time in telling us that he is "a servant of Satan." Drusiana feels that she bears the guilt for this turn of events, simply because of her existence, and she asks God that she may soon die. She dies in the presence of the apostle, who has known nothing about all this up to now (64). When Andronicus explains the reason for her death, the apostle falls silent, deeply disturbed by the "threats of the enemy." The discourse that he then holds is not a funeral discourse addressed to the immediate situation, but a more general exhortation to prepare for one's own death, employing a series of metaphors in §67: the helmsman, the farmer, the runner in the race, and the prizefighter (cf. 1 Cor 9:24-27). The point of comparison is the singlemindedness of their conduct, as well as the difficulties they endure—storms, mildew, vermin—which symbolize the emotions, passions, vices, and daily cares in human life (68). John sums up: the only soul that is to be praised is one that "refused to be inflamed by filthy lust, to succumb to levity, to be ensnared by thirst after money, or to be betrayed by the strength of the body and anger" (69).

In the Tomb

In the meantime, incited by "the polymorphous Satan," Callimachus is not idle, but sees a way to attain the goal of his wishes, namely. through the perversion of necrophilia. He bribes Fortunatus, the steward of Andronicus, with a large sum of money to admit him to the tomb and its innermost chamber. They begin to unclothe the body, mocking her in unison: "What have you gained, unhappy Drusiana? Could you not have done this while you were alive? It need not have grieved you if you had done it willingly" (70). When only the last undergarment covers her nakedness, a serpent suddenly appears, kills the steward with one single bite, wraps itself around the feet of Callimachus and brings him to the ground, then sits upon him (71).

On the following day, the third day after Drusiana's death, John goes to the tomb in the early morning with Andronicus and other brethren in order to break bread (an early example of the Christian adaptation of the third day as the date of a memorial celebration of the dead). The keys to the funeral chamber cannot be found, but the doors are opened by a miracle, and the apostle interprets the lack of keys as providential (thereby also relativizing the importance of the cultic celebration): "For Drusiana is not in the tomb" (§72): In other words, only her mortal wrapping lies there, while her immortal soul has already entered heaven.

When they enter the funeral chamber, the group meets a beautiful young man who smiles. This is not the first time that John sees him (cf. §73: "Do you come before us here also, noble one?"). He announces that Drusiana will be raised from the dead, and then vanishes. It is only now that the visitors see the other "drama" (*theama* in §73; cf. *dramatourgia* in §74): in addition to Drusiana, there are the corpses of two men (Callimachus, too, appears to have died of sheer terror, or to have entered a state similar to death), and a huge serpent sleeping on one of the corpses. Andronicus at once realizes what has happened and explains the situation to the apostle.

The Raising Up of Callimachus and Drusiana

At the request of Andronicus, the apostle first raises Callimachus to life. In his account of the events, the young man attributes to Fortunatus a considerable share of the guilt (§76: "He encouraged me to such madness, after I had already desisted from the ill-timed and dreadful frenzy") and then emphasizes what had particularly impressed him: the apparition of the beautiful young man, who covered Drusiana with his cloak and then told him: "Callimachus, die, that you may live!" Looking back, Callimachus identifies the young man as an angel of God. He knows that he will find new life only when he believes in the true God, whom John preaches, and he earnestly implores the apostle to help him to overcome his earlier criminal inclination and his evil disposition so that he can make progress along the path to the truth.

The apostle replies in §77 with a beautiful prayer of praise addressed to Jesus Christ, which includes both acclamations linked to the context in ActJoh (e.g., "You have kept the grave from shame, and redeemed that man who contaminated himself with blood") and more general acclamations which tell us a great deal about the Christology of the work (e.g., "Father, full of mercy and compassion . . ." [these words are addressed to Christ], or toward the end of the prayer: "Holy Jesus, you alone are God and none else").

The raising of Drusiana has a similar structure but is less spectacular (§§79–80). Andronicus requests this, and the apostle begins with a prayer addressed to Jesus (cf. above all the words: "before whose voice the demons are confounded"; cf. Jas 2:19). After she returns to life, Drusiana is "perplexed." She is briefly informed about what has happened and breaks out in rejoicing and praise.

The "Unsuccessful" Raising of Fortunatus

Drusiana displays great generosity by asking the apostle to restore Fortunatus too to life. Callimachus protests vigorously that the heavenly voice said nothing about this. John appeals to the principle that one should not repay evil with evil (cf. Rom 12:17), a principle demonstrated by the conduct of God or Jesus: one example in the long list in §81 says: "And when we reviled him, he forsook us not, but was merciful." He leaves the decision in this case to Drusiana. She prays to Jesus as "the God of truth" who is the only object of her love, and she mentions the "polymorphous face" which the Lord showed her (§82).

After he is successfully raised from the dead, Fortunatus sees the tableau with the apostle, the married couple, and Callimachus—who has become a Christian—and he has only one wish: "I wish I were not raised, but remained dead, so as not to see them" (§83). He flees from the tomb.

The last three brief scenes belong to the apostle. In a long speech full of metaphors (§84), he laments the profound corruption of human nature which can be seen in Fortunatus, and says that the real author of this corruption is Satan, who ought to keep his distance from the way of life of the faithful, which is described in a long list of twenty-four elements, including the sacred bath, the eucharist, food and drink, the agape celebration, and continence.

This leads into the breaking of bread, which John had originally intended to do. This takes place in §85, but is no longer a memorial celebration of the dead. John formulates a genuine prayer of thanksgiving. Many of the individual acclamations are introduced by "We give thanks" (*eukharistoumen*), others by "We praise," "We bear witness," or "We glorify."

After this, all return to the house of Andronicus. "A spirit in me" prophesies to John (86) that Fortunatus will die a second time as a result of the bite of the serpent, which is described as a spreading "blackness." One of the young men discovers that the poison has already reached Fortunatus' heart and that he has been dead for three hours. John's lapidary comment is: "You have your child, devil!"

4. The "Polymorphous" Earthly Lord (ActJoh 87–93, 103–5)

Bibliography: H. Garcia, "La polymorphie du Christ. Remarques sur quelques définitions et sur des multiples enjeux." *Apocrypha* 10 (1999): 16–55. – **I. Czachesz**, "The Gospel of Peter and the Apocryphal Acts of the Apostles: Using Cognitive Science to Reconstruct Gospel Tradition." Pages 245–61 in *Das Petrusevangelium und die Petrusapokalypse. Die griechischen Fragmente mit deutscher und englischer Übersetzung* (GCS NF 11). Edited by Thomas J. Kraus and Tobias Nicklas. Berlin: 2003. – **E. Junod**, "Polymorphie du Dieu Sauveur." Pages 38–46 in *Gnosticisme et Monde Hellénistique*. Edited by J. Ries. Louvain-la-Neuve: 1982. – **P. J. Lallemann**, "Polymorphy of Christ." Pages 97–118 in *The Apocryphal Acts of John*. Edited by J. N. Bremmer. – **H.-J. Klauck**, *Die apokryphe Bibel: Ein anderer Zugang zum frühen Christentum*, Ch. 7. Tübingen: 2008.

Sections 87–115, which are transmitted in one single manuscript, begin abruptly with words in which Drusiana may be referring to the event just narrated (cf., e.g., §73) or to the earlier crime of Andronicus, to which §63 alludes: "The Lord appeared to me in the tomb in the form of John and of a youth." This brings us to the most important theme of the passages that frame this section, the *polymorphy* of Jesus Christ, who appears as an earthly being to different persons in different forms at one and the same time. (Polymorphy is not the same concept as *metamorphosis*, in which the figure changes in a number of temporal stages, but all the witnesses see this change in the same manner.)

John realizes that he must explain Drusiana's remarkable experience to his hearers, who are not yet solidly established in the faith. He affirms that this polymorphy is neither "strange" nor "paradoxical." In a passage in direct speech, which runs to §104, he presents twelve examples (according to the enumeration by Junod and Kaestli) of the polymorphy which the disciples experienced even before Easter. Not all these examples imply polymorphy in the strict sense, but they help to underline that for the God on earth there is in fact no "normal" mode of appearance:

1. When Jesus calls the first disciples (cf. Mark 1:16-20), James sees a boy standing on the shore who calls and waves to them, but his brother John sees a man who is "fair and comely and of a cheerful countenance" (88).

2. When the two fishermen follow this figure, John suddenly sees him as an almost bald man with a flowing beard, but James sees him as a "youth whose beard is just starting." Both men find this puzzling (89).

3. John experienced other incomprehensible things too: He never saw Jesus close his eyes, not even when they were alone. His eyes were always open (89).

4. Sometimes Jesus showed himself to him as a small, "unattractive" man; at another time, his face seemed to touch the sky (89).

5. "When I sat at table he would take me upon his breast [cf. John 13:23-25] and I held him; and sometimes his breast felt to me to be smooth and tender, and sometimes hard, like stone. . . ." Once again, John is bewildered (89; it is possible that a logion of Jesus has disappeared from the close of this paragraph, e.g., "Be of good courage, it is I."

6. On a mountain, John, James, and Peter see the Lord shining in an indescribably bright light (90; cf. Mark 9:2f.).

7. The transfiguration scene is repeated. The second time, only John, whom Jesus loves (cf. John 20:2, etc.), draws near to the Lord. He sees him only from behind (cf. Exod 33:23), but notes that he no longer wears any clothes and no longer appears human in any way. His feet are whiter than snow and light up the earth around him, and his head reaches the sky. When John cries out in fear, the Lord turns around—and now he is only a small human being. He pulls at John's beard in reproach (so that the apostle's chin is painful for thirty days) and rebukes him: "John, be not unbelieving, but believing, and not inquisitive" (90; cf. John 20:27).

8. Peter and John now come on the scene and ask John: "Who was speaking to the Lord when he was on top of the mountain?" John then meditates on the unity of the Lord, which has so many faces (poluprosôpon, 91).

9. When they spend the night in Gennesaret, John pretends to be sleeping. He sees and hears another man, who looks like Jesus, talking with the Lord: "Jesus, those whom you have chosen still do not believe in you." The Lord replies: "You are right, for they are only human beings" (92).

10. When he attempts to take hold of the Lord and touch him (cf. 1 John 1:1), John sometimes encounters "a material and solid body; and at other times again when I felt him, the substance was immaterial and bodiless and as if it were not existing at all" (93).

11. Jesus accepts an invitation to the house of a Pharisee, with his disciples (cf. Luke 7:36, etc.). Each receives a loaf, but Jesus does not himself eat his bread. He blesses it and divides it among the disciples. All have their hunger satisfied from these fragments, and they do not even touch their own loaves (93; this is obviously reminiscent of the miracles of the multiplication of loaves, but the emphasis is on the fact that Jesus does not take any earthly nourishment).

12. Often, John tried to detect the footprints of Jesus in the dust of the earth—especially because he also saw how Jesus rose up above the earth—but he never succeeded (93). This means that Jesus' body no longer belongs to the earth, but is oriented towards heaven.

When we look for the roots of this idea of the polymorphy of the Redeemer, we must turn first to the narratives of the Easter apparitions of the risen Lord, who appears in a strange form so that he is not immediately recognized (John 21:4; Luke 24:15f.); he seems no longer to be tied to space and time (John 20:19); the disciples think that they are seeing a ghost (Luke 24:37). In the secondary but ancient conclusion to Mark, the actual word "form" is used: "After this he appeared in another form [*morphê*] to two of them, as they were walking into the country" (Mark 16:12). These qualities of the risen Lord are projected back into the life of the earthly Jesus. This means that the Christology proposed here has tendencies to docetism, since it clearly reduces the bodiliness and the humanity of the earthly Jesus.

This is confirmed by the apostle's exhortation, which begins at the close of §93 and originally concluded in §§103–4 (with a brief narrative note in §105). There is a slight tension between the affirmation that the miraculous deeds of the Lord "cannot be uttered nor heard" and 1 John 1:1-3, which is often echoed in this passage.

The *peristasis* catalogue in §103 (i.e., the description of various difficult circumstances) assures those who suffer that their Lord suffers with them in solidarity, and contains some references to specific contexts: "He keeps watch even now over prisons for our sakes, and in tombs, in bonds and dungeons . . . as he is the God of those who are imprisoned." Nevertheless, it is not a human being who is proclaimed by the apostle, but "God unchangeable, God invincible, God higher than all authority, and all power, and older and mightier than all the angels . . ." (104).

5. The True "Passion" of the Lord (ActJoh 94–102)

Junod and Kaestli are not wholly wrong to describe as a "gnostic apocalypse" the passage in §§94–102, which probably once existed as an independent text. It offers a new evaluation of the passion narratives in the gospels, and especially the Gospel of John, from an unmistakably gnostic perspective. The introduction, which includes a vehement anti-Jewish polemic, recalls the beginning of the tradition about the Lord's Supper in Luke 22:15; 1 Corinthians 11:23:

> *Now*, before he was arrested *by the lawless Jews, who received their law from a lawless serpent* [cf. John 8:44], *he gathered us all together and said, "Before I am delivered up to them* [cf. John 18:36], *let us sing a hymn to the Father* [who here, unlike in the rest of the text, is distinguished from Jesus], *and go forth* [cf. Mark 14:26] *to what lies before us."*

The Dance Hymn

Bibliography: B. E. Bowe, "Dancing into the Divine: The Hymn of the Dance in the Acts of John." *JECS* 7 (1999): 83–104. – **A. J. Dewey**, "The Hymn in the Acts of John: Dance as Hermeneutic." *Semeia* 38 (1986): 67–80. – **P. G. Schneider**, *The Mystery of the Acts of John: An Interpretation of the Hymn and the Dance in the Light of the Acts' Theology* (Distinguished Dissertation Series 10). San Francisco: 1991.

There follows a kind of institution narrative, but this is related not to the Lord's Supper, but to a hymn accompanied by a dance. Jesus stands in the middle and speaks or sings the text, while the disciples move in a circle around him and answer every pair of lines with an antiphonal "Amen." It is highly likely that this ritual was in fact practiced in a community, perhaps instead of the Lord's Supper. Many examples of ritual dance with and without song are known from antiquity; it suffices here to recall the Therapeutae of Philo (*Contempl.* 83–85) and the celebration of the mysteries known as *thronismos* in the Olympian discourse of Dion of Prusa (*Or.* 12.33).

The hymn proper begins with several doxologies (§94). In §95, we have first a number of strophes with reciprocal statements in the passive and the active moods: "I will be saved, and I will save," "I will be loosed, and I will loose." The vocabulary of the passion ("I will be pierced, and I will pierce") is used, as is sacramental language ("I will eat, and I will be eaten"; "I will be washed, and I will wash"). In an intermezzo that may be the work of a redactor, the little parable from Matthew 11:17 is translated into action: "I will pipe, dance all of you!"; "I will mourn, lament all of you!" The gnostic eightfold power ("Ogdoad") and the number twelve are mentioned, and then the reciprocal statements resume (in the earliest form of the text?): "I will adorn, and I will be adorned"; "I will be united, and I will unite." The speaker then states that he both has and does not have a house, a place, and a temple (cf. John 2:21; 14:2f.) and closes the hymn proper with a sequence of metaphors to which there are New Testament parallels: "I am for you [singular] a lamp . . . a mirror . . . a door . . . a way" (cf. Rev 21:23; 1 Cor 13:12; John 10:9; 14:6). All these affirmations, including those relating to the passion and to the sacraments, are assuredly meant to be understood spiritually. They indicate the path taken by a gnostic redeemer who is obliged to accept painfully the conditions of the material world in order to free those who belong to him.

Section 98 offers an explanation in elevated language. Despite the difficulties of understanding some individual points, it points in general in this direction: the one who takes part in the dance will be transformed. He will recognize himself in the speaker, but then he will keep silence about these mysteries. As the following passage emphasizes, it is important to have a correct understanding of suffering. What then is the suffering of "the human being" (namely, of the Redeemer and of every gnostic)? The contrast remains as yet unclear, but the true suffering does not consist in an external passion that affects the body. The main theme of the farewell discourses in John, the departure of Jesus, is echoed in the

verse: "Who am I? You shall know when I go away." In keeping
with these words, the speaker says: "What I now seem to be, that
I am not. You shall see when you come." Further doxologies and a
responsorial "Amen" close this section.

The "Passion" Narrative

Bibliography: A. Böhlig, "Zur Vorstellung vom Lichtkreuz in
Gnostizismus und Manichäismus." Pages 473–91 in *Gnosis* (Festschrift
for Hans Jonas). Göttingen: 1978. – **G. Luttikhuizen**, "A Gnostic
Reading of the Acts of John." Pages 119–52 in *The Apocryphal Acts of
John*. Edited by J. N. Bremmer. – **G. H. Stroumsa**, "Christ's Laughter:
Docetic Origins Reconsidered." *JECS* 12 (2004): 267–88.

After the dance, the Lord departs, and the disciples flee in all
directions (cf. Mark 14:50; John 16:32). John goes only as far as a
cave on the Mount of Olives (contrast this account with, e.g., John
19:26). At the very moment of the crucifixion, when darkness covers all the earth, the Lord appears and gives him light, saying:
"John, to the multitude down below in Jerusalem I am being crucified, and pierced with lances and nails [John 19:34; Mark 15:19],
and gall and vinegar is given me to drink [Mark 15:36; Matt
27:34]." But John is to hear what is *really* happening.

The Lord now shows him, in a vision, a cross of light with
apparently cosmic dimensions. What then happens, within the
description of the vision, is both significant and obscure (98):

> . . . and around the cross [of light he showed me] a great multitude
> which had no one form; and in the cross was one form and one like-
> ness [cf. perhaps the "image and likeness" in Gen 1:26]. And the
> Lord himself I beheld above the cross, not having a shape, but only
> a voice. . . .

We can draw on §§99–101, which contain an interpretation of
the vision, to define as follows the three entities around the cross
of light, in it, and above it. The great crowd around the cross are
those persons who have no prospect of redemption. The
Redeemer above the cross has returned to his heavenly homeland.
The problematic middle group refers to the gnostics, who belong
to the upper world because they are related to the Redeemer; but
the process of gathering them together and purifying them is still
in course.

This means that the cross of light has a critical function, and it is defined correspondingly in §98 as a boundary between right and left, above and below (more precisely, the horizontal beam of the presumably T-shaped cross would form this boundary). Only for the sake of human beings, who need vivid concepts, it is also given other names (some of which are typically Johannine), such as *Logos*, reason, Christ, door, way, bread, seed, resurrection, Son, Father, Spirit, life, truth, faith, and grace. In §99, the Lord distinguishes the cross of light from the wooden cross on Golgotha and emphasizes, "I am not he who is on the cross." To suppose this would be "vile and not worthy of me." The following words in §100 have a key function in determining the place of this whole passage in the gnostic myth: "For as long as you do not call yourself mine, I am not that which I was. But if you hear and hearken to me, then you shall be as I am, and I shall be what I was." Through the gathering together of all those destined for salvation, the Redeemer constitutes his own self and returns to the ideal original state, which is characterized inter alia by calm and fullness.

Section 101 continues almost obsessively with the correction of the synoptic and Johannine passion narratives: "I have suffered none of the things which they will say of me." This principle is extended consistently to all the details: "You hear that I suffered, yet I suffered not; . . . that I was pierced, yet was I not wounded; . . . that blood flowed from me, yet it did not flow." The mystery of the true suffering can be spoken of only in enigmatic words. This mystery was displayed in the dance; it refers to the spiritual and mythical path taken by the *Logos*, to whom ultimately all the concepts from the tradition of the passion of Jesus refer symbolically (cf. *sumbolikôs* at the close of §102). What must be spoken of is "the piercing of the *Logos*, the blood of the *Logos*, the wounding of the *Logos*," and so on. We can understand now why John, who now descends and returns to Jerusalem, laughs over everything that he hears there about the suffering of the Lord (102). In other gnostic texts, it is Christ himself who laughs at those who imagine they are crucifying him (on this, cf. Stroumsa).

6. The Death of the Apostle (ActJoh 106–15)

Bibliography: I. Czachesz, *Commission Narratives* 92/122. – **J.-D. Kaestli**, "Le role des textes bibliques dans la genèse et le développement des légendes apocryphes: Le cas du sort final de l'apôtre Jean," *Aug* 23 (1983): 319–36.

Almost 90 percent of the death scene consists of long prayers and speeches by the apostle, broken up by only a few narrative elements. On a Sunday, John begins to speak (§106). He addresses the brethren in words that display an ecclesiological dimension that is less clear elsewhere in the text: "fellow-servants, coheirs, and copartners in the kingdom of the Lord." He reminds them of the many gifts of grace that they have received (fourteen are listed) and on the "mystery of the dispensation" of salvation (*oikonomias*) that has been accomplished for their sake. In §107, many attributes are predicated of "our God Jesus Christ," and the hearers are exhorted to live in such a way that he has joy in them—especially since it is not clear whether those who fall away have any possibility of a renewed repentance. There follows a new prayer, full of anaphoras, in which the apostle asks the Lord to protect the believers always from the wiles of the adversary (108). The breaking of bread in §109 is accompanied by a prayer of thanksgiving and praise which is formulated in the first person plural and contains a great number of metaphors. (According to Junod and Kaestli, this paragraph is part of the gnostic interpolation in §§94–102.)

After the breaking of bread, the apostle takes Verus and two young brothers with baskets and shovels (§110) and goes to a tomb outside the city (§111), where he bids his companions dig a very deep trench. He then takes off his outer garments and lays them "as if they were bedding, at the bottom of the trench." Wearing only his under-garment, he raises his hands for a final prayer in three parts. At the beginning of this prayer (§112), he employs an expression—"O God, who have chosen us for the apostleship among the Gentiles"—that we tend rather to associate with Paul. At the heart of the twenty invocations of the Lord stand all the benefits that he bestows on the soul. This leads to the final petition that he may also take up the soul of the apostle.

In the second part of the prayer (§113), an autobiographical passage is particularly striking. As a young man, John wanted to marry, but the Lord appeared to him and said: "I am in need of you, John." When he attempted this a second time, the Lord prevented him by means of a bodily illness. On his third attempt, the Lord appeared to him "at the third hour on the sea" and said,

"John, if you were not mine, I would have let you marry." He blinds John for two years and restores his sight only in the third year. This means that John's marriage plans will never be realized. We should however note that the single state and the renunciation of sexual intercourse are demanded here only of particular persons; they are not elevated into a general norm. Despite an unmistakable devaluation of the bodily and sexual spheres, despite a culturally conditioned view of the female as defective, and despite a certain preference for sexual continence, the Acts of John do not propagate a universal encratism.

The third and final section of the prayer (§114) looks forward to the path that the apostle's soul will take after his death in order to reach its Lord. It will encounter obstacles—well known as "stage props" from mythical descriptions of what lies beyond the grave—and it must overcome these:

> And as I go to you, let the fire withdraw; let darkness be overcome; let chaos be powerless; let the furnace grow weak; let hell be extinguished, let the angels get behind me; let the demons be afraid. . . . Let the devil be brought to silence; let Satan be laughed to scorn.

After "sealing himself in every part" (with the sign of the cross?), the apostle lies down in the trench and says once again: "Peace be with you, brethren!" He then breathes his last (§115). Clearly, the knowledge that John had died a natural death was so firmly anchored in the tradition that it was impossible to work the story up into a more dramatic death such as martyrdom. Nevertheless, it was at this point that legends began to develop, as we see in the manuscripts of the close of ActJoh. Two of our main witnesses, the manuscripts R and Z, add that the brethren came to the tomb on the following day but could not find the apostle's body: He had been caught up to the Lord. According to another group of textual witnesses, on the following day all that remained were his sandals, but the soil bubbled up (perhaps because the apostle lay sleeping in the grave and moved the earth with his breathing). This reminded them of John 21:22, where Jesus says: "If it is my will that he remain until I come, what is that to you?" This leads directly into later hagiography and to the cult of relics that centered on John's tomb in Ephesus: as long as the church of Saint John stood, miraculous power was attributed to the dust from his grave.

7. Fragments That Cannot be Localized

The editors agree that a papyrus discovery from Oxyrhynchus (P.Oxy 850, from the fourth century; cf. NTApo 6th ed. II: 145f.; Junod and Kaestli, 118–22) belongs to ActJoh. The text on the *verso* side mentions a man named Zeuxis who wants to commit suicide, apparently out of despair (over a sin that he has committed?). John addresses a prayer to Jesus and administers the Eucharist to Zeuxis alone; the others do not dare to take part in the sacrament. The Roman proconsul appears, and letters are brought from the emperor that could concern either Zeuxis or John.

On the *recto* side of the papyrus, a new title mentions Andronicus. John wants to cross a bridge with several brethren. A man in soldier's uniform bars his path and threatens that the apostle will soon fall into his hands. John invokes the Lord, and the man vanishes. Clearly, it was the adversary who concealed himself behind this soldier.

These two episodes are found in this sequence, but in a considerably revised form, in a medieval Irish collection of legends, the *Liber Flavus* (NTApo 6th ed. II: 191–93). They are separated in this text by an intermezzo that relates that elderly women and widows among John's adherents complain that they receive too little of the wealth that the visitors bring to the apostle each day (cf. Acts 6:1). The apostle takes hay in his hand, changes it into pure gold, and has it melted and minted into coins. But then he throws the costly end product into the water, thereby demonstrating his independence and his love of poverty.

Finally, we have the pseudepigraphical letter of Paul to Titus, written in Latin in the fifth century (NTApo 6th ed. II: 147f.; Junod and Kaestli, 136–45), a work of propaganda for a life in virginity which refers three times to ActJoh: (1) It quotes John's thanksgiving that the Lord has preserved him from his childhood untouched by any woman (cf. ActJoh 113); (2) the demons admit to the deacon Dyrus, who may be identical to the Verus of ActJoh (cf. §30), that those who have remained unsullied by contact with women have power over the demons; (3) when he is invited to a wedding, the apostle addresses to the newly wedded couple an extremely vigorous attack on marital intercourse, which is "the experiment of the serpent, the ignorance of teaching, injury of the seed, the gift of death . . . the impediment which separates from the Lord, the beginning of disobedience," and so on. This would have consequences for our evaluation of the encratism of ActJoh, which we would have to judge both consistent and extreme. However, since other textual data contradict this, we must ask whether the specific intention of the author of the pseudepigraphical Letter has led him to intensify the polemic—or indeed, to put it more pointedly, whether John's sermon was a part of the ancient Acts of John at all.

C. Evaluation

Bibliography: P. J. Lallemann, *The Acts of John*. – **R. I. Pervo**, "Johannine Trajectories in the Acts of John." *Apocrypha* 3 (1992): 47–68. – **K. Schäferdiek**, "Herkunft und Interesse der alten Johannesakten." *ZNW* 74 (1983): 247–67. – **P. G. Schneider**, "The Acts of John: The Gnostic Transformation of a Christian Community." Pages 241–69 in *Hellenization Revisited: Shaping a Christian Response within the Greco-Roman World*. Edited by W. E. Helleman. Lanham: 1994. – **T. W. Thompson**, *Claiming Ephesus: The Apocryphal John and the Canonical Paul*. Term paper. Chicago: 2003.

The Christology of ActJoh has been described as a "christomonism" (*Schäferdiek*), and a look back over the preceding section of this chapter will confirm that this term is correct: Christ is the only true God, and this God is no one other than Jesus Christ, to whom the title "Father" also belongs. There is thus no distinction between two, let alone three divine Persons. It is only in the gnostic section that one can discern a measure of differentiation with an adumbration of triadic formulae, but we must ask how seriously the author takes the differentiation between the various names and titles; he may simply be playing with them (cf. Lallemann, 184). This equation between Jesus Christ and God the Father is made all the easier by the lack of any conscious recourse to the Old Testament in ActJoh. This obviates the need to respect the prior claims of the biblical image of God, the God of Israel. The obvious conclusion is that this Christ cannot be a genuine human being, and this is explicitly affirmed in the paragraphs that describe his polymorphy.

The gnostic section also eliminates the cross and physical suffering from the image of Christ. This means that this section fits well into the existing framework of the Acts of John and should not be judged a later interpolation by a different hand. It is more likely that a single author recognized the possibilities offered by the integration of a variety of traditions, for now the passion narrative, reshaped in the spirit of gnosis, casts a new light on the travel narratives. Each episode must be read anew and interpreted in a more decisively spiritual manner. For example, the miracles of raising the dead already possessed a transparency, but a re-reading offers the insight that resurrection happens here and now, in the midst of life on earth, wherever a person acquires knowledge.

It is surprising to see how single-mindedly the passion narrative of John is rewritten and its meaning reversed, since there are also clear affinities precisely to the Johannine theology, for example, in the use of metaphors, the treatment of the concept of *Logos*, and even in the characteristic Christology of ActJoh (e.g., the unity between the Father and the Son expressed in John 10:30 could have contributed to the elaboration of christomonism). This prompts the question whether there are direct historical links. The First Letter of John, which was written only a few decades before ActJoh, attacks an opposing Christology that appeals to the Gospel of John but already tends toward docetism. We see only the beginnings in the First Letter, but the full-blown development in ActJoh. If this is correct, we could trace the history of the Johannine community and of the schism that it has experienced (see 1 John 2:19) beyond the Corpus Johanneum itself into the second century.

This accords with a second characteristic of ActJoh, the focus on Ephesus. This seems intended to deprive the mainstream church of its apostle with his local tradition and to lay claim to him as the founder and hero of the author's own group. Besides this, many passages of the *vita* of John in ActJoh read like a counterfoil to the image of Paul in the Acts of the Apostles (cf. Thompson): It is John, not Paul, who is destined to be the apostle of the Gentile world. On the occasion of his early vocation, he becomes blind for a period. He brings Christianity into a city that clearly had not known it before. In Acts 19, Paul departs, thus evading a public conflict with Artemis of the Ephesians and her adherents, but John succeeds in reducing the entire temple of the goddess to rubble and ruins. He is guided on his path by visions, and once even by a double vision. A central (perhaps the most central) goal of ActJoh is to claim Ephesus for the author's own apostle, in opposition to the tradition of the mainstream church, in order thereby to demonstrate the correctness of his own theology and to ensure the cohesion of his own little group; and this supports the assumption that ActJoh was written in Asia Minor.

D. Later Narratives

The fact that the narratives of the life of John, which we shall now discuss, are later than the ancient ActJoh does not mean that they are dependent upon it; in most cases, the opposite is true. However, they often provided the context in which the surviving portions of ActJoh were transmitted, and they too can have preserved ancient traditional material. They also form the broad transition to the medieval hagiography in which John had a prominent place.

1. The Syriac History of John

Bibliography: **W. Wright,** *Apocryphal Acts*, Vol. 1: 4–65 (text); Vol. 2: 3–60 (translation). – **E. Junod and J.-D. Kaestli,** *Acta Iohannis* 705–17. – **R. A. Culpepper,** *John, the Son of Zebedee.* 223–30. (Gives the contents of this work.)

The *History of John* in Syriac, which according to Junod and Kaestli was composed at the end of the fourth century or perhaps even earlier, begins in Jerusalem shortly after Pentecost and then concentrates on Ephesus, like the ancient ActJoh. When one looks at the individual scenes, one sees that it does not follow ActJoh; but there are points of contact between the material of this work and Pseudo-Prochorus. An important section of the main narrative is set in a public bath in Ephesus, where John works as a servant. He makes the son of the proconsul, who visits the bath in the company of a prostitute, die for a short period. There is also an extensive account of John's clash with Artemis, her temple, her image, her priests, and her cult. Emperor Nero makes an appearance. Peter and Paul come to Ephesus in order to persuade John to write his gospel; the other three evangelists had already sent him their own works. John dies in his hermit's hut at the age of 120 (like Moses).

In its theology, especially trinitarian doctrine, Mariology, and the significance of the cross, the work remains strictly Catholic.

This suggests that its author, who may have been a monk, either did not know the ancient ActJoh or else consciously refrained from using them because of their heterodox views.

2. *The Acts of John* by Pseudo-Prochorus

Bibliography: T. Zahn, *Acta Ioannis* (Greek text). – **E. Junod and J.-D. Kaestli**, *Acta Ioannis*. 718–49. – **A. de Santos Otero**, NTApo, 6th ed. II: 385–91. – **R. A. Lipsius**, *Die apokryphen Apostelgeschichten*, Vol. 1: 355–408. – **R. A. Culpepper**, *John, the Son of Zebedee*. 206–22. (Detailed presentation of contents.)

"Prochorus" is the name of one of the seven "deacons" in Acts 6:5; the tradition sometimes also includes him among the seventy or seventy-two "other disciples" of Luke 10:1. In *The Acts of John* that bear his name and were probably written in the fifth century, perhaps at Antioch (cf. Junod and Kaestli), he also serves the apostle as his companion and secretary. This finds an iconographic echo in the numerous depictions of John dictating to Prochorus, who writes down his words. His work has points of contact with the ancient ActJoh above all in the scene of the apostle's death, as well as in the description of the period in Ephesus (in both instances, however, Junod and Kaestli deny any direct dependence upon ActJoh). Around two-thirds of Pseudo-Prochorus' *Acts of John* have nothing in common with the ancient ActJoh, for the simple reason that they relate events set on the island of Patmos. According to Pseudo-Prochorus (and in contrast to the prevailing opinion), it was on Patmos rather than in Ephesus that the apostle wrote his gospel.

The apostle survives a shipwreck at the very beginning of this work. He then performs many miracles of healing and raising the dead and fights successfully against demons, who are active inter alia in a bathhouse and take on the forms of Roman officers. He preaches and baptizes and brings about the collapse of pagan temples in Ephesus and on Patmos. He is sentenced to exile on Patmos by Emperor Trajan (according to another reading, by Hadrian)—one of the frequent anachronisms in this work—and remains there for fifteen years. Considerable space is given to his duel with the great magician Cynops, who practices his dark arts on the island. The people fear him because of his power, and take him to be a god (cf. Simon Magus in the Acts of Peter and the Pseudo-Clementines). The erotic element is provided by a mother who wants to persuade her twenty-four-year-old son to begin an incestuous relationship with her. When he refuses, she denounces him to the city governor, accusing him of precisely this crime. It is only by means of a massive punitive miracle that the apostle can restore good order. It is striking that the ascetic attitude, which often dominates in other texts, is not found in Pseudo-Prochorus: Existing marriages remain intact.

The somewhat stereotypical plot did not prevent this work from enjoying a great success—as can be seen in the approximately 150 manuscripts of the Greek text and the translations into most of the Christian oriental languages, as well as Latin and Slavonic.

3. *Virtutes Johannis, Passio Johannis*

Bibliography: E. Junod and J.-D. Kaestli, *Acta Iohannis.* 750–834. (With a newly constituted Latin text of the *Virtutes Johannis.*) – **L. Moraldi,** *Apocrifi.* 583–609. (Italian translation of the *Virtutes Johannis*) – **K. Schäferdiek,** "Die 'Passio Johannis' des Melito von Laodikeia und die 'Virtutes Johannis.' " *AnBoll* 103 (1985): 367–82.

The contents of the *Virtutes Johannis* (which is mostly to be found in the larger collection of the *Virtutes apostolorum* of Pseudo-Abdias) and of the *Passio Johannis* (which is attributed to Melito of Laodicea) are not limited to the death of the apostle. Basically, they are short Latin Acts of John from the fifth or sixth century that are either immediately dependent one on the other or else go back to a common (Greek?) original text. The *Virtutes* contain a very exact Latin translation of the episode of Drusiana from ActJoh 63–86 and the death scene from ActJoh 106–15. This basic stock is completed with other individual hagiographical traditions, some of which are ancient: the martyrdom of John in boiling oil, which he survives unharmed (already mentioned by Tertullian), the conversion of a young robber chief (known also to Clement of Alexandria), and the drinking of a cup containing poison, which we shall encounter in the following text as well.

4. The Acts of John in Rome

Bibliography: E. Junod and J.-D. Kaestli, *Acta Iohannis*. 835–86. (With a newly constituted Greek text and French translation.)

This very interesting text, which has received too little scholarly attention, is printed by Bonnet as §§1–14 of ActJoh. In the manuscripts, it is transmitted (in the more reliable of the two versions) together with ActJoh 106–15, but it is an independent unit.

The narrative begins with Vespasian's capture of Jerusalem and Domitian's access to power (Titus is omitted). Domitian plans to expel all the Jews from Rome (2), and they react by distancing themselves from the Christians in a letter that they address to him (3). The emperor now orders a general persecution of the Christians (4) and has John, whose fame has reached Rome, brought by soldiers from Ephesus to Rome (5). On his journey, the apostle lives on figs alone; he eats one fig every two days (6). John pays homage to the emperor with a humble greeting, quoting Proverbs 21:1, "The king's heart is in the hand of the Lord" (7). He must then explain what he means when he says that Jesus will rule as king (8). As evidence that his message is true, he himself asks for a strong poison, which he dissolves in water and drinks (9). Since it does not do him any harm (cf. Mark 16:18), its effectiveness is tested on a prisoner who is condemned to death—he dies at once (10), but John restores him to life (11). The emperor limits himself to banishing John to an island instead of having him executed as his earlier edict had envisaged (12). John goes to Patmos, where he writes the Apocalypse. In the reign of Trajan, he returns to Ephesus. On his death, he leaves Polycarp as his successor in the episcopal office in Ephesus (14).

The author seems to have used Eusebius, especially *Hist. eccl.* 3, for the historical data and the evaluation of imperial rule (cf. the individual details in the tables in Junod and Kaestli, 859f.). This an important indication of the date of the work: fifth century?

Chapter 2

The Acts of Paul

Editions: R. A. Lipsius, AAAp I: 23–44, 104–17, 235–72. – **C. Schmidt,** *Acta Pauli: Übersetzung, Untersuchungen und koptischer Text* (Aus der Heidelberger Koptischen Papyrushandschrift Nr. 1). 2nd ed. Leipzig: 1905. Repr. Hildesheim: 1965. – **C. Schmidt and W. Schubert,** *Praxeis Paulou: Acta Pauli, Nach dem Papyrus der Hamburger Staats- und Universitätsbibliothek* (Veröffentlichungen aus der Hamburger Staats- und Universitätsbibliothek 2). Glückstadt: 1936. – **O. von Gebhardt,** *Passio S. Theclae virginis. Die lateinischen Übersetzungen der Acta Pauli et Theclae nebst Fragmenten, Auszügen und Beilagen* (TU 22, 2). Leipzig: 1902. – **L. Vouaux,** *Les Actes de Paul et ses lettres apocryphes: Introduction, textes, traduction et commentaire.* Paris: 1913. (Greek text.) – **W. Wright,** *Apocryphal Acts,* Vol. 1: 128–69 (Syriac text); Vol. 2: 116–45 (English translation).

Translations: W. Schneemelcher, NTApo 6th ed. II:193–241. – **J. K. Elliott,** *Apocryphal NT.* 350–89. – **W. Rordorf.** Pages 1115–77 in *Écrits apocryphes chrétiens,* Vol. 1. Edited by F. Bovon and P. Geoltrain. (Particularly important because this translation is partly based on hitherto unpublished textual material; Rordorf's new division into chapters is given in square brackets).

Bibliography: J. N. Bremmer, ed. *The Apocryphal Acts of Paul and Thecla* (Studies on the Apocryphal Acts of the Apostles 2). Kampen: 1996. – **A. G. Brock,** "Genre of the Acts of Paul: One Tradition Enhancing Another." *Apocrypha* 5 (1994): 119–36. – **D. R. MacDonald,** *The Legend and the Apostle. The Battles for Paul in Story and Canon.* Philadelphia: 1983. – **W. Rordorf,** *Lex orandi—Lex credendi. Gesammelte Aufsätze* (Paradosis 36). Fribourg (Switz.): 1993. 368–496. – **W. Schneemelcher,** *Gesammelte Aufsätze zum Neuen Testament und zur Patristik* (Analecta Vlatadon 22). Thessalonica: 1974. 154–239.

A. Context

Bibliography: S. L. Davies, "Women, Tertullian and the Acts of Paul." *Semeia* 38 (1986): 139–44. – **A. Hilhorst**, "Tertullian on the Acts of Paul." Pages 150–63 in *The Apocryphal Acts of Paul*. Ed. J. N. Bremmer. – **W. Rordorf**, "Tertullien et les Actes de Paul (à propos de bapt. 17.5)." Pages 475–84 in idem, *Lex Orandi*.

At a relatively early date, ca. 200, Tertullian mentions the Acts of Paul (ActPaul) in his treatise on baptism (*Bapt.*, 17.5). Thanks to problems in the textual transmission, the original text of this celebrated passage is uncertain, and it has even been questioned whether it does in fact refer to ActPaul. The following English translation follows the standard Latin edition of the text by J. W. P. Borleffs (CChrSL 1, 291f.):

> But if certain women defend the Acts of Paul, which are falsely so named, with regard to the right of women [after the example of Thecla] to teach and to baptize, let them know that in Asia the presbyter who compiled that document, thinking to complete Paul's authority by his own authority, was found out. He admitted that he had done it only out of love for Paul, and he laid down his office.

Tertullian and other representatives of the church are moved to anger by disciplinary questions. The presbyter mentioned here, who avoided an imminent deposition by laying down his office, is not accused of heresy. Origen, too, quotes two or three times from ActPaul at this period, without seeing any problem. One quotation not found in the surviving text of ActPaul is in *De principiis* 1.2.3, where Origen is speaking of the Word who has become a person: "And therefore that language which is used in the Acts of Paul, where it is said that 'here is the Word a living being,' appears to me to be rightly used. John, however, with more sublimity and propriety, says in the beginning of his Gospel . . ." (English translation by A. Roberts and A. Donaldson, *Ante-Nicene Fathers*, Vol. 4, Peabody, Mass.: 1994). This last remark preserves the precedence of the writings collected together in the New Testament. Eusebius makes a distinction between ActPaul and the other apocryphal Acts and includes it among the "not indubitably genuine" or "not universally acknowledged" writings. He mentions it in the same breath as the highly respected *Shepherd* of Hermas (*Hist. eccl.* 3.5f.). In the course of the present chapter, we shall cite other mentions in patristic texts that are more critical—especially when we discuss the baptized lion. The picture changes fundamentally only when ActPaul also came to play a role in Manichaeism and in the struggle against this religion.

ActPaul must have been a very extensive work, rather longer than Luke's Acts of the Apostles, because the *Stichometry* of Nicephorus says that it ran to 3,600 *stichoi* (by comparison, in the list of the Codex Claromontanus, Luke's Acts run to 2,600 *stichoi* and ActPaul to 3,650). Over the centuries, however, only parts of the whole work were used and transmitted in various ways. Three large units have survived:

1. The Acts of Thecla (ActThecla) were regarded as an independent work and became extremely popular. About eighty Greek manuscripts containing its text are now known (as opposed to the eleven manuscripts that Lipsius used in his edition) as well as four Latin versions (cf. von Gebhardt) and translations into Christian oriental languages. Although it is a part of ActPaul, ActThecla is not a completely free creation by the author. It goes back to oral and probably written traditions that had grown up around the heroine Thecla. It is also significant that the textual transmission of the Pastoral Letters was influenced by the legend of Thecla. At 2 Timothy 3:11, where the text speaks of the sufferings of Paul in Antioch, the critical apparatus mentions the gloss: "These are the (sufferings) which he endured because of Thecla" (and this is a very benevolent interpretation of Paul's conduct in this situation; see below). The critical apparatus to 2 Timothy 4:19 identifies the members of the household of Onesiphorus as "Lectra, his wife, and his sons Simmias and Zeno"; cf. ActThecla 2.

2. The exchange of letters between Paul and Corinth (3 Corinthians). Via the Syriac canon, 3 Cor became a part of the Armenian New Testament canon. Papyrus Bodmer (P.Bodm) 10, published only in 1959, is evidence of an isolated Greek version of 3 Cor; this has been taken to indicate that the correspondence predates ActPaul and that it was integrated into this work by the author, who provided the introduction and a narrative intermezzo. Novelists, historians, and the authors of forensic discourses all liked to insert epistolary sections of this kind into their work.

3. The Martyrdom of Paul (MartPaul) was a suitable reading on feasts of Paul and therefore survived as an independent text. Four Greek manuscripts are known, as well as translations into

several ancient languages that play a role in the constitution of the text. A more detailed sixth-century Latin paraphrase of MartPaul is attributed by some manuscripts to Linus, the first successor of Peter in Rome (cf. AAAp I: 23–44).

Important progress was made at the beginning of the twentieth century, when Carl Schmidt edited a sixth-century Coptic papyrus from Heidelberg (P.Heid). Although this text is very fragmentary, it is clear that it contained ActPaul in its entirety with a number of new, hitherto unknown scenes. The surprise was that ActThecla, 3 Corinthians and MartPaul were woven seamlessly into the story as a whole. Later, Schmidt edited a Greek papyrus from Hamburg (P.Hamb, written ca. 300) that likewise contains the Martyrdom but also includes a new discovery, material from an episode relating Paul's fight against the beasts in Ephesus. Other papyrus discoveries—which are still being made—overlap in part with texts that are already known (e.g., P.Oxy 6 corresponds to ActThecla 8f.; P.Oxy 1602 corresponds to P.Hamb p. 8, lines 9–26, something the editors of the Oxyrhnychus papyri did not recognize; and P.Ant. 13 to ActThecla 2f.), but they also contribute additional insights at a number of neuralgic points (e.g., at the transition from the main narrative to the account of Paul's martyrdom).

Tertullian is probably correct to say that this impressive work was written in Asia Minor. The author's educational level and knowledge of the Bible are what we could ideally expect in a presbyter of that period. ActPaul must have been written before 200, since it had already attracted attention by then, and the news had reached Tertullian in North Africa. It is probably later than the composition of ActJoh, because it was most likely the latter work, as the oldest representative of this narrative type, that inspired the author to write his novel about Paul. This brings us (bearing in mind the dating of ActJoh) to ca. 170–180.

We conclude this section with a detail that may be coincidental, but is interesting: Schmidt (*Acta Pauli*, 205 n. 1) entertains the possibility that ActPaul was written in Smyrna, because inscriptions from this city contain a number of names that are also found in ActPaul; and it will be recalled that Smyrna also has been suggested as the place of composition of ActJoh.

B. Contents

1. The Beginning of the Acts of Paul (P.Heid pp. 60, 59, 61f., 1–6; P.Ryl.Copt)

Bibliography: W. E. Crum, "New Coptic Manuscripts in the John Rylands Library." *BJRL* 5 (1920): 497–503 (501).

Fragments of the beginning of ActPaul [1] survive in a Coptic papyrus from the John Rylands Library and in P.Heid pp. 59–62 (the high numbering of these pages is due to changes made by Schmidt and subsequent scholars to the order of the pages in the original publication). According to these manuscripts, the work began with a description of the conversion of Saul outside Damascus, followed by his visit to the community in that city, probably including a sermon. After receiving a divine directive, Paul then goes to Jerusalem, where he probably spends some time (inter alia, the name of Peter, with whom Paul had discussions in Jerusalem [Gal 1:18], is clearly legible on p. 59, line 7).

P.Heid pp. 1–6 gives a somewhat clearer account of Paul's activity in Antioch [2], but it is not completely clear whether this is the Syrian or the Pisidian city of this name. (Here, at the beginning of the work, however, it is more likely that Syrian Antioch is meant, both because this follows Jerusalem better, and above all because Pisidian Antioch gets a great scene of its own later on.) Paul incurs the hatred of the local Jews by raising the son of Anchares (or Panchares) from the dead. They chase him from the city with stones. The Acts of Thecla [3–4] begin with the intermediate title "[After the flight from] Antioch, when [he] wanted to go up to Iconium." Fortunately, we have a much broader attestation for ActThecla.

2. The Acts of Thecla [3–4]

Bibliography: C. Büllesbach, "'Ich will mich rundherum scheren und dir folgen': Begegnungen zwischen Paulus und Thekla in den Acta Pauli et Theclae." Pages 125–46 in *Körper und Kommunikation: Beiträge aus der theologischen Genderforschung.* Edited by K. Greschat and H. Omerzu. Leipzig: 2003. – **M. Ebner,** ed. *Aus Liebe zu Paulus? Die Akte Thekla neu aufgerollt* (SBS 206). Stuttgart: 2005. – **A. Jensen,** *Thekla—Die Apostolin.*

Ein apokrypher Text neu entdeckt (KT 172). Gütersloh: 1999. – **S. F. Johnson**, *The Life and Miracles of Thekla: A Literary Study* (Hellenic Studies 13). Washington, D.C.: 2006.

Demas (cf. 2 Tim 4:10) and Hermogenes (cf. 2 Tim 1:15) the coppersmith (cf. 2 Tim 4:14) join Paul on his travels. When one recalls the negative description of these men in the Pastoral Letters, one is not surprised to see that they are portrayed here in §1 as hypocrites who merely pretend to love Paul. Paul, however, shows no signs of noticing this, but tells them above all about the birth and the resurrection of Jesus Christ. His words are directed at weak points in their own understanding of the faith, which is colored by gnosis.

A Portrait

Bibliography: J. Bollók, "The Description of Paul in the Acta Pauli." Pages 1–15 in *The Apocryphal Acts of Paul*. Edited by J. N. Bremmer. – **R. M. Grant**, "The Description of Paul in the Acts of Paul and Thecla." *VigChr* 36 (1982): 1–4. – **A. J. Malherbe**, "A Physical Description of Paul." *HTR* 76 (1986): 170–75; repr. pages 165–70 in idem, *Paul and the Popular Philosophers*. Minneapolis: 1989. – **P. Zanker**, *Die Maske des Sokrates. Das Bild des Intellektuellen in der antiken Kunst*. Munich: 1995.

Onesiphorus (cf. 1 Tim 1:16; 4:19) comes from Iconium with his entire family to meet Paul and welcomes him into his house. Titus has given him a description of Paul's appearance, and he looks carefully at every passer-by to see if he matches this. Section 3 then gives us its very remarkable portrait of the apostle:

> And he saw Paul coming, a man small in size, bald-headed, bandy-legged, of noble mien, with eyebrows meeting, rather hook-nosed, full of grace. Sometimes he seemed like a man, and sometimes he had the face of an angel (cf. Acts 6:15).

The rather unflattering traits of this "mixed" portrait are probably suggested by the way in which Paul's opponents describe his body, as he writes in 2 Corinthians 10:10, "His bodily presence is weak." We should also note that this sketch includes several culturally determined evaluations. We find parallels in the description of an able general (Grant) and in a "wanted poster" on papyrus for an escaped slave (Bollók). Scholars have drawn attention to ancient handbooks on physiognomy, where eyebrows that meet in the middle of the face are a sign of beauty and a hawked nose is a kingly feature (Malherbe). An outstanding example of this is no less a personage than Emperor Augustus: "His teeth were wide apart, small, and ill kept; his hair was slightly curly and inclining to golden; his eyebrows met. His ears were of moderate size, and his nose projected a little at the top and then bent slightly inward" (Suetonius, *Augustus* 79.2; English translation: J. C. Rolfe, Loeb Classical Library, London: 1913). Another cultural link is even more important: what we encounter here is the same "adaptation of the iconography of the apostles to ancient types of philosopher" that we find in the visual arts (Zanker, 284). In the case of Paul, the obvious model is Socrates, who was no exceptional beauty but whose characteristic head established criteria for the way in which a philosopher was expected to look.

In Love with the Word

Bibliography: P. Tohey, "Love, Lovesickness, and Melancholy." *Illinois Classical Studies* 17 (1992): 265–86.

When he arrives at the house of Onesiphorus, Paul breaks bread and proclaims "the word of God about abstinence and the resurrection," which he elaborates in a series of twelve beatitudes (there are thirteen in AAAp I: 238–40, but the second-to-last macarism, the first part of which agrees literally with Matthew 5:7, is missing in P.Heid and may be a later interpolation). Their unmistakable center is sexual continence: "Blessed are those who have kept the flesh chaste . . . Blessed are the continent . . . Blessed are those who have wives as if not having them" (5; cf. 1 Cor 7:29). Even the macarism "Blessed are those who have kept the baptism, for they shall be refreshed by the Father and the Son" (6) can be interpreted as a reference to the renunciation of marriage as a precondition of baptism. The last and longest beatitude, which applies to the virgins, prepares the appearance on the scene of the main person in the following paragraph.

While Paul is speaking, Thecla is sitting in the window of the neighboring house. She cannot see Paul, but she listens avidly to him as he speaks about the virginal life by day and by night (7). After this has gone on for three days, her mother Theoclia alerts

Thamyris, Thecla's fiancé (we should note the alliteration in the names of the characters; this phenomenon recurs in other parts of ActPaul as well). In the account Theoclia gives, she reduces Paul's preaching to one single sentence: "He says one must fear only one God and live in chastity." She describes her daughter's conduct vividly as an inverted form of intense love: "My daughter, clinging to the window like a spider, lays hold of what is said by him with a strange eagerness and fearful emotion" (9). They both speak to Thecla, attempting to win her over, but are unsuccessful. A great lamentation breaks out in the house.

Contrary Measures

Thamyris does not give up so easily. On the street outside the house of Onesiphorus, he encounters Demas and Hermogenes and promises to give them gold. He invites them to a lavish meal in his house, where they summarize Paul's message in one single, highly pointed sentence: "There is for you no resurrection unless you remain chaste and do not pollute the flesh" (12; cf. Rev 14:4). Against this view, they put forward their own version: The resurrection "has already come [cf. 2 Tim 2:18] in the children whom we have, and we rise again, after having come to the knowledge of the true God" (14)—a strange mixture of trust in the sequence of the generations (as a form of bodily resurrection, unless they mean "spiritual" children, i.e. those who have converted to the beliefs held by Demas and Hermogenes) and a gnostic-sounding evaluation of knowledge (as a spiritual resurrection), which at any rate amounts to a realized eschatology. They give Thamyris the concrete advice that he should accuse Paul before the Roman governor Castellius of being a Christian missionary. Here, the mere name of "Christian" seems sufficient grounds for punishment.

In a sequence of scenes that recalls the story of Jesus' passion, Thamyris seizes Paul and brings him to the proconsul. The crowd who arrests him cies out: "Away with the sorcerer, for he has misled all our wives!" (15; they give the impression that he has practiced magic to gain their love). Thamyris demands that the proconsul should ask why Paul "makes virgins averse to marriage" (16). In his lengthy reply (17), Paul does not address this question directly but speaks more generally of the necessity to preach the gospel in order to save those who are lost (a direct reference to the immediate issue can be seen only in the words, ". . . that I may rescue them from corruption and uncleanness and from all pleasure"). The proconsul throws him into prison "until he had time to hear him more attentively" (cf. Acts 24:25).

Thecla visits him in the prison by night. She bribes the gatekeeper with her bracelet and the jailer with a silver mirror (both of which are female accessories) so that she can sit at Paul's feet and listen to his words (18). She kisses his fetters and is later found "riveted" to the place where he taught. In the context, this can perhaps be interpreted as a form of passive resistance ("she rolls herself into a ball," cf. Vouaux, 183).

The First Martyrdom of Thecla

Bibliography: K. M. Coleman, "Fatal Charades: Roman Execution Staged as Mythological Enactments." *JRS* 80 (1990): 44–73. – **D. G. Kyle**, *Spectacles of Death in Ancient Rome*. London: 1998.

In the meantime, Thecla's mother and Thamyris, who have been looking for her, track her down and bring the matter once again before the governor. He first interrogates Paul and "gladly hears him speak about the holy works of Christ" (20), and then questions Thecla, who never averts her gaze from Paul. Her own mother (in this scene an evil mother, as in fairy-tales) is the spokeswoman for the crowd: "Burn the wicked one; burn her who will not marry in the midst of the theater, that all the women who have been taught by this man may be afraid." The governor has Paul flogged and expelled from the city but condemns Thecla to be burned at the stake (21).

Many people throng together to witness this great "spectacle" (we recall here what was said above, with regard to ActJoh 30f., about the "theatricalization" of public life). "But as a lamb in the wilderness looks around for the shepherd, so Thecla kept searching for Paul." She sees the Lord, in the form of Paul, sitting in the crowd, and she is content, although he disappears into heaven.

Meanwhile, young men and women bring wood and straw for the pyre. Thecla is brought out naked—a sight that moves the governor to tears. When she stands on the pyre, "she fulfilled the form (*tupos*) of the cross" (22); a part of the Latin tradition interprets this to mean that she stretches out her arms in the form of a cross, while other textual witnesses say that she makes the sign of the cross upon herself. The fire is kindled and blazes up but does not touch Thecla, because God makes "an underground rumbling, and a cloud full of water and hail overshadowed the theater from above" (22). This cascades down on the crowd so that the floods of water put many of them at risk; some indeed die. The fire is extinguished, and Thecla is saved.

Paul and Thecla Meet Again

A sudden change of scene in §23 takes us into a public cemetery on the road from Iconium to Daphne, where Paul has spent some days (six, as we later learn) with the family of Onesiphorus, fasting. The children are hungry, so Paul takes off his upper garment and sends a boy to sell it and buy bread with the money. When he is making his purchases, the boy sees his neighbor Thecla, who has been searching for Paul since her rescue. The boy leads her to him.

When they enter the cemetery, they hear Paul praying: "Father of Christ, let not the fire touch Thecla, but stand by her, for she is yours" (§24). Thecla responds with a prayer which affirms that the whole point of her rescue was that she might see Paul once more. In great joy, all those present celebrate a community meal with five loaves, vegetables, and water (one manuscript adds salt). Thecla declares: "I will cut my hair off and I shall follow you wherever you go" (§25; cf. Matt 8:19 par.). To cut off her hair would be per se a sign of disgrace for a woman (cf. 1 Cor 11:5f.), but this action may mean here that Thecla wishes to disguise herself as a man so that she may be able to take part in the apostle's itinerant life without hindrance or harassment. Paul seems not to reject this proposal in principle, when he speaks of the evil times, the beauty of Thecla, and the risk of even harder trials. Thecla asks that she may be strengthened for all this with the seal of baptism, but Paul puts her off: "Thecla, be patient; you shall receive the water."

In Antioch: Thecla and Tryphaena

Bibliography: F. Augar, *Die Frau im römischen Christenprozeß: Ein Beitrag zur Verfolgungsgeschichte der christlichen Kirche im römischen Reich* (TU 28.4c). Leipzig: 1905.

Paul sends Onesiphorus with his family back to Iconium and takes
Thecla with him to Antioch (in Pisidia). When they enter the city,
an aristocratic Syrian named Alexander sees them and falls pas-
sionately in love with Thecla. He attempts to bribe Paul with
money and gifts, but the apostle takes his distance: "I know not the
woman of whom you speak, nor is she mine" (§26). Alexander then
embraces Thecla on the open street. She does not accept this and
fights him off after she has looked around in vain for Paul. She
tears off Alexander's upper garment, pulls the garland off his hair
(on which, in keeping with the Syrian custom, there is an image of
the emperor), and makes him a laughingstock.

Filled with love and with shame, Alexander leads Thecla
before the governor, who condemns her to fight against the beasts.
This is to Alexander's advantage because, according to P.Heid, it
was he who had responsibility for holding the games (cf. also §30).
The women of the city are enraged, and cry out: "Evil judgment!
Impious judgment!" (§27). Thecla expresses the wish that she may
remain untouched until her sentence is carried out, instead of
being thrown into a brothel or raped in prison, as might very well
have happened (cf. Augar). In order to accommodate this wish, a
rich woman named Tryphaena (according to some manuscripts,
she was in fact a queen), whose own daughter has just died, takes
Thecla into her house. Historically speaking, an Antonia
Tryphaena is attested to as the daughter of Ptolemy I of Pontus
and the wife or widow of Cotys, king of Thrace, in the first century (cf. KP I, 415). This may have inspired the author to use this
particular name (cf. also Rom 16:12).

In the meantime, to get the crowd into the right mood, a
parade of wild animals is held, with Thecla either sitting on a
lioness (according to the Coptic text) or chained to the cage of a
lioness (according to another version). A tablet with the inscription "desecrator of the temple" displays her guilt (cf. Mark 15:26;
the meaning of this accusation is obscure unless it refers to the
"sacrilege" that Thecla committed when she tore the garland with
the image of the emperor from Alexander's head). All are astonished to see the wild lioness lick Thecla's feet; thus, the gender solidarity encompasses even the world of the animals.

In Tryphaena's house, a mother–daughter relationship develops between the two women. We learn that the deceased daughter, whose place Thecla now takes, was called Falconilla, and that

she has adjured her mother in a dream to take care of Thecla, so "that she may pray for me and I may come to the place of the just" (28). When Alexander fetches Thecla for her fight with the beasts on the following morning, Tryphaena prays for her: "God of Thecla, my child, help Thecla!" (30). Thecla also prays, but not for herself: She asks that Tryphaena, who had compassion on her and protected her chastity, may be rewarded (31).

The Second Martyrdom of Thecla

Bibliography: M. P. Aymer, "Hailstorms and Fireballs: Redaction, World Creation, and Resistance in the Acts of Paul and Thecla." *Semeia* 79 (1997): 45–61. – **K. M. Coleman**, "Launching into History: Aquatic Displays in the Early Empire." *JRS* 83 (1993): 48–74. – **H. Schneider**, "Thekla und die Robben." *VigChr* 55 (2001): 45–57.

Temperatures are already running high in the theater, where the roar of the beasts mingles with the din of the crowd. Some of the women who are present demand the death of the woman who has desecrated the temple, but others deplore the disgraceful spectacle (§32). Thecla is stripped but is given an apron (a concession to the sensibilities of Christian readers?) and is pushed into the stadium, where lions and bears are let loose on her. A lioness (the one from the cage in §28?) lies down at Thecla's feet and tears to pieces a she-bear that tries to attack Thecla. The lioness then engages in combat with a lion which belongs to Alexander and has been trained to fight against human beings; both animals die (§33).

In the meantime Thecla has prayed with outstretched arms. When she looks around after ending her prayer, she sees a great pit full of water (this was used in ancient stadiums e.g. for the staging of sea battles; cf. Coleman) with seals swimming in it (as mentioned also in *Physiologus* 40). Clearly, the seals are regarded as dangerous monsters from the deep, because the women warn Thecla against them, and the governor assumes that they will eat Thecla. (Combats in the circus between bears and seals—improbable as it may sound—are attested in the imperial age; cf. Schneider.) Thecla's reaction is to say, "Now it is time to wash myself," and she throws herself into the water with the words, "In the name of Jesus Christ, I baptize myself on my last day" (§34). The seals see a flash of lightning and float dead on the surface of the water—an ironical sideswipe, since some believed that seals

had the function of lightning conductors. A cloud of fire sur-
rounds Thecla, so that she cannot be seen in her nakedness.

At the next attempt, when other terrifying beasts are let loose
upon Thecla, the women throw nard, cassia, and other spices into
the arena. The beasts are "hypnotized" (by the aromas and herbs?)
and do her no harm. Alexander makes one last suggestion, with a
scarcely veiled sexual aggression that astonishes even this coars-
ened crowd (cf. Vouaux, 217: "The author has really exaggerated
here"). "They bound her by the feet between the bulls and put
red-hot irons under their genitals so that they, being rendered
more furious, might kill her. They rushed forward but the burning flame around her consumed the ropes." Once again, she suffers no harm (§35).

Thecla Is Rescued

Tryphaena, who is watching at the gates of the arena, is so horri-
fied by the sight of this unbridled cruelty that she falls in a faint.
This greatly frightens the governor and Alexander, since
Tryphaena is both a queen—the title is used by her maids here—
and (as Alexander says) a relative of the emperor. If anything happens to her, the emperor will inflict a harsh punishment on the
entire city (§36). The governor summons Thecla and asks her why
the beasts have not touched her. Thecla answers with a confession
of faith (§37). He has clothes brought for her and declares in an
official document: "I release to you the pious Thecla, the servant
of God." All the women join in a grateful acclamation: "One is the
God, who saved Thecla" (§38).

Tryphaena also hears this good news (§39: *euaggelistheisan*) and
confesses her faith that the dead are raised up and that her daughter Falconilla lives. Thecla rests in her house for eight days and
instructs (*katêkhêsen*) those present in the Word of God, so that
not only Tryphaena but also most of her maids come to faith.

The End of the Story

Thecla yearns to see Paul, and when she hears that he is in Myra,
she sews for herself an upper garment like that worn by men and
goes to that city. She tells him, "I have received baptism, O Paul;
for he who worked with you for the [preaching of the] gospel has
worked with me also for baptism" (41; cf. Gal 2:8). After relating

all that has happened to her, she tells him that she intends to return to Iconium. Paul sends her away, charging her; "Go and teach the Word of God" (41).

In the house of Onesiphorus in Iconium, Thecla throws herself to the ground at the place where Paul had sat and *taught the Word of God* (we should note the parallelism between what Paul does and what Thecla does) and addresses a prayer to Jesus Christ who has helped her in all her distress (42). Thamyris is now dead; Thecla addresses conciliatory words to her mother Theoclia, but we are not told how she reacts. Thecla then departs for Seleucia (in Cilicia or Isauria), where she works and then dies peacefully some time later (43). This ending seems abrupt, and it is possible that something has dropped out when the material about Thecla was integrated into ActPaul, such as the actual administration of baptism by Thecla that is presupposed by Tertullian in the text quoted above.

This undramatic conclusion is the point where the legendary elaboration of the story begins already in the manuscripts (texts in AAAp I: 267–72; translations in Elliott, 372–74). We learn inter alia that Thecla was eighteen years old when she fought with the beasts and lived in Seleucia for a further seventy-two years. Her house in that city develops into a place of pilgrimage for women and becomes the center of their ascetic community life. Thecla's successful healings provoke the jealousy of the local physicians, who plan to rape her and thus deprive her of her virginity—the supposed cause of this power of hers. But Thecla finds refuge in a rock, which opens up to receive her. According to one version, she travels under the earth, following Paul to Rome, where she is buried near his tomb.

Although Paul makes one more appearance here, it is clear that he is not the protagonist of the Acts of Thecla. It is she who has the principal role. She grows into an independent herald of the faith. What Paul does—or refrains from doing—often appears in a very dubious light unless the reader decides to interpret his behavior as a pedagogical measure intended to teach Thecla to stand on her own feet. The stage is free for the great appearances of Paul only when Thecla has left it.

3. The Main Body of the Acts of Paul

From this point, we depend primarily on P.Heid and (especially for Ephesus) on P.Hamb, until we come to the Martyrdom of Paul. For the reconstruction of the narrative sequence, we follow NTApo 6th ed. and Rordorf.

In Myra (P.Heid pp. 28–35) [5]

Paul plays an energetic part in another family drama that takes place in Myra, this time involving Hermocrates, his wife Nympha, their elder son Hermippus, and their younger son Dion. Hermocrates suffers from dropsy and asks Paul to heal him. At once a great quantity of water flows out of his body, and he falls down as if dead. Paul takes him by the hand, raises him to his feet, and gives him a loaf to eat as a demonstration that he has been restored to health. Hermocrates and his wife receive the "seal" of baptism.

The elder son, Hermippus, reacts with anger to the healing because he has been looking forward to his inheritance, and he seeks an occasion to kill Paul. The younger son, Dion, hears Paul gladly but falls down from somewhere and dies (cf. Acts 20:7-12). The unhappy mother brings Paul the sad news. Hermippus remains beside the body and begins to lament, but probably only in order to have a further excuse to attack Paul. A page of the manuscript is missing here; it must have related the raising of Dion from the dead, to which Hermippus himself later alludes.

By night, an angel announces to Paul that a combat awaits him but that he will be victorious. In the morning, Hermippus comes with a drawn sword, accompanied by men of his own age carrying cudgels. Paul defends himself in words that include a self-description echoing his portrait in ActThecla 3: "I am alone, a stranger, small and of no significance among the heathen." When Hermippus attempts to rush upon Paul, he is immediately blinded. He repents at once and asks his friends not to abandon him in his distress. Now that he realizes how false his greed was, he confesses his wrong conduct toward Paul and beseeches everyone to ask Paul to heal him.

His friends set him down before the door of the house where Paul has gone to teach. Hermippus humbly touches the feet of all

those who enter, including his own parents. They are are deeply
troubled at this, although there ought in fact to be joy at the raising of Dion, and Hermocrates distributes money among the widows to mark this occasion. Hermippus recovers his health at the
prayers of his parents and Paul. He sees what is happening in a
kind of vision: "Paul came and laid his hand upon me while I wept.
And in that hour I saw all things clearly." The text breaks off at this
point. A whole page is probably missing before the surviving fragment with the concluding lines; this may have contained a lengthy
sermon by Paul.

In Sidon and Tyre (P.Heid pp. 35–40) [6–7]

Paul's departure from Myra causes great grief to the brothers and
sisters. Two married couples, Thrasymachus and Cleon with their
wives Aline and Chrysa, accompany him on his journey to Sidon.
En route, they rest in order to share bread together, apparently at
a place that a pagan deity claims for itself. The concepts "idol"
(eidôlon) and "table of the demons" (cf. 1 Cor 10:21) can be made
out in the fragmentary text, which speaks of a deadly danger and
of the protection bestowed by faith in Jesus Christ. A group of
local inhabitants arrive on the scene. One of them, an aged man,
puts forward the opposite argument: It is precisely the renunciation of the old gods (by Christians?) that has demonstrably led to
death in many cases. Paul's rebuttal, which certainly followed
these words, has not survived.

In Sidon, Paul warns the inhabitants that they must not incur
the punishment that fell on Sodom and Gomorrah (they probably
wanted to assault the foreign visitors in the same way as the inhabitants of Sodom sought to assault the guests in the house of Lot: see
Gen 19). First, however, they shut up the three men (Paul,
Thrasymachus, and Cleon) in the temple of Apollo, the god of the
city, and serve them a rich meal (perhaps because they are later to
be sacrificed). But Paul fasts, prays, and utters lamentations. One
half of the temple—probably where the idol stood—collapses, but
the other part—where the prisoners are kept—remains unharmed.
The eyewitnesses proclaim in the city: "Apollo the god of the
Sidonians has fallen and half of his temple." Paul and his companions weep because they are once again to be made a spectacle (the-
atron, cf. 1 Cor 4:9), and the crowd does in fact shout: "Bring them

to the theater!" We learn no details about the happy outcome of
these events. All that can be gleaned from the surviving text is that
at the end, everyone praises the God who has sent Paul to them,
and that a man named Theudas asks for the seal of baptism.

⋅ It is no longer possible to grasp clearly what takes place in
Tyre. Jews appear; we read the names Amphion and Chrysippus;
and Paul conquers demons in the power of God. A man who had
a son who had been born dumb—with this beginning of a miracle
of healing, the last legible fragment ends. (In Rordorf, there follow two very fragmentary pieces: one that mentions a stay in Tyre
[7] and one that speaks of a journey to Jerusalem, Cilicia, and
Smyrna [8].)

In Ephesus (P.Hamb pp. 1-6) [9]

Bibliography: R. Kasser, "Acta Pauli 1959." *RHPR* 40 (1960): 45–57.
– Idem, NTApo 6th ed. II: 241–43. – Idem, Pages 1151–56 in *Écrits apoc-
ryphes chrétiens*, Vol. 1. Edited by F. Bovon and P. Geoltrain. – Idem **and
P. Luisier**, "Le Papyrus Bodmer XLI en Édition Princeps. L'Épisode
d'Éphèse des Acta Pauli en Copte et en Traduction." *Le Muséon* 17
(2004): 281–384. – **T. Adamik**, "The Baptized Lion in the Acts of Paul."
Pages 60–74 in *The Apocryphal Acts of Paul*. Edited by J. N. Bremmer.
– **H. J. W. Drijvers**, "Der getaufte Löwe und die Theologie der Acta
Pauli." Chap. 10 in *History and Religion in Late Antique Syria* (Variorum
Collected Study Series CS 464). Edited by idem. Aldershot: 1994. – **D.
R. MacDonald**, "A Conjectural Emendation of 1 Cor 15:31-32: Or the
Case of the Misplaced Lion Fight." *HTR* 73 (1980): 265–76. – **C. R.
Matthews**, "Articulate Animals." 206–10. – **B. M. Metzger**, "St Paul
and the Baptized Lion." *PSB* 39 (1945): 11–21. – **W. Rordorf**, "Quelques
jalons pour une interprétation symbolique des Actes de Paul." Pages
251–65 in *Early Christian Voices: In Texts, Traditions, and Symbols*
(Festschrift for F. Bovon) (BIS 66). Leiden: 2003. – **W. Schneemelcher**,
"Der getaufte Löwe in den Acta Pauli." Pages 223–29 in *Gesammelte
Aufsätze*. Edited by idem.

The first five pages of the Greek P.Hamb offer the textual basis for
the period that the apostle spends in Ephesus. For the prior history, we can also draw on a Coptic papyrus from the Bodmer collection. We begin with this fragment.

Paul comes from Smyrna to Ephesus and visits the house of
Aquila and Prisca. The appearance of an angel, who speaks to Paul
in tongues (?) so that those who are present understand nothing,

inspires Paul to a flashback. Shortly after his own conversion, he was making his way to Jericho by night, accompanied by two women and immersed in prayer. A terrifying lion "from the valley of the field of bones" (cf. Ezek 37:1-9) comes toward them but casts itself down at Paul's feet. He asks the animal what it wants, and receives the reply: "I want to be baptized." By a happy chance, there is a river nearby, and Paul descends with the lion into the water. After a prayer:

> I took him by the mane in the name of Jesus Christ and immersed him three times. When he came up out of the water, he shook his mane and said to me: "Grace be with you!" And I said to him: "With you too!" When the lion ran off to the field rejoicing—for this was revealed to me in my heart—a lioness met him, and he did not direct his face towards her, but turned away and ran off towards the woods (§9 of the Coptic text in the enumeration by Kasser and Luisier; the translation follows their French version).

After this exquisite exemplification of the interconnection between baptism and the renunciation of marital intercourse, the narrative switches back to the house of Aquila and Prisca in Ephesus. Paul converts many people in the city. This leads to disturbances that compel the governor Hieronymus to intervene. P.Hamb begins with Paul's interrogation before him: Paul criticizes the vices of human beings and their false gods of bronze, stone, and wood. The governor is impressed but asks the people what they desire. Some propose that Paul be burnt at the stake; the goldsmiths (cf. Acts 19:24) cry: "To the beasts with the man!" The governor has Paul flogged and then condemns him to fight against the beasts. All this happens in the period of Pentecost (cf. 1 Cor 16:8), as the angel had predicted in the Coptic fragment quoted above.

Six days later, the familiar parade with the wild animals takes place. A lion goes past the side door of the arena, where Paul is in prison, and roars so powerfully that the people cry out, "The lion!"—and even Paul breaks off his prayer.

Paul receives visitors in his prison. Eubula (cf. Eubulus in 2 Tim 4:19), the wife of Diophantes, a freedman of Hieronymus, was already a disciple of Paul; Artemilla, the wife of Hieronymus, wants to hear Paul. They visit him in the jail, and this incites their husbands to an even greater anger at Paul. Paul counsels Artemilla to forget her wealth, her beauty, and her jewels and to abandon her idols and sacrifices in order that she may come to the living God.

In the night before the fight with the beasts, which takes place on a Sunday, the two women ask that Artemilla may receive baptism. They plan to call a locksmith to free Paul from his fetters, but he trusts in God, and a handsome boy enters with a smile and unties the fetters. The doors of the prison open of their own accord; the sentries are asleep (cf. Acts 12:6-10). A young man with a luminescent body goes before them on the road to the sea. The sea surges violently, and Artemilla is so deeply affected by the ceremony of baptism that she faints. Paul calls to the young man: "O you who give light and shine, [come to my help, so that the heathen may not] say that Paul the prisoner fled after killing Artemilla." Artemilla comes to herself. Returning to the prison (?), Paul breaks bread, gives her water to drink, and sends Artemilla home to her husband.

The fight with the beasts is scheduled for the next morning. Paul sighs that he is once again to become a laughingstock for a whole city (the Greek verb *thriambeuein* may be an allusion to 2 Cor 2:14). Artemilla and Eubula are so concerned about Paul that they become sick and do not go the theater; but Hieronymus and Diophantes see this as an opportunity for revenge. A particularly fierce lion is let loose upon Paul, but the lion first bows down in prayer, like Paul. Then it rises up in all its leonine splendor—and lies down at his feet, tame as a lamb. It addresses Paul with a human voice: "[Grace be with] you!" Paul replies: "[Grace be with] you too, O lion!" The people cry out: "Away with the sorcerer (*magos*), away with the poisoner (*pharmakos*)!" The lion and Paul look more closely at each other, and Paul realizes that this must be the lion that he had once baptized; this is confirmed in a dialogue between them.

Hieronymus lets other wild animals loose against Paul and sends archers to deal with the disobedient lion. But a heavy hailstorm thwarts all his plans; many people die, and the rest flee and cry, "Save us, O God, save us, O God of the man who fought with the beasts!" The hail tears off one of Hieronymus' ears. Paul and the lion are left in peace and bid each other farewell. Paul goes down to the harbor and boards a ship that will take him to Macedonia, while the lion escapes into the mountains.

The handsome young man (?) comes by night into the bed-chamber of Artemilla and Eubula and assures them that all is well with Paul. Hieronymus asks the God of Paul for help with his ear, which is already beginning to suppurate. In the presence of the helpless physicians, the young man counsels him to treat it with honey but also seems to utter a command that the ear be healed. At any rate, the ear is restored to health (cf. Luke 22:51).

These are the outlines of the famous episode of the baptized and tame lion that was able to speak. In the early church, Jerome made fun of it (*Vir. Ill.* 7); Hippolytus compared it to the biblical narrative of Daniel in the lions' den (*Comm. in Dan.* 3.29.4), and Commodian alluded to it (*Carmen Apol.* 627f.). The staging of a fight against animals in Ephesus may well have been suggested by Paul's remark at 1 Corinthians 15:32, which is meant to be under-stood metaphorically: "What do I gain if, humanly speaking, I fought with wild animals at Ephesus?" (Cf. also 2 Tim 4:17, "I was rescued from the lion's mouth.") The individual details owe much to the celebrated fable of Androclus and the lion, which is found in Aulus Gellius (*Attic Nights* 5.14.5–30), who says that it goes back to Apion of Alexandria. During a fight against animals in the Circus Maximus in Rome, one lion stands out by reason of its par-ticularly muscular body, its long flowing mane, and its terrifying roar. A slave named Androclus is thrown to it, but the lion approaches its intended victim slowly and full of astonishment. It then jumps around him, waving its tail like a pet dog, and licks him from top to toe. The explanation of the riddle is that Androclus had fled from his master in North Africa and concealed himself in a cave. A lion entered this cave, limping with one paw and bleed-ing. It made gestures to Androclus, begging him to help it, and Androclus extracted a large splinter of wood from the sole of its paw and pressed out the pus that had collected there. This was the beginning of a great friendship that lasted for three years until Androclus was discovered, taken captive, and condemned to be thrown to the beasts as a runaway slave. When this story is made known, Androclus is amnestied, and people see him strolling through the city with his lion, whom he leads on a thin leash. Everyone admires him and gives him presents.

A special message is included in this edifying animal story in ActPaul. The lion with its fierceness and power is a symbol of that part of the soul that Platonic terminology calls "desire." In the world of ideas of ActPaul, it embodies the powerful instinct of sexuality that, although it is oriented to procreation, cannot ultimately free human beings from death. Indeed, it is this instinct that provokes death, especially the death of the spirit. It can be redeemed through baptism. In the ideal case, this allows its "taming" and integration in daily living; de facto, however, in ActPaul it implies instead the massive suppression of sexuality. The fact that a man such as Paul had to encounter the lion more than once probably hints that even for him, coping with his own sexuality was not an easily mastered task (cf. Rordorf).

In Philippi (P.Heid pp. 45–50, 41f., 44a; P.Bodmer 10) [10–11]

Bibliography: G. Luttikhuizen, "The Apocryphal Correspondence with the Corinthians and the Acts of Paul." Pages 75–91 in *The Apocryphal Acts of Paul*. Edited by J. N. Bremmer. – **W. Rordorf**, "Hérésie et orthodoxie selon la Correspondance apocryphe entre les Corinthiens et l'apôtre Paul." Pages 389–431 in idem, *Lex orandi*. – **M. Testuz**, *Papyrus Bodmer 10–12*. Cologne: 1959. 7–45.

Paul is now at Philippi. At the same period, Simon and Cleobius are active in Corinth (cf. Eusebius, *Hist. eccl.* 4.22.5) teaching a number of problematical doctrines: (1) there is no resurrection of the flesh, but only of the spirit; (2) the body of the human being was not created by God; (3) the world was not created by God; (4) the existence of Jesus was a mere appearance, and he was not genuinely crucified; and (5) he was born neither of Mary nor of the seed of David (cf. the contrary thesis, which is put forward already in ActThecla 1). The Corinthians are disturbed by this and send two deacons to Philippi with a letter for Paul. This brief epistle is quoted word for word. It adds two further heresies to the list: (6) one ought not to appeal to the prophets; and (7) God is not omnipotent. The Corinthians conclude by asking Paul to visit Corinth.

When this letter arrives, Paul is in prison because of Stratonike, the wife of Allophanes; presumably (true to pattern in the apocryphal Acts) he has persuaded her to stop sleeping with her husband. He replies with many tears (cf. 2 Cor 2:4) in a lengthy letter in which he appeals to the fundamental testimony of the apostles and refutes the erroneous teachings point by point, but thetically rather than argumentatively. He adduces the following illustrations in support of bodily resurrection: the seed that is sown naked in the earth and rises up clothed (cf. 1 Cor 15:37f.), Jonah's rescue from the belly of the fish after three days and nights (cf. Matt 12:40), and the dead man who returned to life when his body touched the bones of Elisha (cf. 2 Kgs 13:21).

In the next narrative fragment, Paul seems to have been condemned to forced labor in the mines (*metallon* can be read with some measure of certainty in P.Heid p. 41, line 8; a little later on, Paul is working together with other prisoners, and soldiers are present). Once again, we meet a family, Longinus with his wife and their daughter Frontina, who seems to have been condemned to death by being thrown from a cliff. Longinus gives Paul the blame for this and wants to throw him down too. Then we are told that prisoners carry the bier on which Frontina lies. At this point in the story, she must still be alive, but unable to move as a result of ill treatment or because of an illness (perhaps for the same reason as Peter's daughter in BG 4: The Act of Peter, namely in order to preserve her chastity). The way in which she meets her death must have been related in a part of the text that has not survived. Paul takes her corpse in his arms and calls her back to life. He then leads Frontina demonstratively by the hand through the city to the house of Longinus, and the whole crowd professes with one voice the greatness of the one God.

In Corinth (P.Hamb pp. 6–7; P.Heid p. 44b, 43, 51f.) [12]

The longed-for visit to Corinth takes place. In the house of Epiphanius, Paul relates what happened to him in Philippi in the "workshops" or "workhouse" (this confirms the suggestion that he had been condemned to forced labor in Philippi). They listen to him for forty days, and Paul takes the opportunity to relate everything that has befallen him up to then. Then the time comes when Paul must leave for Rome. He sees a "furnace of fire" before him, a prediction of his martyrdom. David, who put all his trust in God in his conduct vis-à-vis Saul and Nabal (cf. 1 Samuel 24–25), serves as his biblical paradigm. The Spirit takes hold of Cleobius (who is to be distinguished from the heretic of the same name, unless he has converted in the meantime), who announces that Paul must fulfill the entire plan of salvation and go to his death.

When Paul offers sacrifice (a reference to the Eucharist?), a sign is given: Something (a loaf?) breaks of its own accord (*automatôs*) in pieces. No one can interpret this event until the Spirit comes upon Myrta and she begins to speak: the many pieces mean that Paul will nourish and save countless people in Rome with the Word. An *agape* with the singing of psalms and hymns is held, and Paul departs for Rome on a day of preparation (i.e. Friday).

The Journey to Rome (P.Hamb p. 7-8; P.Heid pp. 79f.; P.Berlin; P.Mich) [13]

Bibliography: G. D. Kilpatrick and C. H. Roberts, "The Acta Pauli: A New Fragment." *JTS* 47 (1946): 196–99. – **W. Rordorf**, "Les Actes de Paul sur papyrus: problèmes liés aux PMich. Inv. 1317 et 3788." *Proceedings of the XVIII International Congress of Papyrology: Athens, 25–31 May 1986, Vol. 1. Athens: 1988. 453–61.* – **H. A. Sanders**, "A Fragment of the Acta Pauli in the Michigan Collection." *HTR* 31 (1939): 73–90 (P.Mich 1317). – Idem, "Three Theological Fragments." *HTR* 36 (1943): 165–67 (P.Mich 3788).

The captain of the ship that will bring Paul from Corinth to Rome is called Artemon (in Acts 27:40, this is the somewhat puzzling designation of a "foresail"). He greets Paul joyfully, because he himself is a Christian. He was baptized by Peter—a link between the two great apostles and the texts that deal with them. Exhausted by his fasting and vigils, Paul falls asleep on the high seas. The Lord appears to him, walking on the sea (cf. Mark 6:48), and awakens him. Paul recognizes him at once and asks why he appears so "gloomy and downcast." The Lord replies: "I am about to be crucified afresh." Paul utterly rejects this idea: "God forbid, Lord, that I should see this!" These words of Jesus, which Origen found in ActPaul and quotes (cf. *Comm. Jo.* 20.12), are added in P.Hamb at the end of page 7 as lines 39f.; there is a corresponding gap in line 31, where they ought to stand. This may be an indication that the author borrowed them from the tradition about Peter, where the reference to death by crucifixion seems more appropriate, and inserted them here. The Lord also charges Paul to exhort the brothers and sisters in Rome to be faithful. He walks on the sea ahead of the ship and shows it the way.

In the harbor, Claudius (cf. Claudia in 2 Tim 4:21) is waiting for Artemon, and when the captain presents Paul to him, Claudius embraces Paul and carries his baggage to Claudius' own house. The brothers and sisters assemble quickly, and Paul begins to speak, addressing them as "soldiers of Christ" (cf. 2 Tim 2:3f.). He paints a broad picture, beginning with the liberation of Israel from the hand of Pharaoh and of the kings Og and Adar (more correctly Arad, see Num 21:1-33). He mentions the prophets who announced Jesus Christ, but were persecuted and killed by the people (a reflection of the Deuteronomist topos about the violent fate met by the prophets). Israel's failure shows the believers how they are not to behave in the great persecution that is now imminent—and that they must endure victoriously. Here, Paul recalls fundamental doctrinal data: how the Spirit came down upon Mary and she bore Jesus Christ; how Jesus proclaimed that the kingdom of heaven was close at hand; how Jesus chose twelve men and performed great miracles, which are listed in a summary.

The smaller papyrus discoveries, especially P.Mich, allow us to locate at this point a piece from the Coptic P.Heid (pp. 79f.), which Carl Schmidt regarded as a fragment from an apocryphal gospel because Jesus himself begins to speak. He gives an extremely detailed account of his miraculous deeds: raising the dead, healing the sick, cleansing lepers, exorcisms, the miraculous feeding, walking on the sea, and the stilling of the storm. He then demands that the disciples have faith, quoting the logion about the faith that can move mountains (cf. Matt 11:23). Simon Peter now asks if there is anything greater than these miracles. The Lord gives an affirmative answer, but Philip protests. Jesus' reply to his objection has not survived.

From the narrative perspective, this final part can be compared to the proclamation of the gospel in ActJoh 87–102. It may seem strange that this should be presented by Paul, of all people, but he is certainly the speaker here; and he may have appealed, for example, to the testimony of Peter, whose change of name is mentioned in the fragment (cf. Gal 1:18).

4. The Martyrdom of Paul [14]

Bibliography: W. Rordorf, "Die neronische Christenverfolgung im Spiegel der apokryphen Paulusakten." Pages 365–74 in idem, *Lex orandi*.

In Rome, Paul meets Luke and also Titus, who has come from Dalmatia (cf. 2 Tim 4:10). He rents a barn outside the city, where he teaches many persons. His adherents include even members of the emperor's household (cf. Phil 4:22). One of these, the cup-bearer Patroclus, arrives late and finds no place in the barn (cf. Mark 2:4). He sits in a high window. The devil, who is jealous of Paul's success, causes Patroclus to fall down from the window and die (cf. Acts 20:9-12). Paul has him brought in. All those present call to the Lord with tears, and the boy begins to breathe again. He is sent home alive (1).

In the meantime, the emperor has been told of the death of his cupbearer. When Nero then learns that Patroclus is alive and "stands at the sideboard," he is filled with a holy dread, and asks who has made him alive. Patroclus replies: "Christ Jesus, the king of the ages" (2). The emperor scents a threat to his own rule, and asks: "Patroclus, are you also fighting for that king?" The boy answers in the affirmative. "Barsabbas Justus [Acts 1:23] the flat-footed and Urion the Cappadocian and Festus of Galatia," high dignitaries at Nero's court, likewise confess that they "fight for him, the king of the ages." Nero has them cruelly tortured and thrown into prison, and he issues an edict ordering the execution of all the "soldiers of Christ" (2 Tim 2:3).

The play on ambiguous political terms that begins here con-tinues in §3. Paul, too, is led in chains before Nero, who at once identifies him as the commandant of the Christian troops and accuses him of secretly infiltrating the Roman Empire and enlist-ing soldiers. Paul coolly suggests to the emperor that he, too, enter the military service of Jesus Christ the King, since otherwise he cannot be saved, and a judgment by fire threatens the world. This merely provokes the emperor to have the Christian prisoners burned at the stake. As a Roman citizen, Paul is to be beheaded; but first he sends a message to the prefect Longus and to Cestus, the centurion of the sentries. The Romans themselves protest publicly before the palace against Nero's raging, and this puts a stop to the persecution for a time.

However, the emperor insists that Paul must be beheaded (4). The apostle announces that he will rise again and show himself to the emperor as proof that he lives for the Lord. Longus and Cestus are charged to carry out the sentence, but they begin a dia-logue with Paul, who speaks once more of the purification of the earth in the fire that is to come. (Rordorf suggests that this is connected with the idea that the fire in Rome was the occasion of Nero's persecution of Christians.) The officers actually offer him his liberty, but Paul refuses: "I am not a deserter from Christ but a faithful soldier of the living God."

Nero becomes impatient and sends Parthenius and Pheretas "to see whether Paul had already been beheaded." Paul exhorts them too to believe in the God who raises up the dead (5), and they declare themselves ready to do so if Paul indeed—as he affirms—dies and rises again. Paul tells Longus and Cestus that they are to come to his grave early in the morning, where Titus and Luke will wait for them and give them the seal. He then utters a lengthy prayer in Hebrew with raised hands, facing the east (P.Hamb pp. 20, 22f. gives the contents of the prayer: "Father of my Lord Jesus Christ, I lay my spirit in his hand, and Lord Jesus Christ, receive it!"). When the executioner finally cuts off Paul's head, milk (not blood) splashes on the tunics of the soldiers.

While the emperor, who is surrounded by philosophers, is still wondering about the things he hears, Paul stands before him at about the ninth hour and says in the presence of witnesses, "Caesar, behold, here is Paul, the soldier of God; I am not dead but live in my God. But upon you, unhappy one, many evils and great punishment will come because you have unjustly shed the blood of the righteous not many days ago" (6; cf. Matt 23:35). Nero is filled with consternation and releases Patroclus, Barsabbas, and their fellow prisoners.

When Longus and Cestus go to the grave on the following morning, they see there two men praying—with Paul in their company (7). The two men, Titus and Luke, are afraid when they see the officers, and want to flee, but Longus and Cestus explain why they are there, and they receive baptism. The final doxology of the Greek manuscripts is not found in P.Hamb, where the *subscriptio* follows immediately after the baptism: "Acts of Paul."

C. Evaluation

Bibliography: M. Aubin, "Reversing Romance? The Acts of Thecla and the Ancient Novel." Pages 257–72 in *Ancient Fiction and Early Christian Narrative*. Edited by R. F. Hock et al. – **R. J. Bauckham**, "The Acts of Paul as a Sequel to Acts." Pages 105–52 in *The Book of Acts in Its Ancient*

Literary Setting. Edited by B. W. Winter and A. D. Clarke. Michigan: 1993. – **C. Büllesbach**, "Das Verhältnis der Acta Pauli zur Apostelgeschichte des Lukas. Darstellung und Kritik der Forschungsgeschichte." Pages 215–37 in *Das Ende des Paulus: Historische, theologische und literaturgeschichtliche Aspekte* (BZNW 106). Edited by F. W. Horn. Berlin: 2001. – **J. V. Hills**, "The Acts of the Apostles in the Acts of Paul." *SBL.SP* (1994): 24–54. – **E. M. Hoe**, "Interpretations of Paul in The Acts of Paul and Thecla." Pages 33–49 in *Pauline Studies* (Festschrift for F. F. Bruce). Exeter: 1980. – **D. Marguerat**, "The Acts of Paul and the Canonical Acts: A Phenomenon of Reading." Pages 169–83 in *The Apocryphal Acts of the Apostles*. Edited by R. F. Stoops et al. – **W. Rordorf**, "In welchem Verhältnis stehen die apokryphen Paulusakten zur kanonischen Apostelgeschichte und zu den Pastoralbriefen?" Pages 449–65 in idem, *Lex orandi.* – **W. Schneemelcher**, "Die Apostelgeschichte des Lukas und die Acta Pauli." Pages 204–22 in idem, *Gesammelte Aufsätze.*

Looking back over the text, we can discern the successive stations in Paul's itinerary: Damascus—Jerusalem (?)—Antioch in Syria—Iconium—Antioch in Pisidia—Myra—Sidon—Tyre—(in the gap, possibly Jerusalem, with a further journey to Caesarea [Rordorf])—Smyrna—Ephesus—Philippi—Corinth—the voyage to Italy—Rome. This one great journey leads from the vocation of the apostle to his death and is conceived as an exhaustive presentation of the path he took. Paul reaches Rome as a free man, not as a prisoner; there is not even a hint of a journey to Spain. The communities that Paul visits as an itinerant missionary were not founded by him, but already exist; this reflects second-century realities. Ministerial structures are not yet highly developed. Prophecy, in which women also share, continues to play a large role; one might almost be tempted to detect a whiff of Montanism here.

It is obvious that this outline differs from that in the Lukan Acts of the Apostles, but comparable structural emphases are equally obvious, such as the two Antiochs in Syria and Pisidia, Ephesus with its theater, and Rome as the final point of Paul's travels. There are striking points of contact on the level of vocabulary. For example, the address of God as "one who knows the hearts" (*kardiognôsta*) in ActThecla 24 is not as commonly attested in early Christian writings as one might think. The two most important parallels are in Acts 1:24 and 15:8 (cf. Hills). The question of the relationship between ActPaul and the Lukan Acts is a matter of keen scholarly controversy, and we cannot avoid discussing it here.

I find it impossible to accept the thesis that ActPaul understands itself as a continuation of the Acts of the Apostles (as Bauckham proposes). It would be more consistent to hold (with Rordorf) that its author did not know the Acts of the Apostles at all, but this hypothesis is not completely satisfactory. The concept of intertextuality (Marguerat) is more helpful. The author of ActPaul does not regard the Acts of the Apostles as a canonical authority. He finds there inspiration for his attempt to sketch an image of Paul for his own period, in which there will be a place for information that is either simply not found or else deliberately passed over in Luke's work. He also knows the Old Testament and most likely had access to the basic stock of the other New Testament writings. This applies above all to the Pastoral Letters. He takes over and amplifies the personal information in these texts. In individual instances, it is difficult to decide where he has recourse to oral tradition about Paul and where he gives his imagination free rein. (For another position, cf. MacDonald's ingenious proposal that the Pastoral Letters are later than ActPaul and that they should be read as a polemical response to the version of Christianity found in ActThecla.)

The observation that the author of ActPaul inserts toward the close a "proclamation of the gospel" that is similar in form (though not in content) to a lengthy section in ActJoh lends plausibility to the suggestion that he knew not only Luke's Acts but also ActJoh. The influence of the Greek novel can be seen inter alia in the "love story" between Thecla and Paul with its sexually aggressive scenes.

Measured against the development of the confession of faith in the second century, the author's theology is mainstream and orthodox—not in the least heretical or gnostic. He explicitly combats gnosis, first in the figures of Demas and Hermogenes and later in 3 Corinthians, where the early gnostics Simon and Cleobius appear. The Christology sometimes shows slightly modalistic tendencies, and the Holy Spirit does not yet appear as a clearly defined Third Person, but that is not in any way unusual in this period.

The obsessive insistence of the author, or of his spokesman Paul, on sexual continence and chastity might be problematical here, but this too was the trend of the times, and it is not easy to define exactly the standpoint taken by ActPaul on this question.

Despite all the exhortations, and despite Thecla's radiant example as the image of an ideal virgin, there is no clear prohibition of marriage anywhere in the text, nor is the renunciation of marriage made a precondition for the reception of baptism. It is possible that Onesiphorus, with his wife and two sons, is intended to function as a model of Christian family life. It seems that the author stops just short of an important boundary line, which he does not cross into a programmatic encratism. This doubtless made it easier for his work to find acceptance.

Tertullian's objections show that it was possible to instrumentalize ActPaul—and in particular, the example of Thecla in this work—to plead for a stronger participation by women in the life of the Christian community. But this has been countered by the objection that the price is too high: Howe points out skeptically that such a participation, on the terms suggested by ActPaul, would entail the renunciation of typically feminine attributes such as jewels, shaving one's head, the renunciation of marriage and motherhood, and a masculinization in outward appearance and conduct. On the other hand, we should not forget the cultural parameters which may have made precisely this appear the only possible form of emancipation and autonomy for women. Here, ActPaul does not speak with one single voice; but the Christian women who appealed to Thecla and kindled Tertullian's ire surely understood one of the author's intentions correctly.

D. Later Narratives

1. Life and Miracles of Saint Thecla

Bibliography: G. Dagron, *Vie et miracles de sainte Thècle. Texte grec, traduction et commentaire* (SHG 62). Brussels: 1978. – **S. J. Davis**, *The Cult of Saint Thecla: A Tradition of Women's Piety in Late Antiquity* (Oxford Early Christian Studies). Oxford: 2001. – **M. Pesthy**, "Thecla in the Fathers of the Church." Pages 164–78 (at 168–71) in *The Apocryphal Acts of Paul*. Edited by J. N. Bremmer.

Scholars once attributed the two-part work *Life and Miracles of Saint Thecla* to the fifth-century bishop Basil of Seleucia, but we know today that it was compiled between 444 and 476 by an anonymous author who worked first as rhetor, then as priest, and was on a collision course with the local bishops. He spent his life in and around the great pilgrimage site—with its many churches, monasteries, and hermitages that had grown up—in Seleucia in southeast Asia Minor where Thecla had spent her last years. Gregory Nazianzen spent four years there when he fled to escape episcopal ordination, and Egeria writes about her visit to the sanctuary, which attracted many pilgrims, in 384.

In the vita in the first part, the author keeps very close to the narrative thread of ActThecla, expanding it above all by means of lengthy discourses which he places on the lips of the characters. He announces both these traits in his preface: "We have kept to the meaning and the order of those things which were once spoken at the time of the martyrdom. . . . Where possible, we have inserted public discourses." He consistently calls his heroine "apostle and martyr"; as the first woman martyr, she is given a place alongside the protomartyr Stephen. The conclusion is also expanded to include an account of the arrival of the saint in Seleucia. The proximity of this city to Tarsus, the hometown of Paul, is emphasized, and we are now told explicitly that Thecla not only taught, but also baptized (28.1f.).

The book of miracles in the second part contains a collection of forty-six accounts of miracles that Thecla worked after her death at her pilgrimage sanctuary—and still continues to work, for in some cases, the author himself experiences her saving intervention or an apparition by the saint (nr. 12, 31, 41). The conflict with local traditions about pagan deities, which begins at the close of the vita, is continued by the first miracles, which are directed against the hero Sarpedon (who is reduced to silence), Athene (who is deprived of her dwelling place), and Aphrodite (who is driven out). Zeus himself, "the head of the demons," is not spared (nr. 4; this passage includes a beautiful description of the reciprocal hospitality between Tarsus and Seleucia). Other miracles reflect the fact that numerous women lived near the sanctuary or visited it. Nevertheless, the author's views about women do not depart from the evaluation customary at that time, and he is more conservative than the original ActThecla (David, 50: "One detects an undercurrent of misogyny in the *Life and Miracles*").

2. A Panegyric on Thecla

Bibliography: M. Aubineau, "Le panégyrique de Thècle, attribué à

Jean Chrysostome (BHG 1720): la fin retrouvée d'un texte mutilé / Compléments au dossier de Sainte Thècle." *AnBoll* 93 (1975): 349–62. – **D. R. MacDonald and A. D. Scrimgeour**, "Pseudo-Chrysostom's Panegyric to Thecla: The Heroine of the Acts of Paul in Homily and Art." Pages 151–59 in *The Apocryphal Acts of Apostles*. Edited by D. R. MacDonald.

This homily, which was included among the works of John Chrysostom but is not from his pen, was delivered on the annual feast of Saint Thecla in September. It is addressed to a purely female congregation. The basic data of the life and the double martyrdom of the saint, which she endured victoriously, are presupposed and are not set out in a detailed narrative. It is possible that depictions on icons in the church also kept alive the memory of her story. The main achievement of the preacher is to project the external sufferings inward and to compare them with the trials endured day and night by all who live in celibacy. The preacher says that temptations and stimuli enter through the eyes and ears, through the imagination and dreams, and oppress us. Thecla too fought against these and won the struggle—and this was her real martyrdom. Her victory gave her a new freedom, since she need not face the difficulties of family life (which the preacher sets out in detail). Despite his eulogy of virginity, and despite his warning that a consecrated virgin who sins commits a particularly grave fault, the author nevertheless accepts marriage as also a Christian form of life. He addresses his counsels not only to widows and virgins, but also to married women.

3. The Acts of Titus

Bibliography: F. Halkin, "La légende crétoise de saint Tite." *AnBoll* 79 (1961): 241–56 (Greek text). – **R. I. Pervo**, "The 'Acts of Titus': A Preliminary Translation." *SBL.SP* (1996): 455–82.

Menologies (collections of vitae of saints for all the days of the church year) contain two recensions of a revised brief version of the Acts of Titus. In their original form, they may go back to the fifth or sixth century. It is clear that the author employed not only the Acts of the Apostles, but also the ancient Acts of Paul, where Titus is mentioned in Rome at the beginning of ActThecla and at the martyrdom of Paul. With all due caution, one can therefore draw on the Acts of Titus to fill in gaps in ActPaul (e.g., a period spent by Paul on Crete?).

"Zenas the lawyer" (from Tit 3:13) is introduced at the beginning as the author. Titus comes from the island of Crete (an inference from Titus 1:5 and the unflattering portrait in Tit 1:12); he is a descendant of the mythical King Minos. In his youth, he studies Homer and the philosophers, until a vision induces him to start reading the prophet Isaiah. The proconsul of Crete, who is his uncle, sends him with a delegation to Jerusalem because he has heard of Christ. Titus is a witness to the deeds of Christ, his death, and his resurrection. He is one of the 120 disciples of Jesus mentioned in Acts 1:15 and the "Cretans and Arabs" of Acts 2:11.

Some years later, the apostles send him out as a missionary, together with Paul. It is in these sections (3–4) that there are points of contact with ActPaul, although the sequence is partly different. The son of Anchares (P.Heid pp. 1–6) is here given the name "Barnabas." The forced labor in Philippi (P.Heid p. 41) seems to find confirmation in §4. Paul and Titus come to Crete while Rustillus, a brother-in-law of Titus, is the Roman governor. His son dies and is raised to life by Paul. The next episode is Ephesus and the fight with the beasts. The earthly pilgrimage of Paul ends under Nero in Rome.

From §7 onward, the narrative concentrates on the activity of Titus on Crete, where he establishes the ecclesiastical hierarchy and is victorious in his fight against pagan deities, until he reaches the age of ninety-four and angels come to fetch him. His last resting place develops into a sanctuary where human beings find healing and liberation from demons (§12).

4. The Letter of Pelagia

Bibliography: E. J. Goodspeed, "The Epistle of Pelagia." *AJSL* 20 (1903/04): 95–108.

At the beginning of the twentieth century, when the discovery and publication of P.Hamb was still a long way off, the baptized lion, which had achieved a measure of fame, was as yet known only from allusions in the church fathers. Paul's fight with a lion in Ephesus was also known from the late *Church History* of

Nicephorus Callistus; this fourteenth-century author has recourse, not directly to the Acts of Paul, but to a panegyric of Paul by the tenth-century Nicetas of Paphlagonia (which was not published until 1931). This made the publication by Goodspeed of a virtually undatable Ethiopic apocryphal text, the *Letter of Pelagia*, all the more welcome. The princess Pelagia herself plays only a marginal role here, but we learn of a connection between two events that had previously appeared unrelated. Near Caesarea, Paul meets a lion in the mountains and has a conversation with it. At the lion's request, he baptizes it (the baptism is mentioned only indirectly in the text, but this may be due to a translation error in the underlying Coptic text). When Pelagia follows Paul's teaching and refuses to sleep with her husband, Paul is condemned to fight against the beasts. In the arena, he meets his lion once again. They pray together, have a conversation, and are then sent away in peace by the crowd.

P.Hamb, with the Coptic papyrus from Geneva, has brought us a decisive step closer to the original form of this edifying two-part story.

Chapter 3

The Acts of Peter

Editions: R. A. Lipsius, AAAp I: 45–103. – **L. Vouaux,** *Les Actes de Pierre: Introduction, textes, traduction et commentaire*. Paris: 1922.

Translations: W. Schneemelcher, NTApo 6th ed. II: 243–89. – **J. K. Elliott,** *Apocryphal NT*. 390–438. – G. Poupon, Pages 1039–1114 in *Écrits apocryphes chrétiens*, Vol. 1. Edited by F. Bovon and P. Geoltrain.

Bibliography: M. C. Baldwin, *Whose Acts of Peter? Text and Historical Context of the Actus Vercellenses* (WUNT II/196). Tübingen: 2005. – **J. N. Bremmer**, ed. *The Apocryphal Acts of Peter: Magic, Miracles and Gnosticism* (Studies in the Apocryphal Acts of the Apostles 3). Louvain: 1998. – **J. Flamion**, "Les Actes apocryphes de Pierre." *RHE* 9 (1908)–12 (1911). (A series of ten articles.) – **F. Lapham**, *Peter: the Myth, the Man and the Writings: A Study of Early Petrine Text and Tradition* (JSNTSup 239). Sheffield: 2003. 34–70. – **C. Schmidt**, *Die alten Petrusakten im Zusammenhang der apokryphen Apostelliteratur untersucht. Nebst einem neuentdeckten Fragment* (TU 24.1). Leipzig: 1903. – **C. M. Thomas**, *The Acts of Peter, Gospel Literature, and the Ancient Novel: Rewriting the Past.* New York: 2003.

A. Context

Bibliography: J. N. Bremmer, "Aspects of the Acts of Peter: Women, Magic, Place and Date." Pages 1–20 in idem, *The Apocryphal Acts of Peter.* – **B. P. Grenfell and A. S. Hunt**, *The Oxyrhynchus Papyri Part VI.* London: 1908. 6–12. – **P. J. Lallemann**, "The Relation between the Acts of John and the Acts of Peter." Pages 161–77 in *The Apocryphal Acts of Peter.* Edited by J. N. Bremmer. – **T. Nissen**, "Die Petrusakten und ein bardesanitischer Dialog in der Aberkiosvita." *ZNW* 9 (1908): 190–203, 315–28. – **G. Poupon**, "Les 'Actes de Pierre' et leur remaniement."

ANRW II: 25.6 (1988): 4363–83. – **W. Rordorf**, "The Relation between the Acts of Peter and the Acts of Paul: State of the Question." Pages 178–91 in *The Apocryphal Acts of Peter.* Edited by J. N. Bremmer. – **C. Schmidt**, "Zur Datierung der alten Petrusakten." *ZNW* 29 (1930): 150–55.

Luke's Acts of the Apostles is based only in its first part on information about Peter, the spokesman of the Twelve; its second part concentrates entirely on Paul. The lacuna which opens up here is filled in other texts with various traditions. These already include the two pseudo-Petrine Letters in the New Testament, 1 and 2 Peter; it is especially the second of these that offers biographical reminiscences (cf. 2 Pet 1:16-19). The Pseudo-Clementines also belong in this category, and we will study this much neglected body of writings in Chapter 7 below.

The Acts of Peter (ActPet) also belong here. The earliest unambiguous evidence of their existence is in Eusebius, who mentions them with the Gospel of Peter, the *Kerygma Petri* (see below), and the Apocalypse of Peter as texts that were not Catholic and could not be quoted (*Hist. eccl.* 3.3.2). In this context, he also cites Origen (3.1.2f.), who knew that Peter had asked to be crucified with his head downward; this testimony would take us back to the period before 230. However, Origen does not explicitly name "Acts of Peter," and it is possible that he knew this piece of information through oral tradition (like Clement of Alexandria, who knows of the martyrdom of Peter's wife: cf. *Strom.* 7.11.63).

This brings us to a problem that is almost more acute in the study of ActPet than with any of the other apocryphal Acts, namely the lack of a textual basis. Thanks to its use in the liturgy, the Martyrdom of Peter has survived, and three Greek manuscripts are known. One of these begins—in today's enumeration—at §30, the other two with the martyrdom proper in §33. This Martyrdom was also translated into all the oriental liturgical languages. Taken on its own, however, it does not allow us to speak of "Acts of Peter."

Here, the so-called *Actus Vercellenses*, which became available to scholarship in 1891, seem to offer help. This name comes from a codex in the Capitular Library of the city of Vercelli in northern Italy. In a strange late Latin, partly with local forms and partly erroneous, this rather carelessly written codex from the sixth or seventh century contains the Pseudo-Clementine *Recognitions*, followed by a narrative that begins with the departure of Paul from Rome. It then deals with the conflict between Peter and Simon Magus in Rome and concludes with the martyrdom of Peter. Scholars have identified this Latin text with the ancient Acts of Peter and have argued that we thus possess about two-thirds of the original text, which (according to the *Stichometry* of Nicephorus) ran to 2,750 *stichoi*. Support for this hypothesis was found in the fourth-century vita of Abercius, bishop of Hierapolis in the second century, where Greek parallels to §§2, 7, 20, and 21 of the *Actus Vercellenses* were discovered (cf. Nissen).

Notes of caution were sounded from two sides. Gérard Poupon put forward the thesis that the original narrative sequence of ActPet is found in the Actus Vercellenses only in a revised and expanded form. Like Vouaux before him, he believed that the mention of Paul in §§1–3, 30, and 41 is the result of an interpolation made in North Africa in the third century, and he detected traces of this revision also in §§4, 6, and 10. Matthew Baldwin's criticism is even more fundamental. He demonstrates by means of very detailed textual comparisons that the *Actus Vercellenses* cannot simply be understood as the faithful translation of a Greek original. Rather, the first step in interpreting this text must be to see it as an independent new version that came into existence in the late fourth century when the text was translated from Greek into Latin in North Africa or Spain; and it must be interpreted in the context of the Pseudo-Clementines, to which it is linked in the Vercelli codex. He concludes from this that the ancient *Acts* of Peter should be dated relatively late, to the period after 250 (i.e., after the persecution by Decius); however, *traditions* about Peter were in circulation earlier than this.

In view of this discussion, P.Oxy 849 takes on a special importance. Although it is included among the papyri found at Oxyrhynchus, this is a leaf from a parchment codex with a Greek text that corresponds to parts of §§25 and 26 of the *Actus Vercellenses*. As far as I know, no scholar questions its provenance from the Acts of Peter. The editors date the fragment to the early fourth century, but only because of the ink that is used; they affirm that the handwriting of the manuscript would also allow a dating in the late third century (cf. Grenfell and Hunt). Unlike a documentary text, a literary or subliterary text needs a certain time before it leaves traces in textual discoveries in Egypt. I believe that we can go back to ca. 250 as the latest date for the composition of ActPet.

Once again, it was the pioneering investigations of Carl Schmidt that led scholars to see a Coptic fragment that deals with Peter and his daughter as part of the lost first third of ActPet. Here too, however, vigorous objections have been made in recent years, and we shall look at this question when we present this episode.

Further help might come from a definition of the relationship of ActPet to the other apocryphal Acts. The probable dependence on ActJoh can be demonstrated in some passages (cf. Lallemann). The situation with regard to ActPaul is different. It is true that the *Quo vadis* scene seems better placed in ActPet than in ActPaul, but it need not have been taken over from a complete text of ActPet. It is conceivable that it formed part of a free tradition, as a logion of the Lord with an apophthegmatic framework. Poupon regards the mention of Paul in ActPet as a later interpolation. If this is true, his appearance in the text says nothing about a dependence of ActPet on ActPaul (cf. Rordorf).

Bearing in mind all these arguments, the composition of a first identifiable form of ActPet ca. 200 (cf. Schmidt) still seems a plausible assumption. Various suggestions have been made about the place of composition: Bithynia (where a former praetor named Marcus Granius Marcellus functioned as proconsul in the first century; cf. the discussion of ActPet 8 below), Asia Minor in general, Alexandria, Greek-speaking Syria, Jerusalem, or even Rome (a suggestion that raises questions about the author's local knowledge) or northern Italy. The likeliest place is probably a large city in Asia Minor (cf. Bremmer, 16) or Syria.

B. Contents

1. *Actus Vercellenses*

Bibliography: A. Hilhorst, "The Text of the Actus Vercellenses." Pages 148–60 in *The Apocryphal Acts of Peter*. Edited by J. N. Bremmer. – **C. H. Turner**, "The Latin Acts of Peter." *JTS* 32 (1931): 119–33.

Paul Bids Farewell

In the Vercelli codex, the Acts of Peter begin, paradoxically, with Paul. In §1, he is a prisoner in Rome, where he first converts

Candida, the wife of Quartus (cf. Rom 16:23), one of the sentries. Then, through his wife, he converts Quartus himself, who offers Paul the freedom to leave Rome. Paul prefers to wait for instructions from heaven. After he has fasted for three days, the Lord appears to him and says, "Paul, arise, and be a physician to the Spaniards with your personal presence [*corpore tuo*, with Vouaux]." The brethren (*fraternitas*) begin to lament, since they believe that they will never again see Paul alive (cf. Acts 20:37f.). They recall with gratitude the debates he held with Jewish teachers about the Sabbath, fasting, feast days, and circumcision. Finally, they all beseech him to stay away for no more than a year. A loud voice from heaven confirms that Paul will "be perfected under the hands of Nero": This is a prediction of his death as a martyr in Rome.

A Eucharist is celebrated with bread and water (2). Rufina also wishes to receive the Eucharistic gifts from the hands of Paul, but he rejects her: She is unworthy because she has risen from beside an adulterer in order to come to the celebration. Satan will punish her in her body for this, and unless she repents, a consuming fire and everlasting darkness await her. Rufina immediately collapses, paralyzed on her left side from head to foot and unable to speak. This causes a general uncertainty about whether God, "the searcher of hearts" (cf. Acts 1:24; 15:8), has truly forgiven the newly baptized their sins. Paul calms them by listing nine former vices from which they must abstain and fourteen virtues with which they must arm the inner human being. In a prayer, Paul looks back on the radical breach in his own biography (cf. 1 Tim 1:13): "Once I was a blasphemer, but now I am blasphemed; once I was a persecutor, now I suffer persecution from others; once I was an enemy of Christ, now I pray to be his friend." The sisters and brothers must support his plans with their prayer, and they do so with the wish, "O Lord Jesus Christ, be with Paul, and bring him safely back to us."

Paul is brought to the harbor, accompanied by many people, including numerous women, a senator, and members of the emperor's household (Phil 4:22). The threat of a storm postpones his departure for several days, and the Roman Christians take this opportunity to make a pilgrimage in large groups to the harbor, where they pray with Paul and provide him with the food and equipment he will need, until he finally succeeds in setting sail.

Simon Appears on the Scene

Bibliography: S. Haar, *Simon Magus: The First Gnostic?* (BZNW 119). Berlin: 2003. (Esp. 112–16.) – **A. Ferreiro**, *Simon Magus in Patristic, Medieval and Early Modern Tradition* (Studies in the History of Christian Tradition 125). Leiden: 2005. – **G. P. Luttikhuizen**, "Simon Magus as a Narrative Figure in the Acts of Peter." Pages 39–51 in *The Apocryphal Acts of Peter.* Edited by J. N. Bremmer. – **C. R. Matthews**, "The Acts of Peter and Luke's Intertextual Heritage." *Semeia* 80 (1997): 207–22.

The stage in Rome is now free for the appearance of Simon Magus. As yet, he is in Aricia (4), a town on the road from Puteoli to Rome, but his fame precedes him. Even in the Christian community, it is related that he has called himself "The great power of God" (cf. Acts 8:10), and people are asking whether he may be the Christ. The recollection of Paul and of his miracles still suffices to keep such questions at bay. However, some persons have invited Simon to come to Rome "with great acclamation": "You are God in Italy, you are the savior of the Romans; hasten to Rome as quickly as possible" (these acclamations may be borrowed from the imperial cult). Simon replies that he will fly over the gate into the city at the seventh hour on the following day.

The Roman Christians also want to see this spectacle, and they are present when a mighty cloud of dust, smoke, and fiery rays appears in the distance punctually at the seventh hour. It disappears over the city gate, and suddenly Simon stands there in the midst of the crowd. The members of the community have been left alone—not only by Paul, but also by Timothy and Barnabas, who are on a journey in Macedonia—and they become "exceedingly disturbed"; some begin to call Paul "a sorcerer and a deceiver," and finally only a core is left around the presbyter Narcissus (cf. Rom 16:11). This faithful remnant also includes two women who have come to Rome and dwell "in the hospice of the Bithynians," as well as four other persons who can no longer leave their houses because they are ill or feeble. They stay at home and devote themselves unceasingly to prayer.

Peter Arrives

Bibliography: R. von Haehling, "Zwei Fremde in Rom: Das Wunderduell des Petrus mit Simon Magus in den Acta Petri." *RQ* 98 (2003): 47–71.

At this time, Peter is in Jerusalem, where God had commanded him to spend twelve years (the same number is found also in the *Kerygma Petri*). He has already been victorious in a confrontation with Simon Magus, and now he is prepared for his future task (5). In a vision, the Lord tells him that Simon is turning away the faithful in Rome, not as the "power of God," but as the "power of Satan." Peter must go there at once. A ship lies ready for departure in Caesarea, with a friendly captain named Theon (cf. the "kind treatment" [*philanthrôpôs*] by the centurion Julius in Acts 27:3 and, indeed, Paul's whole journey to Rome in Acts 27–28). Peter fasts during the voyage, but after some days Theon invites him to share his early meal (*prandium*) with him. He relates that in the previous night, a voice called him twice by name and told him to treat Peter well: Thanks to his presence on board, the journey will have a happy outcome.

Peter takes this opportunity to instruct Theon in the Word of God. The wind drops, and the ship is detained. All the other passengers and sailors are drunk and fall asleep, and Peter lets himself down from the deck by a rope and baptizes Theon by immersing him in the sea. When they return to the cabin, Peter gives thanks and shares the Eucharistic bread with Theon. At once, a moderate wind arises and brings the ship to Puteoli in six days.

Theon goes to the inn of Ariston, where he usually stays. Ariston has been a Christian for a long time and, when he hears of Theon's baptism, greets him all the more joyfully (6). Ariston informs Theon at once of the disastrous activity of Simon in Rome: Through his magic spells (*magico carmine*), Simon has even succeeded in seducing the Christians. Ariston himself has been waiting impatiently to see Peter, whom Paul had mentioned; a vision has told Ariston that Peter would come to the city.

Theon leads Ariston to the ship, where he falls down before Peter and begs him with tears to go to Rome as quickly as possible. Peter too weeps and replies, "He who tempts the world by his angels" (i.e., Satan) "forestalled us"—but Christ will show that he is stronger. Theon objects that the path to Rome is long and arduous; Peter has fasted throughout the sea voyage, and so he ought to rest first. But Peter refuses to wait. His delay would cause further scandals, and he must therefore shoulder his responsibility at once so that no millstone may be hung around his neck and he be thrown into the depths of the sea (Mark 9:42

par.). Theon and Ariston accompany Peter to Rome, where their first call is on the dwelling of Narcissus.

Peter's First Sermon in Rome, in Two Parts

Bibliography: R. F. Stoops, "Patronage in the Acts of Peter." *Semeia* 38 (1986): 91–100.

All at once the rumor (*fama*) of Peter spreads among the Roman Christians; the text suggests that it reaches precisely those who were in the process of shaking off their ties to the community (7). On the first day of the week, they come together in great numbers and hear a lengthy sermon in which Peter speaks of the temptations that face those present and of the weaknesses of human beings in general. He then deliberately proposes his own person as an example. He was present when Jesus performed his signs and wonders. But he too knows what doubts are and what they mean— it is enough for him to think back on his own attempt to walk on the lake (Matt 14:29f.). He denied the Lord three times and then shed bitter tears. But—he adds almost by way of excuse—the devil had "deceived" him, and he was surrounded by "wicked dogs, just as the prophet of the Lord said" (cf. Ps 22:17, understood as a prophecy by David). The Lord forgave him everything, and this should give his hearers courage and hope. If Satan could "subvert" Peter, the first of the apostles, in such a manner, is it surprising that the new converts in Rome do not fare better? But the way to repentance is open for them too.

The hearers begin to repent and tell Peter about the most important recent development: Simon has won over the senator Marcellus and resides in his house. This Marcellus was an influential and wealthy patron of the community and occupied a key position. His house was a place of refuge for all the widows, orphans, foreigners, and poor persons. This had already come to the notice of the emperor, who had refused to appoint him to any high office lest, for example, he might plunder a province over which he was set as proconsul in order to give gifts to the Christians. The community tells Peter that Marcellus' radical change of mind was an important factor in their own defection from the faith. Marcellus now has all petitioners beaten and thrown out.

Peter begins the second part of his first sermon in Rome, a

rhetorically stylized invective against Satan, who has always played a fateful role in the history of damnation (8):

> You enticed the first man to evil lust . . . You have forced my fellow disciple and co-apostle Judas to act wickedly and betray our Lord Jesus Christ . . . You hardened the heart of Herod and kindled Pharaoh and made him fight against Moses, the holy servant of God; you emboldened Caiaphas to deliver our Lord Jesus Christ to the cruel multitude; and now you are still firing your poisonous arrows at innocent souls.

Peter prays that deepest darkness may swallow up Satan and his adherents. He must desist from attacking the servants of Christ. He must no longer knock at doors that do not belong to him and carry off, like a ravening wolf, sheep that belong to Christ (cf. John 10:9-12).

The First Miracle: or, the Return of Marcellus

Bibliography: J. E. Spittler, *Wild Kingdom*. Chap. 4.

This tirade succeeds in its purpose: Even more souls that were in peril, or seemed already lost, return to the Lord. At the request of the sisters and brothers, Peter seeks a direct confrontation and goes to the house of Marcellus (9). In the presence of numerous witnesses, he charges the doorkeeper to go in and tell Simon, "Peter, on whose account you left Judea, awaits you at the door!" The doorkeeper replies that Simon is aware of Peter's arrival and that he has given instructions, "Whether he comes in the day or at night or at whatever hour, say that I am not at home." Peter is not so easily deceived. He announces that an extraordinary miracle will take place. He unties a huge dog that lies chained in the court-yard. The dog immediately enquires with a human voice how he may be of service to Peter, who tells him to enter the house and say to Simon, "Peter sends word to you to come outside. For on your account I have come to Rome, you wicked man and destroyer of simple souls." The dog runs off, stands on his hind legs before Simon, and hands on this message word for word. Simon is speechless, and all the others who are present are astonished (like the speaking lion from ActPaul, the speaking dog is also mentioned by Commodian in his *Carmen Apologeticum* 626).

One of those who witness this miracle is Marcellus (10), and this is enough for him: He rushes to the gate, prostrates himself before Peter, and defends himself in a lengthy speech. He admits all his sins. For example, he has let Simon persuade him to erect a statue to him with the inscription "To Simon, the youthful god." (This is probably based on Justin, who writes in *Apol.* 26.2 that a statue was erected on an island in the Tiber with the inscription "To Simon, the holy god" [in Latin: *Simoni Sancto Deo*]. This in turn goes back to a confusion, because we know since the discovery of the base of a statue on the island in 1574 that the inscription in fact ran *Semoni Sanco Deo Fidio Sacrum* and was dedicated to an ancient Sabine god of oaths called *Semo Sancus*.) Marcellus appeals for clemency, recalling Jesus' words about the faith "as small as a grain of mustard-seed" in the field (Matt 17:20) and reminding Peter of his own doubts when he walked on the water (see above)—doubts that Simon has in fact adduced as proof of Peter's lack of faith. He concludes his *apologia pro vita sua* with the noncanonical logion of Jesus: "Those who are with me have not understood me" (cf. ActJoh 92). Peter can do nothing other than grant Marcellus' request. The Lord, "the Shepherd of the sheep which once were scattered," will receive his sheep Marcellus, who went astray for a time, back into the flock.

A young man in the crowd laughs, and Peter at once diagnoses this as a grave case of demonic possession (11; for this entire paragraph, cf. *Vit. Apoll.* 4.20). When the demoniac is called to account, he rushes into the atrium and hurls himself against a wall. The demon speaks out of him and describes what is happening in the house, thanks to its superhuman knowledge: The dog has spoken again to Simon about other mysterious matters and will die at Peter's feet once it has carried out what it was told to do. Peter commands the demon to come out of the young man. It is obliged to obey, but as it departs it kicks to pieces a large marble statue in the atrium. Because this is a statue of the emperor, Marcellus fears the worst—the emperor's spies will inform him of this, and he will punish it as lèse-majesté. (The historical M. Granius Marcellus, mentioned above, was accused before Tiberius of dealing disrespectfully with statues of the emperor: cf. Tacitus, *Ann.* 1.74.3.) Peter interprets this anxiety as a form of vacillating faith but does not take up the problem of the sacred value of an image of the emperor; he uses this event to put Marcellus' faith to the test. If he has truly repented and believes from the depths of his heart, then— as what we might call an adaptation to this situation of Jesus' words about the faith that "moves mountains"—he is to take some of the water that bubbles up from the well and sprinkle it over the fragments in the name of Jesus Christ. Marcellus speaks a prayer that ends with the words, "If it is your will, O Lord, that I live and receive no punishment from Caesar, let this statue be whole as before." He carries out the action, and this "baptism" restores the statue to wholeness. Peter is proud, and Marcellus rejoices.

Further Miracles: or, *the Duel Begins*

In §12, we learn something of what the dog said to Simon in the house. When Simon replies evasively: "Tell Peter that I am not in," the dog begins a verbal attack. As "a dumb animal, which received a human voice" (this alludes, via 2 Pet 2:16, to the story of Balaam's ass in Numbers 22), it will convict Simon of deceit. The dog remarks ironically that Simon took an extraordinary amount of time for reflection before he replied "I am not in" and threatens him with the punishment of eternal fire and darkness. It then runs back to Peter in the atrium and relates what has happened. It also predicts that he will have a hard struggle, but will be victorious in the end. The dog then dies at the apostle's feet (after this solo role, a return to a normal dog's life would probably have seemed too banal). Some of the crowd are impressed, but others demand further signs (cf. Mark 8:11), for after all, Simon too has performed many miracles—that is the only reason why they have followed him.

Peter sees a smoked fish or salted cod (*sardam*) hanging in the window (13). He asks the crowd if they would be willing to believe, if this dried fish would once again swim; they reply in the affirmative. He throws the fish into a pool (perhaps the *impluvium* of the house), and at once it swims around. In order that this may not seem to be a sensory deception (*fantasma*) like the miracles of Simon, the fish remains alive and attracts many visitors, who feed it with pieces of bread. Two points emerge clearly from this scene: A genuine miracle has a probative function in the author's eyes, but it is not always easy to distinguish it from the so-called magic tricks of the adversaries. There is something to be said for the hypothesis that the miracle with the fish also points to a more enigmatic dimension, that is, to the fish as a symbol of Christ or of the Christians and to Peter as the fisher of human beings (cf. Bremmer, 12).

Marcellus now throws Simon out of his house (14). The slaves, who had suffered under Simon, take the opportunity to mock him with words and to ill-treat him physically. (Astonishingly enough, this echoes the mockery of Jesus in the passion narrative and becomes even more relevant a little later on, in §16, when Jesus is portrayed in a vision as one "who was reviled, despised, and spat upon.") Simon hastens to the house of Narcissus and stands at the door, issuing a challenge to Peter: He will prove to Peter that he believes merely in "a Jewish man and the son of a carpenter." Peter sends a woman with a seven-month-old suckling child to Simon (15; cf. Matt 11:25 par.). The infant addresses Simon in the voice of a grown man: "You abomination before God and men, O destroyer of truth!" and utters colorful threats. On the following Sabbath, Simon will experience his own doom. Until then, he is to be deprived of speech and must leave the threshold of the house and the city of Rome. Once again, Simon finds that he cannot speak, but this time the effect lasts longer. He lodges outside Rome in a stable (cf. Zechariah's falling silent and the birth of Jesus in a stable in Luke 1–2; it is possible that these strange borrowings from the story of Jesus are meant to stylize Simon as the Antichrist, who, as is well known, imitates the Messiah on many points).

A Flashback

In the following night, Jesus appears, laughing and clothed in a radiant garment (§16). He makes known to Peter what the infant has announced to Simon: The duel will take place on the following Sabbath, and he promises his support. Once again, we are told that Satan is the father of Simon and the driving force behind all that he does.

On the next day, in §17, the narrator uses the account of the vision for a complicated flashback. We learn that Peter once drove off Simon in Judea. Simon was staying in Jerusalem in the house of Eubola (cf. the Eubula in ActPaul), a highly respected, wealthy woman who possessed gold and pearls. With two invisible helpers, he used magic to get hold of these treasures and carried them off. Eubola suspected her servants of having taken advantage of the visit of the "divine man" (*hominis deifici*) to steal her property and had them tortured. In a vision, Peter saw two of his former catechumens and a naked, fettered boy who gave him a wheaten loaf. (The symbolism is difficult to decipher even if one assumes that this boy is meant to be Jesus; it is possible that this time, his attributes hint at the distress of Eubola, who needed to be "unbound" and given spiritual nourishment [cf. Vouaux, 323].) The boy told Peter how the theft had actually taken place. On the third day, at the ninth hour, he would see Simon's two companions in crime at the gate that led to Neapolis (in Samaria, which was Simon's native land, according to Acts 8): they would be offering the goldsmith Agrippinus the chance to buy a statue of a child satyr. The statue was small, but of massive gold, overlaid with precious gems. Peter was not to touch the pagan statuette lest he incur impurity, but he was to inform Eubola's slaves about these events.

Peter visited Eubola, who sat at home with her garments rent and her hair disheveled, and told her to be of good cheer, since she was to recover her property. However, she must do penance for her sins and renounce the world in order to come to the eternal place of rest (*refrigerium*). He instructed her what her servants were to do two days from thence, explained how the theft had taken place, and confronted her with the choice between the living God and Jesus Christ on the one hand and the magician Simon, a "deceitful demon," on the other. Her decision was made easier by the miraculous proof, that is, the return of her stolen treasures.

Next, the goldsmith Agrippinus was informed of the plan. When Simon's two helpers attempted to sell him the golden statue, they were arrested. Eubola went to the Roman governor Pompey (the author may perhaps be thinking of Pompey the Great, who conquered Jerusalem in the first century BCE). Under torture, the two helpers admitted their guilt and betrayed the hiding place of Eubola's treasures and other stolen goods, an underground cave outside the city gate. They were brought in chains to this place. Simon, who was also making for the gate, immediately grasped what was happening and fled. Eubola gave all her possessions to the poor, especially to widows and orphans, and she has since died.

The link to the narrative present is formed by an appeal in §18 to fast and pray in preparation for the trial of strength between Simon and Peter which will take place on the following Sabbath.

A Proclamation of the Gospel, Framed by Miracles

Marcellus informs Peter that he has sprinkled all the rooms and corridors of his house with water accompanied by formulae of blessing, thus removing every trace of Simon (§19). He has also invited all the widows and elderly women into the house, so that he can give each of them a gold coin. All is now ready for a dignified act of worship, made all the more glorious by the presence of Peter. Peter therefore returns to the house of Marcellus, with Narcissus and the other brothers and sisters.

When he enters, Peter sees a blind widow whose daughter leads her by the hand (§20). In the name of Jesus, who gives a share in his "unapproachable light" (1 Tim 6:16), he tells her: "Open your eyes, see and walk on your own." This symbolic miracle is followed by a proclamation of the gospel, which has points of contact with ActJoh 87–105 and is intended to open the eyes of those present to how "the holy scriptures of our Lord," from which they are reading at that moment the transfiguration scene (Mark 9:2-10 parr.; cf. 2 Pet 1:17f.), "must be explained." Peter has written down these words to the best of his ability, taking into account the weakness of human flesh. The form in which the Lord appears on earth corresponds to this: He shows himself as "the image of man" (*effigie hominis*), and "each of us saw him as his capacity permitted."

These words are followed by the core of the sermon, an account of the transfiguration from Peter's perspective. At first, Peter believed that the Lord wanted to deprive him of his sight through the overwhelming splendor of light, and he was indeed ready to accept this, but the Lord took him by the hand and set him on his feet so that he could see him once again, as far as he was able. This is one example of how "the merciful God" (as Jesus is called, with reference to John 10:38) has borne our weaknesses and sins (cf. Isa 53:4). The accommodation goes even further: It was only "on our account" that "he ate and drank though he was neither hungry nor thirsty." We discern a slight polymorphy on the Redeemer's part, when Peter describes Jesus as "this Great and Small One, this Beautiful and Ugly One, this Young Man and Old Man . . . whom a human hand has not grasped, yet is held by his servants" (e.g., in the bread of the eucharist). The antitheses continue for several lines, and are followed by a series of eighteen christological metaphors, most of which are borrowed from the Gospel of John, and more immediately from ActJoh: he is "the door, the light, the way, the bread, the water, the life. . . ." A doxology concludes the sermon.

The widow whom Peter healed at the beginning of this chapter is not the only old and blind widow present, and the others also hope for a miracle (§21). The response is not a simple healing but a re-enactment of the transfiguration of Jesus at the ninth hour (a traditional hour of prayer). Peter tells the widows that their bodily eyes, which will in any case be closed again at death, cannot see anything other than human beings, animals, and matter; but with the inner eyes of faith, they would be able to see Jesus. Nevertheless, he asks the Lord for their bodily healing too. The room in which they are present is lit up by an indescribable, supernatural light. At this point, the text suddenly shifts briefly into the first-person plural in the narrative: "a sight which illuminated us so brightly that we were dazzled with bewilderment, and we cried to the Lord. . . ." Only the widows remain standing, because their blindness means that they cannot initially perceive the light. But it penetrates their eyes and restores their sight. In the testimonies that they then give, the polymorphy that the author borrows from ActJoh emerges even more clearly: Some have seen an old man, others an adolescent, and others a boy. Peter concludes by interpreting the various modes of seeing Jesus as a consequence of the sovereign greatness of God.

A Very Significant Dream

Bibliography: P. Habermehl, *Perpetua und der Ägypter, oder: Bilder des Bösen im frühen afrikanischen Christentum* (TU 140). 2nd ed. Berlin: 2004. – **B. D. Shaw**, "The Passion of Perpetua." *PaP* 139 (1993): 3–45.

The act of worship apparently leads into an *agape*; at any rate, Peter and the other brothers serve the Christian virgins to whom Marcellus offers his house as a dwelling place (§22). He also asks them to spend the night in prayer, because the duel between Peter and Simon is scheduled for the following day, a Sabbath. Platforms have already been erected in the forum, and people are saying, "Tomorrow at break of day two Jews must contend here concerning the worship of God." Nevertheless, Marcellus falls into a brief sleep and has a very significant dream, which he relates to Peter in the morning:

> In my sleep I saw you sitting in an elevated place and before you a great multitude and a very ugly woman, in appearance an Ethiopian, not an Egyptian, but very black, clad in filthy rags, who danced with an iron chain about the neck and a chain on her hands and feet. When you saw her you said to me with a loud voice, "Marcellus, this dancer is the whole power of Simon and of his god; behead her."

The stylization of the female dancer as a demonic figure speaks for itself and needs no commentary. In Peter's interpretation, Simon, his "great power" (cf. §4), and Satan as the author of this "power" merge into one another; the dreaming compresses the symbols and makes them polyvalent. In his dream, Marcellus objects that he is a noble senator and has never yet killed anyone, not even a sparrow. Peter therefore calls on Christ, "our true sword" (cf. Rev 19:15). A man who looks like Peter (i.e., Christ as Peter's *doppelgänger*, cf. ActJoh 87) appears and kills the demonic figure with a sword. Peter understands this dream as announcing his forthcoming victory. (Perpetua in Carthage likewise dreams on the evening before her martyrdom that she is victorious in the fight against an ugly Egyptian: cf. *Passio Perpetuae* 10 and the comments by Shaw and Habermehl. The question is whether Perpetua may have known ActPet.)

The Preliminary Skirmish

The whole of Rome assembles in the forum, including the senators, prefects, and officials; a seat on the platform costs a gold coin (§23). The spectators call to Peter; they designate themselves as "lovers of the gods" (cf. the description of the Athenians in Acts 17:22) and demand that he authenticate himself by means of a miracle. Simon also enters the arena but seems "dismayed" and gazes at Peter as if fascinated by him.

The duel is initially fought with words, and Peter begins. He recalls the theft of Eubola's treasures; the discovery of this crime had forced Simon to flee from Judea (cf. §17). He adds that Simon had prostrated himself in Jerusalem before him and before Paul— who had carried out healings by the laying on of hands—and had offered them a large sum of money, begging them to lay their hands on him and transmit this miraculous power to him (cf. Acts

8:14-24; the localization and some of the persons involved have been changed). Simon now objects that Jesus the Nazarene, whom Peter preaches, is only a human being, the son of a carpenter (cf. Mark 6:3 par.). He appeals to the Romans with an effective argument that convinces many: "Is a God born? Is he crucified? Whoever has a master is no God."

Peter meets this challenge in §24 with a chain of twelve (?) quotations, all of which point prophetically, but mysteriously, to the coming and the dignity of Christ. A number of problems arise in points of detail, since besides well known passages (such as Isa 53:2.8, 7:13f.; Ps 118:22; Dan 2:34, 7:13), we also find texts that come from apocryphal writings (e.g. from Ascension of Isaiah 11.14: "We neither heard her voice, nor did a midwife come") and other texts of unknown provenance, (e.g., the following two quotations: "In the last days a child shall be born of the Holy Spirit; his mother knows not a man and no one claims that he is his father," and "He came not out of the womb of a woman, but descended from a heavenly place" [taken on its own, this last text must be called docetic]). Peter knows that this *catena* will convince only insiders. He finishes by challenging Simon to act.

The First and Second Tests

Bibliography: I. Karasszon, "Agrippa, King and Prefect." Pages 21–28 in *The Apocryphal Acts of Peter*. Edited by J. N. Bremmer. – **C. M. Thomas**, "Revivifying Resurrection Accounts: Techniques of Composition and Rewriting in the Acts of Peter cc. 25–28." Pages 65–83 in *The Apocryphal Acts of Peter*. Edited by J. N. Bremmer.

The author employs variations on a single theme when he describes the competition in miracles. He relates three raisings of the dead. The first two are interwoven in a rather strange way, while the third is intended as a climax.

Agrippa, the city prefect (Agrippa I and Agrippa II from the Herodian dynasty inspired his figure and his name) selects one of his young servants and tells Simon to kill him. He then tells Peter that he is to raise him from the dead and tells the crowd that they must decide who is pleasing to God, "he who kills, or he who revives" (§25). Simon whispers something into the boy's ear, and the boy dies (this already implies that Simon, as the representative of evil, has only destructive powers, not creative powers).

Peter cannot attend to this matter at once, because another element slows down the action by introducing a second plot. One of the widows from Marcellus' house addresses him and collapses at his feet. She has lost her only son, the support of her old age (cf. Luke 7:12). Peter tells young men to bring the widow to her son and then to bring her back with the dead man (cf. Acts 5:6.10). When they arrive at the house, they first thing they do is to establish that the son has really died.

Meanwhile, in the forum, the prefect becomes impatient. Even the emperor was fond of the young man who was the first victim, and Agrippa had agreed to have him killed only because he trusted in Peter and in Peter's Lord (26). The resurrection takes the form of a concerted action: Peter asks the Lord that it may take place "in your power and through my voice." But Peter asks the prefect to hold the right hand of the boy, and through this gesture, it is the prefect himself who raises the boy from the dead (we have encountered similar raisings of the dead "at second hand" in ActJoh). The people acclaim: "There is only one God, the God of Peter" (*Unus Deus, unus Deus Petri*).

It is only now that the widow's plea is answered. She has returned to the forum with her dead son (27). In his prayer, Peter appeals explicitly to the words of the Lord, which he simply repeats: "Young man, arise!" (cf. Luke 7:14). Now that he has returned to life, the young man must first look after his mother; later, he will enter the ecclesiastical ministry as deacon and bishop (or as the bishop's deacon?). Once again, the people are filled with amazement and praise the God and Savior who works through Peter.

The Third Test

The news spreads through the entire city, and moves the mother of a deceased senator to come (§27). We learn later that he is called Nicostratus; he is several times referred to as "boy" or, better, as "son" (a senator had to be at least twenty-five years old). Peter demands that the mother believe in the possibility of a miracle, and she replies emphatically, "I believe, Peter, I believe" (*credo, Petre, credo*). She rushes home and organizes a solemn cortège to bring the corpse. Young men with caps on their heads (as a sign that they had been set free by the death) accompany the bier to the forum and carry the burial objects and funeral gifts.

This third heat must decide the contest, for Simon is not yet defeated. The crowd joins Peter in challenging him, and Simon takes up the gloves: "Romans, when you see that the dead man is raised [through me], will you cast Peter out of the city?" The people reply: "We shall not only cast him out but also burn him at once." Simon approaches the head of the dead man, bends down three times and perhaps also whispers mysterious words into his ear. The dead man raises his head, opens his eyes, and bows to Simon. The people start to collect wood for the pyre on which they will burn Peter, but he stops them, pointing out that the dead man has not even got up as yet. Now the dead man is to get up, loose the band around his head (cf. John 11:44), wave to them, and give other signs, without Simon standing close to him. But Simon is not able to do any of these things: His magical power is insufficient. The disappointed prefect pushes Simon away, and now the people want to burn Simon instead of Peter. But Peter does not allow this, since it would contradict the command to love one's neighbor; besides this, one must wait to see whether Simon will do penance (cf. Acts 8:22-24) or whether he falls completely into the hands of his father, the devil.

Before performing the miracle, Peter negotiates some concessions from the mother: The freed slaves will remain free members of her household and receive a portion of the funeral gifts, while the rest is to be given to the widows. Peter touches the side of the dead man and says only, "Arise!" At once, the dead man does everything that he could not do at Simon's bidding: He rises, unties the bands, and begins to speak. In the sleep of death, he has seen how Christ spoke with Peter and charged him to lead the young man to him. The raising to life attains its real goal only when it results in faith: Peter makes this clear to the Romans who had come to see a spectacle (*spectaculum*) but are now summoned to repentance.

Now it is Peter, instead of Simon, who is honored as a god (§29). The sick are laid at his feet, so that he may heal them, but the prefect, who finds Peter's popularity disturbing, prevents this. The young man remains with Peter in Marcellus' house. The grateful mother brings two thousand gold coins for the Christian virgins, and the young man adds four thousand coins. He declares that he is "a living sacrifice to God" (cf. Rom 12:1).

The conflict with Simon is not yet completely over, and the Latin text in the Vercelli codex goes further. But we prefer to follow the Greek text, which is available in one manuscript from §30 onwards, when we turn to the martyrdom of Peter, which begins, strictly speaking, in §33.

2. The Martyrdom of Peter

Bibliography: R. J. Bauckham, "The Martyrdom of Peter in Early Christian Literature." *ANRW* II: 26.1 (1992): 539–95.

A kind of intermezzo in §30 presents a service of worship at which Peter preaches. Highly placed persons are present, including a woman nicknamed Chryse, "the Golden one," because she has used only vessels of gold since she was born. In a vision, the Lord has instructed her to give ten thousand gold coins to Peter, and she does so. Some of those present object that she is a woman of ill repute: She has several lovers and even sleeps with her own slaves. The money must be returned to her! But Peter merely laughs. He has no problems with taking the money if this is how the Lord cares for his servants.

Simon's Deep Fall

A summary account of other miracles of healing wrought by Peter forms a bridge to the final confrontation with Simon. All that Simon can do is a feeble imitation of Peter's miracles (§31). He summons up spirits who have no genuine existence, he makes sick persons appear well for a short time, and he makes corpses move in the manner of Nicostratus (in the Greek text, a reversal of the two halves of his name makes him "Stratonicus"). Peter follows Simon like a shadow and shows up the ineffectiveness of his magic tricks. In his frustration, Simon summons up his strength for the final showdown, and announces:

> Tomorrow I shall . . . take refuge with God above, whose power I am, though [I now seem] enfeebled. If, therefore, you have fallen, behold I stand. I ascend to the father [cf. John 20:17], and I shall say to him, "Me, your son who stands, they desired to bring low."

Like "the power of God," "the one who stands" is also a title of majesty that belongs to the deity, who alone has permanent exis-

tence in his immutability; it is applied to Simon elsewhere too. He
had initially won over the Romans through his miraculous arrival,
flying through the air (32). His last attempt at flight echoes this
first miracle. Peter was not present then—but he is present now.
Besides this, the author gives Simon's flight the form of a blasphe-
mous parody of Christ's ascension. (Hippolytus gives a different
account: Simon has himself buried alive and announces that he
will rise from the grave on the third day [*Haer.* 6.20.2].)

The crowd gathers on the following day at the Via Sacra.
Simon stands on an elevated place and provokes Peter anew by
declaring that the Jews have killed his God, "And they stoned you
who were chosen by him" (cf. e.g., Acts 14:19)—where then is the
power of this God? Simon then rises up into the air and can be
seen above the city of Rome with its temples and hills, an "incredible spectacle" (*paradoxon theama*). The Christians look at Peter,
full of fear and of expectation. He calls on the Lord for help:
Unless action is taken, everything will have been in vain. Simon
must fall down, but not die: "let him be disabled and break his leg
in three places." This is exactly what happens. Simon lies helpless
on the ground, and the spectators contemptuously throw stones at
him in a mirror reversal of what Simon had earlier said. Even
Gemellus, one of his adherents, ironically throws his earlier
provocation in Simon's face: "If God's power is broken, shall not
that God, whose power you are, be darkened?" Gemellus then
becomes a disciple of Peter.

The end comes quickly and unspectacularly. Simon finds a few
faithful adherents who bring him on a stretcher by night to Aricia,
and from there to Terracina, where he stays with Castor, who had
been obliged to leave Rome because he had practiced sorcery.
Doctors attempt an emergency operation, an amputation, but this
only leads to Simon's death.

The Price of Chastity

Bibliography (especially on *Quo vadis*): **R. F. Stoops**, "The Acts of Peter
in Intertextual Context." *Semeia* 84 (1997): 57–86 (at 77–81). – **C. M.
Thomas**, "Canon and Antitype: The Relationship Between the Acts of
Peter and the New Testament." *Semeia* 84 (1997): 185–205 (at 198–200).

Agrippina, Nicaria, Euphemia, and Doris, four concubines of the
prefect Agrippa, now come to Peter (§33) and hear "preaching

concerning chastity and all the words of the Lord." They resolve that they will no longer sleep with Agrippa but will live in sexual continence (the text does not raise the question whether it was at all possible for slave women to take such a decision). As one might expect, Agrippa reacts with intense anger. He discovers that Peter is the one responsible for this change of heart, and he threatens the women that he will kill them and have Peter burned alive.

This instance involves irregular sexual unions, but §34 concerns a regular marriage. Albinus, a friend of the emperor (a Lucceius Albinus replaced Festus as governor in Judea in 62 CE, and was otherwise active in provincial administration: cf. Tacitus, *Hist.* 2.58.1–59.1), has a beautiful wife named Xanthippe. Influenced by Peter, she refuses to sleep with her husband, who consequently "rages like a beast" (an expression that implicitly designates the frustrated sexual instinct as something "animal"). "Many other women," we are told in a summary, "delighted in the preaching concerning chastity and separated from their husbands, and men too ceased to sleep with their wives." Albinus and Agrippa decide together to take revenge on Peter in the name of all the husbands and lovers who have been affected: He is to pay with his life for the consequences of his recommendation of sexual continence.

Xanthippe sends a warning to Peter, and the sisters and brothers persuade him to leave Rome because they do not want to lose him altogether (35). This is the setting for the famous *Quo vadis* scene (cf. John 13:36), which was also included in ActPaul. Disguising his appearance, Peter goes alone out to the gate. The Lord comes to meet him, on his way into the city. Peter asks, "Lord, where are you going?" He replies, "I go to Rome to be crucified." Peter asks, "Lord, are you being crucified again?" And the Lord replies, "Yes, Peter, *again* shall I be crucified." Peter gets the point; the Lord departs to heaven, and Peter returns to the city. This episode is not only meant as a mild rebuke of Peter; it is also intended to illustrate the conviction that in every martyr, Christ himself as it were suffers death anew.

The Passion of Peter

Bibliography: J. Bolyki, " 'Head Downwards': The Cross of Peter in the Lights of the Apocryphal Acts, of the New Testament and of the Society-transforming Claim of Early Christianity." Pages 111–12 in *The*

Apocryphal Acts of Peter. Edited by J. N. Bremmer. – **B. McNeil**, "A Liturgical Source in Acts of Peter 38." *VC* 33 (1979): 342–46. – **A. Orbe**, *Los primeros herejes ante la persecución: Estudios Valentiniano*, Vol. 5 (AnGr 83). Rome: 1956. 176–212. – **M. Pesthy**, "Cross and Death in the Apocryphal Acts of the Apostles." Pages 123–33 in *The Apocryphal Acts of Peter*. Edited by J. N. Bremmer.

The sisters and brothers are sad to see him return, but Peter explains to them that the will of the Lord must be done in all things (36; cf. Mark 14:36). Four soldiers (the same number that is presupposed in John 19:23) seize him and bring him before Agrippa, who condemns him to crucifixion because of godlessness (a typical Roman accusation leveled at the Christians). The believers and the crowd, "rich and poor, widows and orphans, able-bodied and disabled alike," protest, but Peter himself calms them and offers a half-excuse for Agrippa, who is only "a servant of the power of his father." This enigmatic description means that now it is no longer Simon but Agrippa who carries out the plan of Satan.

The crucifixion gives Peter the opportunity to hold two profound discourses, with which our author imitates the crucifixion scene from ActJoh. This explains their philosophical—sometimes almost gnostic—veneer, which however remains purely external (despite the penetrating analysis by Antonio Orbe, who detects the redeemer myth of Valentinian gnosis in the background). Peter holds his first discourse in §37, standing in front of the cross. He affirms that he has now completely grasped the hidden mystery of the cross: It is not what the sensory perception takes it to be, the instrument of a shameful execution. The deeper insight of faith perceives it to be a participation in the suffering of Christ, which leads to salvation. Finally, Peter asks his executioners to crucify him with his head downward (cf. Seneca, *Consolatio ad Marciam* 20.3: "I see there beams of torture, though not all of one and the same kind . . . some are crucified with their head towards the earth . . . others have spread out their arms on the cross").

Hanging on the cross in this fashion, Peter begins his second discourse, which begins in §38 by interpreting his apparently strange wish. It is not (as the common opinion has it) a gesture of humility, in the sense that the apostle did not regard himself as worthy to die in exactly the same way as his Lord. Rather, Peter's upside-down position symbolizes fallen human nature. Through the sin of the first human being, everything in the world has been turned upside down and distorted: Right appears to be left, and bad appears to be good. This is why the Lord said (in an agraphon): "Unless you make the right as the left and the left as the right, and the top as the bottom and the front as the back, you shall not know the kingdom" (of God; cf. Gos. Thom. 22). Under the conditions of sin, this reversal signifies the reestablishment of the original, correct order of things. The cross of Christ is a manifest expression of the divine-human nature of the Redeemer and of his spreading out into the world as the Word of God. It is only via his cross—in other words, through conversion and penance—that the human person can find the path back to his authentic being.

After thus revealing the allegorical meaning of the cross, Peter begins a prayer of thanksgiving (39), but he no longer wishes to utter this with a human voice that gives birth both to truth and to lies, but with a voice that is heard only in silence. This is the voice of the Spirit in the believer, and it is this Spirit who establishes the communication with the exalted Lord, whom Peter calls his father, mother, brother, friend, servant (cf. Phil 2:7), and steward (cf. Luke 12:42). He promises the believers who are present that they will be able to attain through Christ what "eye has not seen, nor ear heard, neither has it entered into the heart of man" (1 Cor 2:9; Gos. Thom. 17). With the closing Amen, in which the multitude joins loudly, Peter breathes his last (§40).

Marcellus has Peter buried with great luxury. He bathes the corpse in milk and wine, and anoints it with a huge amount of costly spices. He fills the precious sarcophagus in which the body will rest with Attic honey. Peter rebukes him for this by night, recalling Jesus' logion: "Let the dead be buried by their own dead" (Matt 8:22 par.). But Marcellus pays heed only to the fact that Peter has appeared to him. This is sufficient proof to him of the continued existence of the soul of Peter, and he feels himself strengthened in faith.

In a brief postlude, Emperor Nero himself appears (cf. the MartPaul). He would have preferred to inflict an even harsher punishment on Peter and attempts to destroy the Christians; but an apparition in a dream strikes him and warns him to keep his hands from them. Nero is terrified, and this is the beginning of a period of peace for the community in Rome.

This appearance by Nero adds one more anachronism to the others in the narrative. According to §5, Peter left Jerusalem for

Rome twelve years after the resurrection and ascension of the Lord. He must therefore have reached the capital under the reign of Claudius, and this too is the period—according to Justin (*Apol.* 26.2)—at which Simon Magus came to Rome. The martyrdom must have taken place shortly after this. But in this final paragraph, which belongs to a second or third stage of revision, we see the victory of the other tendency, namely to have Peter and Paul suffer martyrdom together in Rome under Nero.

3. The Act of Peter (BG 4)

Bibliography: H. M. Schenke, *Nag Hammadi Deutsch*, Vol. 2: *NHC V,2–XIII,1; BG 1 und 4* (GCS.ns 12). Berlin: 2003. 845–53. – **J. Brashler and D. M. Parrott**, "The Act of Peter. BG, 4:128.1–141.7." Pages 473–93 in *Nag Hammadi Codices V, 2–5 and VI with Papyrus Berolinensis 8502, 1 and 4* (NHS 11). Edited by D. M. Parrott. Leiden: 1979. (With English translation.) – **A. L. Molinari**, *"I Never Knew the Man": The Coptic Act of Peter (Papyrus Berolinensis 8502), Its Independence from the Apocryphal Acts of Peter, Genre and Legendary Origins* (BCNH.E 5). Quebec: 2000. – **C. Schmidt**, *Die alten Petrusakten.* – Idem, "Studien zu den alten Petrusakten." *ZKG* 43 (1924): 321–48; 45 (1927): 481–513.

The *subscriptio* to the fourth and last writing in the Coptic Papyrus Berolinensis 8502, also known as Berolinensis Gnosticus (BG), calls it "The Act (*praxis*) of Peter" (ActusPt). The individual deed (or misdeed) performed by Peter is given particular prominence.

The narrative, which is probably set in Jerusalem, begins with numerous healings that Peter performs on a Sunday. A man in the crowd puts into words a question that has occurred to them all: Why does not Peter help his own daughter, who has grown into a beautiful young woman? She lies helpless in a corner, paralyzed on one side of her body. Peter replies with a smile that he would certainly be able to restore her to health with the help of God and substantiates this claim by commanding her to stand up and come to him. She does so, but after this demonstration, Peter returns her to her former condition, and his daughter lies once again immobile in her corner.

In view of this cruel conduct, the crowd (which represents the readers of the text) begins to weep, and Peter realizes that he must justify what he has done. He explains that on the day of his daughter's birth, the Lord had told him in a vision that the girl would pose a danger to many souls, because of her beauty, if she remained healthy. When she was ten years old, Ptolemy, a rich man, caught a glimpse of her while she was bathing with her mother (either in the sea or in public baths) and became obsessed by the idea of getting her as his wife.

At this point, a leaf written on both sides is missing in the codex. This passage must have related how Ptolemy abducted Peter's daughter and sought to make her his wife by force, but at the last moment, thanks to the prayer of her parents, she became paralyzed and thus could no longer marry. The text resumes at the point where Ptolemy's servants set her down before the door of Peter's house. Peter and his wife find her, paralyzed from head to foot. They bring her in and praise the Lord, who in this dramatic fashion has "saved his servant from defilement, [and] pollution, and [destruction]."

The remainder of the text, in a more edifying style, relates what happened to Ptolemy. He sheds so many tears in repentance that he becomes blind and resolves to end his life by hanging himself (cf. Matt 27:3-5). But a bright light illuminates his house, and he hears a voice that rebukes him and charges him to go to Peter's house, where he regains his sight. When he dies, he leaves a field to Peter's daughter, for it was thanks to her that he became a believer. Peter sells the field in her name, and the entire proceeds are given to the poor (cf. the contrasting picture in Acts 5:1-11).

Peter's behavior toward his daughter seems so scandalous that it is easy to overlook another piece of information in this text, viz. that Peter was a married man who had a daughter with his wife—and that all this clearly occurred during his activity as an apostle after Easter (we should note that it is the exalted Lord who announces the birth of his daughter to him in a dream). This narrative fragment excludes a fundamental rejection of marriage.

The Letter of Pseudo-Titus about chastity (NTApo 6th ed. II: 54f., 258) relates a similar story. Peter prays that the virginal daughter of a gardener may receive whatever is most useful for her soul, and the girl drops down dead. Her enraged father persuades Peter to call her back to life—but a visitor seduces her only a few days later, and both she and he disappear.

Carl Schmidt presented strong arguments for holding that both episodes, but above all ActusPt, belong to the lost first third of the ancient Acts of Peter; the designation as an individual *Act* already suggests this. Another argument is the allusion in Augustine, *Contra Adimantum* 17.5, where the author speaks of *apocrypha* and mentions stories "about the daughter of Peter, who was paralyzed at the prayer of her father, and about the gardener's daughter, who died at the prayer of the same Peter." Recently, Andrea Lorenzo Molinari has energetically argued against this view on the basis of numerous acute observations. We must leave this question open (cf. also the cautious evaluation of the arguments in H. M. Schenke's review of Molinari's book, in *JAC* 45 [2002]: 247–53). In general terms, we know less about the ancient Acts of Peter than earlier scholarship often supposed.

Molinari's remarks about the genre of the miracle that is "turned upside-down" are helpful here. The narrative in ActusPt recalls a type of rhetorical *exempla*, which he calls "chastity stories." These have the following structure: A father rescues his daughter from a threat to her honor—or else reestablishes her honor by killing her. One early Roman example that scholars have often discussed is the story of Verginius and his fifteen-year-old daughter Verginia, whom one of the *decemviri* stalks and seeks with every means at his disposal to seduce (Molinari, 128–56). The fact that Peter's daughter is "only" paralyzed (instead of being killed outright) is a poor consolation to a Christian reader; but a Christianization of the basic pattern can be discerned in the fact that vengeance is not taken on the evildoer. On the contrary, he is forgiven.

4. Later Narratives

Bibliography: A. de Santos Otero, NTApo 6th ed. II: 392–99. – **H. Achelis**, *Acta SS. Nerei et Achillei: Text und Untersuchung* (TU 11.2). Leipzig: 1893. – **A. L. Molinari**, "I Never Knew the Man." 61–80. – **C. M. Thomas**, *The Acts of Peter*. 42–46.

As in the case of MartPaul, we possess an expanded Latin version of MartPet, which claims to have been written by Linus, Peter's episcopal successor in Rome. It may have been written in ca. the fourth century in Rome (AAAp I, 1–22), at the same period as a Christian interpolation in a Latin translation of Flavius Josephus' *Jewish War*, under the name of (Pseudo-)Hegesippus (3.2.1; ed. in CSEL 66, pp. 183–87), which relates Peter's struggle against

Simon. Nero has Peter executed because he regards him as responsible for the death of his friend and helper Simon. The martyrdom of Paul is juxtaposed with that of Peter.

The martyrdoms of the two apostles are combined in other later works from the fifth century onwards, e.g. in Pseudo-Marcellus, *Passio sanctorum apostolorum Petri et Pauli* (AAAp I, 118–77), a work that is further expanded with the same pseudepigraphical attribution in the *Acta Petri et Pauli* (AAAp I: 178–222), which contains an account of Paul's journey from Malta to Rome. Considerable space is devoted in both versions to Simon Magus; inter alia, we read that Nero kept Simon's dead body in his palace for three days because he believed that Simon would rise again from the dead. A wide manuscript attestation and translations into numerous languages demonstrate the popularity of these variable versions of the legend of the apostle.

In the present context, it is particularly interesting to look briefly at the fifth- or sixth-century Acts of Nereus and Achilleus, because they present the story of Peter's daughter in a new form. Nereus and Achilleus are brothers whom Peter baptizes. They are members of the court of Flavia Domitilla, who belongs to the imperial family, and they succeed in persuading their young mistress, who wishes to contract a marriage in keeping with her high rank in society, that a life in virginity is preferable. The narrative takes many twists and turns and ends with Flavia's exile by Domitian to an island. Nereus and Achilleus accompany her into exile, where they at once meet two pupils of Simon Magus and must fight against them. They send a letter to the Roman governor Marcellus (whom we know from ActPet), asking him to declare the truth about Simon.

Marcellus grants this request in his answering letter, which incorporates various Petrine traditions. One unusual feature (also found in Pseudo-Marcellus) is the mention of a personal friendship between Simon and Nero. A raising of the dead is described, and the speaking dog plays a role (though somewhat different from its role in the *Actus Vercellenses*). Here, Peter's paralyzed daughter is called *Petronilla* in a superficial assimilation to the name "Peter" (in fact, the name Petronilla is connected to *Petro, Petronius*). Peter heals her at the request of Titus, but her beauty immediately attracts the attention of the Roman official Flaccus, and Petronilla escapes from this situation only thanks to a gentle death. Flaccus chooses Felicula as his next victim, but when she persistently refuses his advances, he has her tortured to death; and the old priest Nicodemus, who was a kind of spiritual adviser to the two young women, meets a similar fate. At this point, the letter, which establishes a link to the tradition about Peter, ends. The Acts continue with an account of how Nereus and Achilleus, Domitilla, and other martyrs meet their deaths (cf. the table of contents in Achelis, 37–39). This passage tells us nothing more about the figure of Peter; nevertheless, it would be highly desirable to have a translation into a modern European language and a commentary.

5. The *Kerygma Petri*

Bibliography: W. Schneemelcher, NTApo 6th ed. II: 34–41. – **J. K. Elliott**, *Apocryphal NT*. 20–24. – **M. Cambe**, *Kerygma Petri: Textus et Commentarius* (CChr.SA 15). Turnhout: 2003. – **E. von Dobschütz**, *Das Kerygma Petri kritisch untersucht* (TU 11,1). Leipzig: 1893. – **H. Paulsen**, "Das Kerygma Petri und die urchristliche Apologetik." *ZKG* 88 (1977): 1–37.

We now turn briefly to another "Petrine" writing, the *Kerygma Petri* or "Preaching of Peter," although it is not directly connected to ActPet (cf. however Elliott, 21: "should perhaps be classified as part of an apocryphal acts"). It is considerably older than ActPet, and may have been written ca. 100/110 CE (thus, Cambe, 383, although I find this dating almost too early). Unfortunately, only fragments survive, mainly thanks to quotations of connected texts by Clement of Alexandria in the *Stromateis*. Origen also quotes the *Kerygma Petri* twice. He in turn appeals to Heracleon, the author of a commentary on John; Origen himself is more skeptical than Clement about the Petrine provenance of this text.

Peter presents his preaching as the spokesman of the Twelve; this is why the first personal plural predominates. He is addressing Christians and his most important subject is the correct worship of God, which is demarcated vis-à-vis both Greeks and Jews. We should note the negative theology that is a consequence of the profession of faith in the one creator God: He is invisible, uncontainable, and needs nothing; he is incomprehensible, eternal, imperishable, and uncreated (*Strom.* 6.5.39: in Greek, these seven adjectives are formed with the so-called alpha privative). As is common in Jewish apologetic, the Egyptian cult of animals is presented as the embodiment of Greek polytheism: Material things— wood, stone, and precious metals—are shaped into images of the gods, and animals that are meant to be eaten are both venerated and—paradoxically—offered in sacrifice. But the author criticizes Judaism too, alleging that the Jews serve, not the true God, but "angels and archangels, the month and the moon" (a reference to the weekly and annual Jewish feasts: *Strom.* 6.5.41; cf. Gal 4:8-11).

The Christians form the "third race" or a "third type," because they belong to the new covenant that is announced in Jeremiah 31 (cf. Heb 8:8-13; 10:16f.). In two brief scenes, the foundations of the Christian proclamation are traced back to words that the risen Jesus addressed to the Twelve, including the command (presupposed in ActPet 5) to wait for twelve years before going out into the world (*Strom.* 6.5.43). In a kind of hermeneutical reflection, Peter explains that the development of the "apostolic" theology was the outcome of the study of Scripture. In the books of the prophets, "sometimes expressed by parables, sometimes by riddles, and sometimes directly and in so many words," the apostles read about Jesus' activity on earth, his death on the cross, and his ascension. Accordingly, "without the scripture we say nothing" (*Strom.* 6.15.128).

C. Evaluation

Bibliography: A. G. Brock, "Political Authority and Cultural Accommodation: Social Diversity in the Acts of Paul and the Acts of Peter." Pages 145–69 in *The Apocryphal Acts of the Apostles*. Edited by F. Bovon et al. – **C. Grappe**, *Images de Pierre aux deux premiers siècles* (EHPhR 75). Paris: 1995. – **J. Perkins**, "Healing and Power: The Acts of Peter." Pages 124–41 in idem, *The Suffering Self*. – **C. M. Thomas**, "The 'Prehistory' of the Acts of Peter." Page 39–62 in *The Apocryphal Acts of the Apostles*. Edited by F. Bovon et al.

As we have seen, the search for the text of the ancient ActPet yields little apart from what is contained in the *Actus Vercellenses*, which offers what we might call a snapshot that "freezes" one specific constellation within a continuing process; the later narratives show us something of the rich subsequent history of these traditions, but for their prehistory, we are dependent on literary-critical reconstructions and hypotheses. Traditions about Simon Peter circulated at an early date, as we see in the New Testament itself. Around 200, these took the form of an alternative narrative in which Paul was as yet missing, but Simon Magus from Acts 8 had already become the great opponent of the apostle Peter. The other characters are borrowed—without any concern for historical accuracy—either from early Christian traditions (including New Testament writings) or from secular history.

It is obvious that Simon does full justice in ActPet to his nickname "Magus." His activity is primarily that of a magician, and the principal area in which he competes with the apostle is that of miracles. Traits that associate him with Satan, the real adversary, and perhaps even give him the appearance of the antichrist, are only hinted at; nor do we find clear references to his role as the founder of all the gnostic heresies—his primary role in the eyes of Irenaeus of Lyons, who wrote at roughly the same period (cf. *Adv. Haer.* 1.23.1–4). Despite some echoes, above all in Peter's discourses at his crucifixion, ActPet does not teach a gnostic theology. Nor is ActPet genuinely anti-gnostic: indeed, the whole question of gnosis seems not to interest the author. He is content with a Christianity that delights in miracles and promotes asceticism and that can be regarded as the lowest common denominator of various tendencies.

Once again, we see an ambivalent attitude toward marriage and the family. Although it is Peter's preaching about sexual continence that ultimately leads to his martyrdom, he has not demanded the renunciation of marriage on principle; the episode of his daughter (if it is acceptable to adduce this here) displays the same ambivalence since it demonstrates that Peter was in fact a married man with a wife and a child, although he treats his daughter with such great rigor.

This observation can be extended to the social and cultural criteria of value that are implied in ActPet. There can be no doubt that the worldview that is propagated in the crucifixion scene—a world that is upside-down and must be put aright—has societal consequences (cf. Perkins), including the discernible sympathy with the situation of the slaves in the houses of Marcellus, Eubola, and Nicostratus. Nevertheless, the general tendency appears somewhat more conciliatory than that in ActPaul (cf. Brock); senators such as Demetrius or Marcellus can be integrated into the

Christian group in this text more smoothly than would be possible in other apocryphal Acts. A statue of the emperor that is smashed is repaired, and Peter accepts the money of the non-Christian Chryse although he is informed about her immoral way of life.

This again brings us to a fundamental affirmation of ActPet as a whole, viz. the message that forgiveness is possible always and in all situations—even in the case of Simon Magus! Almost all the Roman Christians have fallen away from the pure doctrine, but they can all receive forgiveness at any time and without too much trouble. Peter is a particularly appropriate spokesman of this tolerant position because he was its first great beneficiary. He was forgiven for his lack of faith, his threefold denial, and finally his flight from Rome (although he was aware of the gravity of this action). We may suspect that this has contemporary relevance: The author is indicating the proper treatment of the *lapsi*, those Christians who had revoked their confession of faith during the persecution but now wanted to return to membership in the community.

Chapter 4

The Acts of Andrew

Editions: M. Bonnet, AAAp II: 1. 1–64. – **J. M. Prieur**, *Acta Andreae* (CChrSA 5–6). Turnhout: 1989. (With French translation.) – **D. R. MacDonald**, *The Acts of Andrew and the Acts of Andrew and Matthias in the City of the Cannibals* (SBLCA 1). Atlanta: 1990. (With English translation.) – **L. Leloir**, *Écrits apocryphes*, Vol. 1: 228–57. (French translation of the Armenian version.)

Translations: J. M. Prieur and W. Schneemelcher, NTApo 6th ed. II: 93–137. – **J. K. Elliott**, *Apocryphal NT.* 231–302. – **J. M. Prieur**, Pages 887–972 in *Écrits apocryphes chrétiens*, Vol. 1. Edited by F. Bovon and P. Geoltrain. – **D. R. MacDonald**, *The Acts of Andrew* (Early Christian Apocrypha 1). Santa Rosa: 2005.

Bibliography: J. N. Bremmer, ed. *The Apocryphal Acts of Andrew* (Studies in the Apocryphal Acts of the Apostles 5). Louvain: 2000. – **J. Flamion**, *Les Actes apocryphes de l'apôtre André. Les Actes d'André et de Mathias, de Pierre et André et les textes apparentés* (RTCHP 33). Louvain: 1911. – **D. R. MacDonald**, *Christianizing Homer: The Odyssey, Plato, and The Acts of Andrew*. New York: 1994. – **P. M. Peterson**, *Andrew, Brother of Simon Peter. His History and His Legends* (NovTSup 1). Leiden: 1958. – **L. Roig-Lanzillota**, *Acta Andreae Apocrypha: A New Perspective on the Nature, Intention and Significance of the Primitive Text* (COr 26). Geneva: 2007.

A. Context

Bibliography: J. N. Bremmer, "Man, Magic, and Martyrdom in the Acts of Andrew." Pages 15–34 in idem., *The Apocryphal Acts of Andrew.* – **P. J. Lalleman**, "The Acts of Andrew and the Acts of John." Ibid. 140–48. – **J. M. Prieur**, "Les Actes apocryphes d'André: Présentation des diverses traditions apocryphes et état de la question." *ANRW* II: 25.6 (1988): 4384–4414. – **L. Roig-Lanzillota**, *Acta Andreae.* 3–100.

Like the other apocryphal Acts we have studied in the previous chapters, the Acts of Andrew (ActAndr) have not survived in their original form but have left so many traces in hagiography, piety, and art—and not least in the polemic directed against them—that we must conclude that they were very well known and widely diffused. They seem to have been for a time the most popular representative of the genre "apocryphal Acts of Apostles," especially in dualistic and ascetically-minded circles. Eusebius, the first to give clear testimony to their existence, attacks them in the same breath as he mentions them (*Hist. eccl.* 3.25.6f.), whereas the Manichaean Psalter quotes them approvingly several times, for example, in the section on the "ten virgins" in the Psalms of Heraclides: "A shamer of the serpent is Maximilla the faithful. A receiver of good news is Iphidama her sister also, imprisoned in the prisons" (192.26–28). We shall meet both these women in the course of the narrative. Catholic revisions allowed the mainstream church to accept parts of the work. It is only in the ninth century that we lose track of them in the East; in the West, there is no trace of them after the sixth century.

Originally, the Acts of Andrew consisted of two parts: the travels of the apostle, beginning in Pontus in Asia Minor, with the main emphasis on Philippi; and his activity and his death in Patras in Achaea, the goal of his voyages. He leaves Patras for an excursion to Corinth, Megara, and Sparta. (We may compare the definition of the Manichaean apocryphal texts about Andrew that we find in Philaster of Brescia, *Diversarum hereseon liber* 88f., written in 390: "These are deeds [*Actus*] which he performed when he went from Pontus to Greece and which were then written down by the disciples who followed the blessed apostle.") They must have been considerably lengthier than the other apocryphal Acts, but they seem to have been written at one go, so to speak. In other words, it is not possible to identify older, autonomous parts; a single author has created the work with great literary skill on the basis of a small amount of traditional information. This insight, however, is the outcome of a laborious work of reconstruction that is obliged to work with disparate materials.

We must begin with the *Book of the Miracles of Blessed Andrew the Apostle*, compiled on the basis of a Latin version of the complete ActAndr by Gregory, bishop of Tours, ca. 593, shortly before his death. He writes that he has omitted the lengthy discourses and concentrated on the miracle stories; he has also corrected, in a Catholic sense, whatever seemed theologically offensive. His work still reflects the geographical structure of the underlying ActAndr, and we can also compare some episodes with traditions recorded elsewhere (for an overview, see Elliott, 234f. and Prieur, 59–65). The point at which Gregory abbreviates most radically, toward the end of the narrative, is where the other textual witnesses begin.

The principal text for the activity of Andrew in Patras is found in two manuscripts from Sinai (S) and Jerusalem (H) discovered by Jean-Marc Prieur. For §§33–50, before the martyrdom, a Vatican manuscript (V; AAAp II: 1, 38–45) contains the better (because more detailed) text. The martyrdom itself in §§51–65 was transmitted independently (as was so often the case) in a variety of recensions, paraphrases, and free elaborations. Here we should mention a still unpublished manuscript from Ann Arbor (C); the so-called *Martyrium alterum* (AAAp II: 1, 58–64); the "Letter of the presbyters and deacons of Achaea" (originally written in Latin, but also translated into Greek: cf. AAAp II: 1, 1–37); and a document known from its initial words as *Conversante et docente* (*AnBoll* 13 [1894]: 373–78). Some details seem to have been preserved only in the Armenian passion (cf. Leloir), which is therefore particularly important. The following texts begin at an earlier point in the narrative sequence: the *Martyrium prius* (AAAp II: 1, 46–57; Prieur, 684–703); a *Vita* written by the monk Epiphanius after 815 (PG 120, 215–60); the *Laudatio* by Nicetas of Paphlagonia, which is based (though not exclusively) on Epiphanius' work (*AnBoll* 13 [1894]: 309–52); the *Narratio* (*AnBoll* 13, 353–72); and, as always, the late collection of legends about the apostles in Pseudo-Abdias, book 3.

On this basis, it is possible to reconstruct a text that comes close to the ActAndr in its earliest form; but when we employ this reconstruction, we must not forget that we are looking at a mosaic or jigsaw puzzle that has been assembled from individual pieces by the skill of scholars (even more skeptical on the history of tradition of the Acts of Andrew is L. Roig-Lanzillota, who accepts only the fragment in V as a reliable part of the older form of this work).

In addition to internal indications and external attestation, the relationship to the other apocryphal Acts helps to date ActAndr. There is some evidence that the author knew ActJoh and that he may have adopted the form from this work (cf. Lalleman). In the

crucifixion scene, there are obvious parallels to ActPet (or to earlier literary or tradition-historical stages in the formation of what
subsequently became the text of ActPet). Here too, it seems that
the author of ActAndr is drawing on an earlier work for his own
purposes. It is often assumed that ActPaul draws on ActAndr, but
there is no compelling reason to accept this hypothesis. Jan N.
Bremmer has put forward a significant argument based on internal evidence: The abandonment of military service because of the
Christian faith, which is an explicit theme in the Coptic Utrecht
fragment, seems to have become a problem only ca. 200. All this
suggests that ActAndr was composed in the first decade of the
third Christian century.

Various suggestions have been made about the place of com-
position, from Achaea (Flamion) via Asia Minor and Syria to
Egypt (Prieur). Once again, Asia Minor, and perhaps specifically
Pontus, seems the most likely place (cf. Bremmer, 16).

The author of ActAndr remains unknown. It is certain that he
had a measure of rhetorical and philosophical education, which
allowed him to transmit an enigmatic message in a good style,
which indeed sometimes shows traces of hard work or is recher-
ché. It is possible that he was formerly a pagan philosopher, who
then discovered the Christian faith—like Justin Martyr. In this
context, it is interesting to note that Pope Innocent I, writing
against the use of ActAndr by the Priscillianists in Spain, says that
it was written by the philosophers Xenocharides and Leonidas.
(However, the text-critical basis of this passage is not reliable: cf.
NTApo 6th ed. II: 95 with n. 9.)

B. Contents

1. Gregory of Tours, *Book of the Miracles of Blessed Andrew the Apostle*

Bibliography: Text (following Bonnet) and French translation in **J. M. Prieur**, *Acta Andreae*. 564–651. – Text and English translation in **D. R. MacDonald**, *The Acts of Andrew*. 207–317.

After a preface in which he explains the reasons for writing as he
does (i.e., his concentration on the miracles and the elimination of
the verbose speeches), Gregory begins in §1 by speaking of the

division of the missionary territories among the apostles. Andrew was assigned the province of Achaea (in Eusebius, *Hist. eccl.* 3.1.1, he is assigned Scythia). Gregory then traces the path taken by Matthew (*Matthaeus* in Gregory, rather than *Matthias*) to the cannibals in Mermidona. Andrew has to rescue him before he can take up his own task in §2.

On His Journey

The miracles and the places in which they are performed are presented in rapid succession. In Amasia Andrew heals a blind man and brings back to life a young Egyptian slave, who has died of a fever (§3). The mother of Sostratus, a young Christian, wants to commit incest with him; when he refuses to sleep with her, she accuses him before the proconsul of committing precisely this crime. The apostle clears up the matter in time, and it is the mother who is executed (§4; it is worth asking whether this story reflects the accusation of incest that was leveled against the Christians).

In Sinope, the son of Gratinus is violently attacked by a demon in a women's bathhouse (where he ought not to have been present). Gratinus sends word to Andrew, asking him for help—for he too has a fever, and his wife suffers from dropsy. Andrew expels the demon and then speaks to the parents: they are suffering justly, because the husband had visited a prostitute and the wife had committed adultery with other men. Their bodily healing goes hand in hand with their moral conversion (§5). In Nicaea, Andrew is confronted with seven demons, who throw stones at passers-by from wayside tombs (§6; cf. Mark 5:1-20 par.). He forces them to show themselves to the people in the form of dogs and then sends them away into desolate, barren regions (cf. Matt 12:43-45 par.).

This exorcism has consequences, as we see in Nicomedia (§7). At the city gate, Andrew encounters a funeral cortege with an elderly married couple who are bearing their son (probably their only son) out to be buried (cf. Luke 7:11-17). Andrew questions them and learns that seven dogs killed the young man with their bites; he realizes at once that these "dogs" were the demons from Nicaea. The father promises to give Andrew the most precious of all his possessions, his son. Andrew summons the young man back to life and takes him with him to Macedonia. The crossing to

Byzantium (§8), which Gregory has presumably abbreviated, is relatively undramatic, but Andrew must still a storm at sea (cf. Mark 4:35-41 par.).

Angels of God are active in the next two scenes. On the way to Thrace, a troop of men with swords and spears attempt to attack Andrew and his companions (9), but an angel of the Lord, surrounded by radiant light, hurls them to the ground. In Perinthus, a harbor town, an angel tells Andrew which ship he should board for Macedonia (10).

In Philippi

Bibliography: J. E. Spittler, *Wild Kingdom*. Chap. 2 (on the scenes with animals).

Philippi, the first station in continental Europe, is an important center for the apostle's activity. In the city, all the preparations have been made for a double wedding between two brothers and two sisters, who are their paternal cousins (§11; Leucippe and Cleitophon, the couple whose names form the title of the novel by Achilles Tatius, are likewise the children of two brothers). Andrew prevents these marriages, because they are incestuous. (This reason for the apostle's action is probably no older than Gregory of Tours, who found a more fundamental rejection of the planned marriages in the original text and introduced into the text the canonical legislation governing marriage in his own period.)

A rich young man from Thessalonica now appears (§12), throws himself at the apostle's feet, and asks for instruction about the path of life (cf. Mark 10:17-22 par.). His parents want to bring him back home, but when no agreement is reached on this question, they set fire to the house where Andrew is lodging. (The Manichaean Psalter alludes to this: "Andrew the apostle—they set fire to the house beneath him" [142.20].) But all their assaults are thwarted, and they leave Philippi without being reconciled to their son. Fifty days later, they both die within one hour, and the son distributes the money that he inherits to the poor and the needy. He accompanies Andrew to Thessalonica and preaches in the theater in that city (§13; he is the only person whom the author of ActAndr allows to preach); but it is Andrew who heals another son of the family, who has been paralyzed for twenty-three years. The next miracle concerns a boy who is possessed by a demon. The demon realizes that it will shortly be expelled, and so it throttles the boy beforehand (§14). The father brings the body into the theater, where Andrew restores the boy to life, and all who see the miracle definitively embrace the faith. The "theatricalization" of public life is well advanced here.

The father-and-son stories continue. The father of a son who has been crippled for twenty-two years asks Andrew to come back to Philippi (§15), but first the apostle must free nine persons who are in chains under deplorable conditions. After their wounds have been treated for three days, he heals the paralyzed son. A summary account then tells us that the son himself heals other sick persons; this means that both preaching and the working of miracles can be delegated to post-apostolic office bearers.

The next distressed father wants to bring the apostle to his daughter in a golden carriage with four white mules and four white horses (§16). Before healing her, Andrew holds a discourse in which he points to the true, i.e. invisible, values. An exorcism leads in §17 to a remarkable reaction. The crowd demands, "Tell us, man of God, who is the true God, in whose name you heal our sick?" Philosophers too hold discussions with him, "and no one could resist his teaching" (Acts 6:10).

This brings us to the lengthy §18; we shall discuss the parallels in the Coptic Utrecht papyrus below. Andrew is accused before the proconsul Virinus: "He says the temples should be destroyed and ceremonies done away, and all the ancient law abolished." The proconsul three times sends soldiers to arrest Andrew, but each time in vain. One soldier from the third group, which regards Andrew as a magician, is possessed by a demon and dies when it comes out from him. This provides the occasion for Andrew to raise the man from the dead in the presence of the proconsul, who has by now come to the place of these events. While the people react, "Glory to our God!" (*Gloria Deo nostro!*), the proconsul cries: "Believe not the sorcerer!" On the following morning, he three times orders that wild animals be stirred up to attack Andrew: first a boar, which does nothing; a bull, which tramples two professional animal-fighters (*venatores*) to death and then itself falls down dead; and finally a leopard, which leaps into the proconsul's lodge and kills his son. Andrew restores him to life and prevents the crowd, all of whom are on his side, from killing the proconsul. (It is possible that P.Oxy 851, a fragment with a few lines in Greek, may come from this episode.)

The proconsul's wife certainly had a larger role in the original ActAndr but makes only a brief appearance in §19. The apostle charges her to raise to life a child that had been killed by the poison of a huge snake. The apostle rebukes the snake, which is wreaking havoc on a rural estate, for all the evil it has brought upon humankind since the beginning (cf. Genesis 3). The snake coils around an oak tree, vomits poison and blood, and dies.

A vision in the following night prepares Andrew for his martyrdom (§20). He sees himself standing with Peter and John on a high mountain, illuminated by a radiant light (cf. the transfiguration of Jesus). John says to him: "You will soon drink Peter's cup," and he speaks of the cross "whereon you shall hang shortly." (On the literary level, this may reflect a dependence of ActAndr on the traditions in ActJoh and ActPet.)

In Achaea

The group set sail in two ships for Achaea and reach their destination after twelve days; en route, the apostle shows that the wind and the waves are subject to him (§21). The province is governed by the proconsul Lesbius (historically speaking, however, the proconsul's seat was in Corinth, not in Patras). He seeks to kill Andrew, but he is so badly beaten in the night by two demonic figures, who look like dark-skinned Ethiopians, that he lies sick on his bed (§22). Andrew heals him, and Lesbius becomes a believer.

As a consequence, Lesbius' wife Calisto (whose name means "the most beautiful one") feels neglected, and she readily believes a spurned lover of Trophima—who once was the mistress of Lesbius but now accepts the apostle's preaching about sexual continence—when he asserts that Trophima has resumed her relationship with Lesbius (§23). Calisto has Trophima put into a brothel, where she lays a book of the gospels on her body in order to protect herself from harassment by clients (in the novel *Historia Apollonii regis Tyri*, 33–36, the daughter of Apollonius likewise succeeds in preserving her chastity in a brothel). One particularly brutal client catches sight of an angel and falls down dead; Trophima raises him to life. In the meantime, Calisto and another man have entered the public baths, where an ugly demon kills them both. Calisto's old nurse succeeds in moving the apostle to compassion, and he raises her to life—despite the initial opposition of her husband Lesbius.

Andrew is walking along the shore with Lesbius when a corpse is washed up before their feet (§24). After he is raised up, we learn that the dead man, whose name is Philopater, and his thirty-nine companions had been searching for the apostle in order to hear his message with their own ears, but they all perished in a storm. The apostle's prayer brings all the other corpses ashore. He himself sees only to the raising of Varus, a foster-brother of Philopater. He then bids the two brothers restore the other thirty-eight to life.

Andrew is summoned to Corinth, where a woman who has conceived the child of a murderer cannot give birth although she has already asked her sister to pray to the goddess of childbirth, Diana/Artemis (§25). These demonic powers cannot help, but the apostle can: The child is born dead and remains dead, but the mother's life is saved. There is a happy outcome to Andrew's meeting with Philopater's father in Corinth (§26), and Andrew performs two exorcisms in a public bathhouse (§27), which is a favorite lodging for demons.

An old man named Nicolaus comes to the apostle (§28); we may already be in Sparta, which is mentioned in §29. Although he is seventy-four years old and appears in principle to be a believer, he regularly visits the brothel for immoral purposes. Andrew weeps for three hours, fasts for several days, and prays for him with all the believers: This brings about the miracle of his repentance. After fasting severely on bread and water, Nicolaus dies six months later, and a heavenly voice confirms that he has been saved. Andrew frees a household in Megara from especially persistent demons, thereby winning Antiphanes, the master of the house, and his wife as reliable helpers in the work of preaching (§29).

In Patras

Bibliography: D. W. Pao, "Physical and Spiritual Restoration: The Role of Healing Miracles in the Acts of Andrew." Pages 259–80 in *The Apocryphal Acts of the Apostles*. Edited by F. Bovon et al.

In §30 Andrew returns to Patras, where Aegeates is now proconsul. His sick wife, Maximilla, sends her maid Iphidama to fetch Andrew. He frees her from her fever but rejects the hundred silver pieces which the proconsul (who thinks that he is a doctor) wants to pay him; and the proconsul does not forget this.

Andrew now quickly heals a lame man (§31), a blind family (§32), and a man with a particularly severe and repulsive skin disease, who lives on a dunghill by the harbor (§33). Some brief concluding paragraphs present further events concerning Maximilla, her husband, his brother Stratocles, and the maid Iphidama, but here we have much more detailed Greek textual witnesses. In §37, Gregory himself observes that he need not say much about the martyrdom, "because I find it well done by someone else." His final words in §38 take the form of a prayer.

As the Latin title of Gregory's work (*Liber de Miraculis Beati Andreae Apostoli*) shows, the central role played by the apostle's miracles is intentional. They must, however, have played a considerable role in the original Acts as well, and we shall encounter further examples. In comparison to the other apocryphal Acts, we miss some elements, such as the animals which speak and act in a miraculous manner. In their original context, the miracles are not merely events; they also communicate messages (cf. Pao). They are employed as weapons in the fight against evil; they symbolically portray the salvation of the spiritual person; and they are employed to confirm ethically desirable modes of conduct.

2. Three Coptic Fragments

Bibliography: J. M. Prieur, *Acta Andreae*. 21–25, 653–71. Edited by R. van den Broek. – **J. Barns**, "A Coptic Apocryphal Fragment in the Bodleian Library." *JTS* NS 11 (1960): 70–76. – **G. Quispel**, "An Unknown Fragment of the Acts of Andrew." *VC* 10 (1956): 129–48. – **T. S. Richter**, "P. Ien. inv. 649: Ein Splitter vom koptischen Text der Acta Andreae." *APF* 44 (1998): 275–84.

The *subscriptio* of a fourth-century Coptic papyrus, which is now in Utrecht, reads: "The Act (*praxis*) of Andrew." The intention seems to be to present a single episode from ActAndr. The first eight of a total of fifteen pages are missing, as are pages 11 and 12, but a narrative structure can be discerned in the remaining text which is partly parallel to §18 in Gregory of Tours. It tells of a confrontation with the proconsul Varianus (the Coptic has a more appropriate form of his name) and the military might of Rome.

One of the four soldiers who are sent out against the adherents of the apostle proves to be possessed by an evil spirit. Andrew compels the demon to relate everything that has happened up to that point (we hear nothing of this in Gregory). The soldier had a virginal sister who devoted herself zealously to an ascetic life. A great magician in the neighboring house wanted to make her his own, and he employed supernatural powers against her—but in vain. Instead, one of the demons seems to have entered the brother; and the sister, with tears, told the story to a woman who was her friend and adviser. This confidante announced that Andrew would heal the brother. Other "hidden mysteries" are revealed to her, and it is clear that the demon had the opportunity to eavesdrop on her.

This brings us back to the main narrative. Without any further resistance, the demon leaves the soldier, who takes off his uniform and throws it to the ground. Despite the punishment with which he is threatened, he insists on giving up his military service. He has recognized that the greater power lies with the apostle Andrew.

Two leaves from a Coptic parchment codex, which also comes from the fourth century (Barns), present a textual fragment that may belong to the beginning of ActAndr. Jesus appears to Andrew and addresses him as "pillar" (cf. Gal 2:9). Andrew emphasizes that he has abandoned his parents, his children, and his wife in order to take up the cross every day and to carry it behind Jesus.

Another Coptic fragment, which is all that remains of the first page of a parchment codex from the fourth or fifth century, is important for a more formal reason (cf. Richter). The surviving text corresponds to §1 of the Martyrdom narrative in Bonnet (§51 in Prieur) and thus attests that the Martyrdom had become an independent literary unit at a very early date.

3. Andrew in Patras (Greek Text)

Bibliography: Text and French translation in **J. M. Prieur**, *Acta Andreae*. 443–549. – Text and English translation in **D. R. MacDonald**, *The Acts of Andrew*. 319–441. – German translation by **Gregor Ahn** (without enumeration of the paragraphs) in NTApo 6th ed. II: 123–37. – **L. Roig-Lanzillota**, *Acta Andreae*. 101–35 (text and translation of the fragment in the Vatican manuscript V); 137–90 (analysis and comments). – **S. Schwartz**, "From Bedroom to Courtroom: The Adultery Type Scene in the Acts of Andrew." Pages 267–311 in *Mapping Gender in Ancient Religious Discourse* (BIS 84). Edited by Todd Penner and Caroline van der Stichele. Leiden: 2007.

The Greek textual tradition in manuscripts S and H, in a connected account which includes the martyrdom, begins in §1 with the arrival in Patras of Stratocles, a brother of the proconsul Aegeates, who is on his way to Rome. (In Gregory of Tours, the parallel is in §34. From now on, we follow Prieur's enumeration. §1 of the independent Martyrdom narrative printed in Bonnet corresponds to §51 in Prieur.)

The Conversion of Stratocles

Stratocles had persuaded the emperor to free him from the obligation of military service (with a play on words in the Greek, since the name *Strato-klês* indicates "glory in battle") so that he may devote himself entirely to philosophy. His sister-in-law Maximilla greets him warmly, and she knows what must be done when a demon takes possession of a favorite young slave of Stratocles and the philosopher is completely distraught (2; a homoerotic relationship between the two men is probably implied): Andrew will help—and at that very moment, he too enters the praetorium (3). The situation is dramatic. The young man lies on refuse, twisting and turning and foaming at the mouth—Stratocles is threatening to commit suicide—and his servants take Andrew for a hobo and want to throw him out. The apostle makes his way, smiling and calm, to the one who needs his help; Stratocles says that the slave, named Alcman after a famous poet, has become "a spectacle" (4). From this point on, the miracles are accompanied by the discourses and prayers that have mostly been missing in Gregory. Andrew explains that magicians and charlatans were not able to help the slave because they themselves are "kindred" to the demons. When he commands it to leave the slave, the demon replies with a man's voice, "I flee, servant of God!" Alcman regains his senses and is astonished to see so many people present (5).

Maximilla brings her brother, the apostle, and all the sisters and brothers into her bedroom (6), where Andrew holds a profound discourse (7) in which he appeals to the "new self" in Stratocles. He has already bidden farewell to his earlier belief in the pagan gods and to philosophy, and has desired to worship God in truth. This new self must be born, like a child, with the help of the apostle—for he understands the art of midwifery (these words are an unmistakable allusion to Socrates). With a deep sigh, Stratocles declares his intention of never leaving the apostle's side from then on (8). In the days that follow, he puts an endless stream of questions not only to Andrew but also to the other brothers. Andrew makes a humorous comment on this behavior (the translation in NTApo 6th ed. incorrectly suggests that he rebukes Stratocles), developing a comparison that he has already made (9): A pregnant woman consults other women who have already experienced the mystery of giving birth. The child wants to come into the world and must do so—and the other women know best how one should look after the child once it is born. This is Stratocles' situation: His new existence in the midst of the fellowship of believers is gradually taking shape. Alcman also joins this fellowship (10).

Andrew holds another sermon, rounding off this section, on the occasion of the sealing of the newly converted men with the seal of baptism (11–12). This seal must be kept pure so that it can also be an effective defense against the power of evil. If we return to the Lord the "deposit" of faith that has been entrusted to us (cf. 1 Tim 6:20), he will give us himself as friend, father, and brother. Some of the hearers are moved to tears, while others exult. The neophyte Stratocles renounces all his worldly goods.

The Conflict Draws Near

Bibliography: I. Czachesz, " 'Whatever Goes into the Mouth . . . .' " Pages 56–69 in *The Apocryphal Acts of Andrew*. Edited by J. N. Bremmer. – **M. Pesthy**, "Aegeates, the Devil in Person." Ibid. 47–55.

The brothers and sisters are assembled on a Sunday in Maximilla's house, when Aegeates returns from his journey. Andrew therefore prays that the Christians may be able to leave the house unnoticed (13). Aegeates feels stomach pains and withdraws with a chamber pot for "a long time" (a detail in the narrative that clearly helps to degrade him and make him ridiculous: cf. Czachesz). Later, he enters Maximilla's bedroom because he desires her. He finds her at prayer and thinks that she is praying for him, because he has overheard his own name (14); but she had in fact said: "Rescue me at last from Aegeates' filthy intercourse." When he attempts to kiss her, she rejects him. He withdraws for the moment so that he may sleep after his long journey. Maximilla summons Andrew (15). In a prayer, he speaks of Aegeates as "that insolent and hostile snake," equating him with Satan (16). He asks that Maximilla may be preserved from the "disgusting pollution" of intercourse with her husband and may be united with "her inner husband."

A Problematical Interim Solution

Maximilla has an idea: She calls Euclia, a very pretty—and "exceedingly wanton"—young slave woman and prepares the marital bedroom for her. She succeeds in disguising Euclia in such a way that Aegeates sleeps with her without noticing that she is not in fact his wife (17). This plan succeeds for eight months, but then Euclia begins to make ever greater demands (18). She wants her freedom, gold, and jewels. Nor is this all: She boasts of her role to her fellow slaves and proves the truth of her assertions.

Maximilla thinks that all is going well, but Andrew, with whom she spends most of her time, is warned in a dream (19). The other slaves try their hand at blackmail (20), and Maximilla pays them a thousand denarii to keep silence (21), but finally, "at the instigation of their father the devil," they go to Aegeates and tell him everything. Euclia admits her guilt under torture (22). Aegeates has her tongue cut out, mutilates her, and throws her out of the house, where the dogs eat her. He has three other slaves crucified, in order to protect his wife's honor. We note that the author has no qualms about letting other persons pay a very high price for Maximilla's chastity; and the matter is not made any more acceptable by the fact that they are morally dubious characters.

A Declaration of Love

In his despair, Aegeates throws himself at his wife's feet and begs her, in the name of the twelve years that they have spent together as husband and wife, to tell him whether there is another man in her life; if this is so, he is ready to forgive her (23). Maximilla's reply remains necessarily ambiguous for him. It is only the reader who grasps the true meaning, not least because of the neutral form:

> I am in love, Aegeates. I am in love, and the object of my love is not of this world and therefore is imperceptible to you. Night and day it

kindles and enflames me with love for it. You cannot see it for it is
difficult to see, and you cannot separate me from it, for that is impossible. Let me have intercourse with it and take my rest with it alone.

Aegeates tells his brother Stratocles of his suffering and mentions
that his wife comes from a much more noble family than he himself (24). A young slave informs him that Stratocles is also involved
in this affair. He tells of the miraculous healer who wanders
around in all of Achaea; both Maximilla and Stratocles have fallen
under his spell—Stratocles indeed to such an extent that he completely forgets his dignity as the brother of the proconsul and buys
his vegetables in person and brings them home (25). While the
slave is still speaking, he sees Andrew far off and runs to him and
brings him to Aegeates (26). The proconsul at once identifies him
as the man who had healed Maximilla but had refused to accept
any payment for this (cf. §30 in Gregory's vita). He throws Andrew
into prison.

Aegeates himself informs Maximilla of what has happened
(27). Filled with anxiety, she charges her maid Iphidama to discover where Andrew is being kept prisoner. Iphidama succeeds in
reaching Andrew without being detected. He is preaching to his
fellow prisoners in the dungeon (28). He tells Iphidama that she
must return in the evening with Maximilla; the prison gates will
not bar their way (29).

When she hears this, Maximilla shows her resolute determination: Even if an entire legion were to encircle them and keep them
under observation, it could not prevent them from visiting the
apostle (30). Aegeates knows what his wife is planning. He does
not send a whole legion against her, but he does post four soldiers
in front of her bedroom and four others at the prison gate (31).
However, the two women become invisible and leave the house
unnoticed. At the prison gate, a beautiful child is waiting for them
and leads them through the doors, which open of their own
accord, to the apostle (32). In Evodius of Uzala (*De fide contra
Manichaeos*, 38), this child, who represents Christ, then enters the
bedroom of the two women and imitates a conversation between
them. Aegeates, who is eavesdropping, is convinced that they have
not left the room.

From this point on, we have another manuscript in addition to
H and S, viz. Codex Vaticanus 808 (V; German translation in
NTApo 6th ed. II: 117–22; the paragraph numbers of this section

are given in brackets). In §33[1], it is only V that offers the fragment of a lengthy discourse by the apostle. All three manuscripts agree in §34[2] in their description of the undisturbed comings and goings that take place in the prison for days on end. What follows has a literary model in Plato's *Phaedo*, where Socrates, who is facing death, has deep conversations in the circle of his friends about what awaits the soul after death.

A Bitter Choice

Bibliography: K. Cooper, *The Virgin and the Bride*. 45–49. – **K. C. Wagener**, " 'Repentant Eve, Perfected Adam': Conversion in The Acts of Andrew." *SBLSP* 30 (1991): 348–56.

The peace does not last long. During another trial, Aegeates suddenly recalls that he has unfinished business with Andrew (35[3]). He rushes home and confronts his wife with a choice (36[4]): If she resumes marital intercourse with him and is ready to bear children (we note here that the marriage is childless even after twelve years), he will release the foreigner who sits in prison. Otherwise, he will not do any harm to his wife herself, but he will torture her through the treatment that will be meted out to the prisoner whom she loves.

Maximilla goes to Andrew. "Putting his hands on her eyes and then bringing them to her mouth, she kissed them and began to seek his advice" (37[5]). His answer is clear: Maximilla must not yield in any way to Aegeates' proposal. He then locates their two roles in a broad salvation-historical perspective: In them, the fate of the first human couple is repeated, but the outcome is different. In Maximilla, Eve repairs her fault, and Adam does the same in Andrew. Implicitly, the original sin is equated with sexual intercourse, and consistent sexual continence leads to the overcoming of this sin, as we read explicitly in 39[7] in H and S: "Just as Adam died in Eve through his complicity with her, so also I now live in you through your observing the commandment of the Lord." Andrew looks ahead unflinchingly to the terrible forms of capital punishment envisaged by Roman law (as yet, he does not mention crucifixion): "Let him throw me to the beasts, burn me with fire, and throw me off a cliff."

In the other passages of direct speech, which are found above all here in V, there is noticeable tendency to form *catenae*. The

new, inner human being is described in four macarisms or acclamations of praise introduced by *euge*, "You have done well . . . ,"
and in twelve attributes such as "immaterial, holy, light, heavenly,
translucent, pure . . ." (38[6]). Fifteen adjectives, most of them
with an alpha privative, are applied to Maximilla: "unsullied, unal-
loyed, unbroken, undamaged, unweeping, unwounded . . ."
(40[8]). When Andrew addresses Maximilla as a "wise man"
(41[9]), it may be due to a general patriarchalist tendency, but one
must also bear in mind that in gnostic thinking, the female soul
needs a male counterpart if it is to attain to perfection.

Farewell Scenes

From §42[10] onward, Andrew turns to the second person in need
of consolation, Stratocles. He begins (in V) by firing off a battery
of brief questions at him, approximately fifty-five in all. These are
intended to uncover the spiritual dispositions of Stratocles and to
see whether he has truly come to an affinity of spirit with the apostle. Stratocles insists in his answers that this is the case. The words
of the apostle have kindled a blazing fire in him (44[12]). But he
wonders what will happen to him when the apostle is no longer
there. Andrew announces that on the following day, Aegeates will
condemn him to be impaled on a stake (45[13]).

In the meantime, Maximilla has told Aegeates that she refuses
to accept his offer. Aegeates, whom we know to be an agent of
Satan, has decided that Andrew will die by crucifixion. The Lord,
who this time takes on the form of Andrew (46[14]), leads
Maximilla once again to the prison, where she finds the apostle
delivering an exhortatory discourse. His preaching, which seeks
not to teach people but only to remind them (this too is a reminis-
cence of Socrates), leads those whose being is related to the Word
that is preached to the knowledge of their own true nature
(47[15]). In a world where everything is transitory and in flux, they
find a solid ground on which they can build (48[16]). They must
not let themselves be disturbed by the violent fate that awaits the
apostle (49[17]), since this is only a typical snare that the devil with
his "children" lays for the true believers. The main danger is that
evil appears under the mask of friendship; but now, the devil realizes that he has been unmasked by the apostolic preaching
(50[18]).

The Crucifixion

Bibliography: V. Calzolari, "La version arménienne du Martyre d'André." Pages 149–85 in *The Apocryphal Acts of Andrew*. Edited by J. N. Bremmer.

Section 51[1] marks the beginning of the Martyrdom, which is attested not only in our principal manuscripts H and S as well as in an unpublished manuscript from Ann Arbor (C), but also in a number of variants in further bearers of the tradition (hence the double enumeration of the paragraphs).

Aegeates begins by informing Andrew scornfully that he will now give him an appropriate gift in return for all that the apostle has done to him by taking his wife away from him. He then has him whipped with seven scourges and orders the soldiers who execute him not to nail him to the cross but to tie him to it. His limbs are not to be cut or broken (cf. 54[4]) in order that his painful death may be prolonged as long as possible. (The x-form of the so-called Saint Andrew's cross is a medieval addition that is not found in the ancient Acts.)

The city, which sides with the apostle, is in uproar. Stratocles intervenes and actually assaults the soldiers physically (52[2]). He snatches Andrew away from them and leads him by the hand to the place of crucifixion beside the sea, but the apostle rebukes him gently for this conduct: He ought to show a greater equanimity. At this point, the Armenian translation (cf. Calzolari) introduces the allegory of the eagle, which (at least in its first part) may belong to the original text. If the eagle does not fly high in the sky but remains too close to the earth, its wings become heavy, and it loses its majestic nature. So too the soul is at home in heaven, not on the earth; it wants to ascend, not to remain a captive here below (cf. the flight of the soul in Plato, *Phaedrus* 246c).

When he arrives at the place of execution, Andrew greets the cross, which has long been waiting for him, as "pure, radiant, full of life and light" (cf. the cross of light in ActJoh 97–102). This address to the cross, which echoes ActPet 37, is much more detailed in the Armenian translation and in other versions of the martyrdom (cf. Prieur, 737–45; MacDonald, 409–15). Andrew speaks of the form of the cross, which in its vertical beam unites things below the earth, things on the earth, and things in heaven (cf. Phil 2:10) and in its horizontal beam unites opposites such as right and left. Once again, we find a series of praises of the cross, introduced by *euge*. At the close, most of the textual witnesses agree in presenting the following narrative element: Andrew asks that the sentence be carried out. As Aegeates has ordered, he is only tied to the cross (54[4]).

The Sermon on the Cross

When Stratocles asks why Andrew, who is hanging on the cross, smiles whereas everyone else feels like weeping (55[5]), Andrew replies with his first discourse from the cross, which is addressed to everyone: "Men who are present with me, women, children, old, slaves, free, and any others who would hear" (56[6]).

The first part of his sermon contains nine (or ten, if we follow the Armenian translation) sentences with protasis and apodosis, for example: "If you understand the conjunction of the soul with a body to be the soul itself, so that after the separation [of the two] nothing at all exists, you possess the intelligence of animals and one would have to list you among ferocious beasts" (we note the Platonic color of the anthropology). In general, Andrew teaches that an attachment to earthly things prevents us from clearly seeing that which is spiritual and has a completely different kind of reality.

In the second part (57), we find twenty negative descriptions of earthly life as painful, vain, foolish, boastful, empty, transient, etc., and an appeal to follow the example of Andrew. In the third part (58), the apostle says that he is going away in order to "prepare routes" to heaven for his adherents (cf. John 14:2f.). But first, he must overcome the hostile powers embodied not only in the devil and demons, but also in worm, fire, and shadows. The demons dance around in a veritable shower of verbs: They "fly out, become agitated, rush forth, take wing, ravage, fight, conquer, rule, wreak vengeance, smile, etc."

Attempted Rescue and Death

The hearers do not move from the spot, and Andrew speaks to them from the cross for three days and three nights (59). On the fourth day, the crowd is so overwhelmed that they rush to the tribunal and demand that Aegeates set the apostle free:

> What is this judgment of yours, O proconsul? You have judged
> wickedly! You have made an unjust decision! . . . What crime did the
> man commit? What evil has he done? The city is in uproar! You are
> wronging us all! You are grieving us all! . . . Grant us this God-fear-
> ing man! Do not kill this man possessed of God! . . . Even though he
> has been hanging for four days, he is still alive. Although he has eaten
> nothing, he has nourished us with his words. Bring the man down
> and we will all become philosophers.

Aegeates initially attempts to ignore this demand (60[7]), but when
he sees that there are about two thousand (in another version,
twenty thousand) persons present whom he cannot intimidate, he
himself begins to be afraid, and declares himself ready to set the
apostle free. This causes a general rejoicing, which comes to the
ears of those who are still standing at the place of crucifixion.

Only one person is unhappy—the apostle himself, who com-
plains of the lack of understanding on the part even of his closest
associates (61[8]) and wonders what may be the source of this
enduring love of the flesh (i.e., of life here on earth). Aegeates now
comes to the cross, and the apostle asks him why he has come (62):
Does he wish to untie one who has tied himself (to the Lord), one
who has already escaped and been set free? Andrew says that the
Lord, to whom he is now making his way, has warned him against
Aegeates, calling him an enemy, corruptor, deceiver, seducer, slanderer, charlatan, murderer, flatterer, magician, etc. When
Aegeates nevertheless draws near to the cross in order to untie
Andrew, the apostle cries with a loud voice (63[9]):

> O Master, do not permit Andrew, the one tied to your wood, to be
> untied again. O Jesus, do not give me to the shameless devil, I who
> am attached to your mystery [i.e., to the cross]. O Father [he is still
> addressing Jesus], do not let your opponent untie me, I who am
> hanging upon your grace. May he who is little [i.e., the devil, or
> Aegeates] no longer humiliate the one who has known your great-
> ness. But you yourself, O Christ . . . receive me, so that by my depar-
> ture [Greek: *exodos*] to you there may be a reunion of my many
> kindred, those who rest in your majesty.

With these words, Andrew gives up his spirit (cf. Jn 19:30).
The narrative continues in the first person plural: "We wept and
everyone grieved at his departure . . ." (64[10]). Maximilla and
Stratocles bury him. We are told that Aegeates, whom Maximilla
definitively leaves, kills himself some time later by hurling himself

down from a great height (into the sea?). His heir is Stratocles—the author underlines here the fact that Maximilla and Aegeates had no children—but he does not touch the property which he inherits.

A "Hermeneutical" Concluding Word

Bibliography: F. Bovon, "The Words of Life in the Acts of Andrew." Pages 81–95 in *The Apocryphal Acts of Andrew*. Edited by J. N. Bremmer. – **G. Luttikhuizen**, "The Religious Message of Andrew's Speeches." Ibid. 96–103.

The work ends with a closing personal observation in the first person singular: "Here let me make an end of the blessed tales . . ." (65[11]). The most significant element in this passage is the hermeneutical information that the work contains not only the narration of deeds (*diêgêmata* and *praxeis*) but also mysteries (*mustêria*), which it is difficult—or even perhaps impossible—to relate. This means that the work is to be read on two levels, "the obvious and the obscure, comprehensible only to the intellect." This ambiguous work explicitly demands to be read in two stages, for only such a reading can communicate to the reader the salvation that is its central concern.

C. Evaluation

Bibliography: D. R. MacDonald, *Christianizing Homer*. – **L. S. Nasrallah**, " 'She Became What the Words Signified': The Greek Acts of Andrew's Construction of the Reader-Disciple." Pages 233–58 in *The Apocryphal Acts of the Apostles*. Edited by F. Bovon et al. – **D. W. Pao**, "The Genre of the Acts of Andrew." *Apocrypha* 6 (1995): 179–202. – **J. M. Prieur**, "La figure de l'apôtre dans les Actes apocryphes d'André." Pages 121–39 in *Les actes apocryphes des apôtres*. Edited by F. Bovon et al. – **L. Roig-Lanzillota**, *Acta Andreae*. 190–272. – **C. T. Schroeder**, "Embracing the Erotic in the Passion of Andrew. The Apocryphal Acts of Andrew, the Greek Novel, and Platonic Philosophy." Pages 110–26 in *The Apocryphal Acts of Andrew*. Edited by J. N. Bremmer.

The concluding words of ActAndr demand that the entire narrative be understood allegorically. In his controversial, but instructive and entertaining book, Dennis Ronald MacDonald has defined the second layer of meaning intertextually: Readers who are "in the know" (and *only* such readers) would have no difficulty in recognizing that ActAndr, including the "Acts of Andrew and Matthias" (see below), offers a Christianized retelling of Homer's *Odyssey*, drawing partly on the *Iliad* and borrowing from Euripides and Plato. This thesis is untenable in its full-blown form, but MacDonald has certainly made a number of correct observations. The author of ActAndr had a classical education, and there can be no doubt that his portrait of Andrew resembles the figure of Socrates, as this is mediated above all in Plato's dialogues *Theaetetus* and *Phaedo*.

In formal terms, this philosophical element agrees with the observation that although ActAndr has novelistic traits and is similar in genre to ActJoh, it recalls the biographies of philosophers more strongly than do the other apocryphal Acts (cf. Pao). The primary frame of reference for its contents is Middle Platonism. Scholars have also referred to Neo-Platonism, but this poses problems of dating. Neo-Pythagoreanism and Stoicism have also been mentioned, but it is not in fact necessary to be too precise on this point, since the philosophical systems at the end of the second and the beginning of the third centuries were increasingly eclectic. The Stoic doctrine of the soul penetrated Platonism, there was a rapprochement between Plato's world-soul and the Stoic providence, and so on. Our author breathes the intellectual climate of his age, and this explains much of his dualism, his contempt for the body, his desire to leave the world behind, his asceticism, and even to some extent his encratism.

Although the author decisively rejects sexuality, even in marriage, he does not however reject love, as we see in Maximilla's confession in §23: "I am in love, Aegeates, I am in love." She rejects the advances of her husband with horror, since that would be (in Platonic language) the lower, sexual love. Her love is directed in the first instance toward Andrew, who begins a real competition with Aegeates for Maximilla; and her love is directed beyond Andrew to a spiritual, heavenly reality. It is the Platonic, divine *eros* that speaks out of her (cf. Schroeder).

This explains why so many scenes are set in Maximilla's bedroom, which Aegeates no longer enters. This room no longer serves for marital intercourse and the procreation of children; its purpose now is spiritual fertility. The Word that is preached encounters persons who are essentially related to it (*suggenês* is a central word in the whole text) and awakens in them the inner, new human being who wishes to take shape and to assume the leadership (on the transformative power of the Word, cf. for example, §46[14]: Maximilla "became what the words themselves had signified"). This too is an act of procreation, calling for all the skill of the apostle as obstetrician or midwife, his Socratic maieutic. He himself can achieve perfection and be set free from his body only when he has saved as many souls as possible in this way through the living Word (cf. §40[8]: Andrew can attain "rest" only if Maximilla does not "give herself up to that which is opposed [to her]"). In their remaining period of earthly life, the redeemed must practice sexual continence, the renunciation of material goods, a very simple way of life, and frugal nourishment. It is not by chance that one is reminded of Manichaeism here.

In the theology of ActAndr, the world as God's creation plays scarcely any role; the same is true of the earthly life of Christ and his death and resurrection. Docetism lies outside the interests of the author, who does not even touch on such christological questions. Although Christ appears as a small child and in the form of Andrew, there is no genuine polymorphy because it does not happen very often and never before more than a single person. On the other hand, we can speak of a christomonism in ActAndr (as in ActJoh), because Christ is once called "Father," but the term "Son of God" is never used (other than in textual variants). There is nowhere any trace of a clear distinction between the divine Persons. Redemption means the return of the human person to the state before the fall, as we see in the parallels that are drawn between Andrew and Maximilla on the one hand and Adam and Eve on the other. To a greater extent than in the other apocryphal Acts, the apostle, as the earthly mediator of redemption, has a role similar to Christ—or more precisely, a role that is not played by Christ. The sacraments are not mentioned, with the exception of the mysterious "seal." It is possible, but not certain, that this denotes baptism. We can scarcely speak of an ecclesiology; even the simplest ecclesiastical structures are lacking.

We must ask whether the anthropology and theology that I have sketched here deserve the label "gnostic." ActAndr has often enough been judged gnostic, but when one compares this text with the other apocryphal Acts, our first observation is that it is less gnostic (and much less polemical) than ActJoh—at least as far as the gnostic passage in ActJoh 94–102 is concerned—but much closer to gnosis than ActPaul and ActPet. The intention of leading human beings to the knowledge of their true situation, and of unmasking and shattering the dominion of the demonic powers that want to keep them in ignorance, would fit well into a gnostic system; the same is true of the idea that the human person is essentially related to the Word and of the dependence of the redeemer figure (here: the apostle) on the salvation of those who are to be redeemed.

On the other hand, it appears that everyone, not only a chosen group, has access to the transforming Word. ActAndr does not present cosmogonic speculations about a fall before time began or about the work of a demiurge. Nor do we hear of the ascent of the soul through a succession of heavens. It is not possible to attach ActAndr to any of the known gnostic schools; it is thus best to describe its theology with the open term "close to gnosis" (L. Roig-Lanzillota also uses "gnostic" as characterization of the portion in V); but it is still within the margins of what seemed acceptable to the mainstream church, especially since the entire construction of systems was still fluid. ActAndr crossed the borders of what was acceptable, not so much in its theology, as in its ethics, that is, through its strict encratism.

D. Later Narratives

1. The Acts of Andrew and Matthias

Bibliography: M. Bonnet, AAAp II: 1. 65–116. – **J. K. Elliott**, *Apocryphal NT.* 283–99. – **D. R. MacDonald**, *The Acts of Andrew.* 61–177. – **F. Blatt**, *Die lateinischen Bearbeitungen der Acta Andreae et Matthiae apud anthropophagos. Mit sprachlichem Kommentar* (BZNW 12). Giessen: 1930. – **A. Hilhorst and P. J. Lalleman**, "The Acts of Andrew and Matthias: Is it a Part of the Original Acts of Andrew?" Pages 1–14 in *The Apocryphal Acts of Andrew.* Edited by J. N. Bremmer. – **D. R. MacDonald and J. M. Prieur**, "The Acts of Andrew and Matthias and the Acts of Andrew." *Semeia* 38 (1986): 9–39. – **L. Roig Lanzilotta**, "Cannibals, Myrmidonians, Sinopeans or Jews? The Five Versions of the *The Acts of Andrew and Matthias* and Their Sources." Pages 221–43 in *Wonders Never Cease: The Purpose of Narrating Miracle Stories in the New Testament and its Religious Environment* (Library of New Testament Studies 288). Edited by M. Labahn and B.J. Lietaert Peerbolte. London 2006.

The epitome of ActAndr in Gregory of Tours overlaps at the beginning with another narrative that is known as the "Acts of Andrew and Matthias in the City of the Cannibals." The linguistic style and contents of this text are so clearly different from the Greek ActAndr that (despite MacDonald's arguments) it can scarcely have formed the lost beginning of the apocryphal Acts. It was composed in the fourth or fifth century.

When the missionary territories are assigned to the individual apostles, Matthias is sent to Myrmidona (according to the Latin version, with variants), to the region of the cannibals (according to the Greek version). The inhabitants of this city live, not on bread and water, but on human flesh and blood. When Matthias arrives, they deal with him as they deal with all their visitors: They blind him and give him a magical potion to drink, so that his mind will be confused and he will live like an animal on grass and hay. They also stamp a date on his hand, in order to check when thirty days have passed—for that is when they will eat him. The apostle's mind remains clear, and the Lord restores his sight, but now twenty-seven days have elapsed.

At this precise time, the Lord commands Andrew to set out with his disciples (who are probably two in number; see below) to set Matthias free. A little ship lies ready on the shore, with Jesus as captain and two angels as sailors; all are in human form, and Andrew does not recognize them. During the voyage, Andrew and the captain speak inter alia about the miracles of Jesus and the puzzling lack of faith on the part of the Jews. In paragraphs 11–15, which may be a later interpolation, Andrew relates a strange experience: Jesus entered a pagan temple with the twelve disciples and the Jewish chief priest. At his command, the statue of a sphinx in the temple not only came to life but went to Mamre, summoned the twelve patriarchs from their graves, and brought Abraham, Isaac, and Jacob back to the temple. Despite this, the chief priests refused to believe in Jesus.

During this conversation, Andrew's companions have slept. We learn later that their souls were on a journey to heaven, where they saw the patriarchs, the apostles, and the angels all gathered around the heavenly throne.

Andrew too falls asleep, and the little group is transported in sleep by the angels to the city to which they are traveling, where they arrive on time. The Lord appears in the form of a marvelously beautiful child, reminds Andrew of the task he must fulfill, and announces that he must suffer for a period. Andrew meets no obstacles when he enters the prison and comes to Matthias. He restores the other prisoners to their normal state of mind and leads them all out of the city to a great fig tree. A cloud carries off Matthias with the disciples of Andrew, who are identified in some texts as Alexander and Rufus (cf. Mark 15:21), to a mountain where Peter is teaching. They are not mentioned again in the narrative.

Andrew remains in the city and thwarts every attempt of the inhabitants to get hold of human flesh for their consumption. The devil appears in the form of an old man and tells the people who is responsible for their present situation. Andrew reveals himself, and the furious inhabitants drag him by a rope through all the streets of the city, so that his skin, flesh, and hairs stick to the cobbles. This is done three times on three successive days. By night, the demons mock him but cannot kill him, because he bears a seal on his forehead.

On the third day, things begin to take a turn for the better. Trees bearing fruit grow up out of the shreds of Andrew's flesh that remained on the streets. The Lord restores him to health in the prison and bestows on him the power to perform miracles. A statue on a pillar begins to spew out a water that corrodes human flesh like a sharp acid and soon fills the entire city. The inhabitants cannot escape because the archangel Michael has erected a fiery rampart around the city. They turn to Andrew for help. After sending some evildoers who bore a particularly heavy responsibility down to Hades, he prays for the others, and the water dries up. Human beings and animals return to life. He baptizes the inhabitants and instructs them. The Lord bids him to remain with them for another seven days; after this, he departs.

2. The Acts of Peter and Andrew

Bibliography: M. Bonnet, AAAp II: 1. 117–27. – **J. K. Elliott,** *Apocryphal NT.* 299–301. – **X. Jacques,** "Les deux fragments conservés des 'Actes d'André et de Paul.' Cod. Borg. Copt. 109, fasc. 132." *Or.* 38 (1969): 187–213. – **E. Lucchesi and J. M. Prieur,** "Fragments coptes des Actes d'André et Matthias et d'André et Barthélemy." *AnBoll* 96 (1978): 339–50.

The "Acts of the holy apostles Peter and Andrew" pick up the thread of the narrative which we have just summarized, and seem to have been conceived as its immediate continuation. After his activities, Andrew is also transported to the mountain where Peter, Alexander and Rufus are. A parable about the farmer who rests from his toil when the fruit is ripening is then enacted. After receiving a commission from on high, the four go to the "city of the barbarians" where they meet a farmer sowing outside the gates. When he goes off to fetch bread for the travelers, they continue his work; when he returns, the corn has already ripened. He then takes the travelers to be gods but willingly accepts instruction and joins them.

The leading men of the city are not convinced: they assume that magic is involved. They have also heard that these "Galileans" cause husband and wife to separate. In order to frighten off the "haters of women," they place a shapely, naked prostitute at the city gate; but Michael seizes her by the hair and leaves her dangling in mid-air. She cries out in her pain, reviles the municipal governors, and asks the apostles to forgive her. They perform miracles of healing in the city, and the number of believers grows.

A rich man named Onesiphorus would like to perform such miracles but shrinks from abandoning his wife and his possessions. Peter responds by quoting the logion about the camel and the eye of a needle (Mark 10:25) and, when pressed, demonstrates what these words of Jesus mean: The eye of a little needle that is placed in the earth opens up to the size of a gate, through which a camel passes. It then returns to its original size. Since Onesiphorus still talks about magic, Peter repeats the miracle under tighter control. Onesiphorus wants to do the same, in the name of Jesus and of the apostle, but he comes only half-way because he is not yet baptized. This finally convinces him.

The former prostitute, who is still dangling in the air, promises to turn her house into a convent for virgins and returns to earth unharmed. A church is built; bishops, priests, and deacons are appointed; the city has been Christianized successfully.

There are other legends about the apostle Andrew, some of them considerably later (cf. also NTApo 6th ed. II: 403–6). We mention only the "Acts of Paul and Andrew" (cf. Jacques), where the form of the apocryphal Acts supplies the framework for a journey by Paul to the underworld, which begins with a leap into the sea from a ship. Paul also meets Judas in hell and learns the details of his fate.

Colorful narratives that lead the reader to exotic countries and peoples, with elements of horror and eroticism, and with an obvious moral—all this makes these texts both fascinating and edifying. However, they are far removed from the intellectual profundity and the literary elegance of ActAndr. They form a group on their own, which expand and continue ActAndr in various ways, but contribute little to the reconstruction of the original text.

Chapter 5

The Acts of Thomas

Editions: M. Bonnet, AAAP II: 2. 99–288. – W. Wright, *Apocryphal Acts*, Vol. 1: 171–333 (Syriac text); Vol. 2: 146–298 (English translation). – P.-H. Poirier, *La version copte de la prédication et du martyre de Thomas* (SHG 67). Brussels: 1984.

Translations: G. Bornkamm, NTApo 4th ed. II: 297–372. – H. J. W. Drijvers, NTApo 6th ed. II: 289–367. – A. F. J. Klijn, *The Acts of Thomas: Introduction, Text, and Commentary* (NovTSup 108). 2nd ed. Leiden: 2003. – J. K. Elliott, *Apocryphal NT*. 439–511.

Bibliography: G. Bornkamm, *Mythos und Legende in den apokryphen Thomas-Akten. Beiträge zur Geschichte der Gnosis und zur Vorgeschichte des Manichäismus* (FRLANT 49). Göttingen: 1933. – J. N. Bremmer, ed. *The Apocryphal Acts of Thomas* (Studies on the Apocryphal Acts of the Apostles 6). Louvain: 2001. – J. M. LaFargue, *Language and Gnosis: The Opening Scenes of the Acts of Thomas* (HDR 18). Philadelphia: 1985. – M. Lipinski, *Konkordanz zu den Thomasakten* (BBB 67). Frankfurt am Main: 1988. – G. W. Most, *Doubting Thomas*. Cambridge, Mass.: 2005.

A. Context

Attestation and Transmission

Bibliography: G. Garitte, "Le Martyre géorgien de l'apôtre Thomas." *Muséon* 83 (1970): 497–532. – Idem, "La Passion arménienne de S. Thomas l'apôtre et son modèle grec." *Muséon* 84 (1971): 151–95.

The Acts of Thomas (ActThom) is the only one of the ancient apocryphal Acts that has survived completely, although not in its oldest version. It is not often attested in early Christian writings.

Augustine, who knows that the Manichaeans use ActThom, several times employs the punitive miracle from the second Act as an argument against them (e.g., in *Contra Faustum* 22.79). The allusion to ActThom in the Manichaean Psalter has already been mentioned in the Introduction to the present work. Epiphanius discusses its encratism critically (*Pan.* 47.1.5; 61.1.5). The followers of Priscillian in Spain also read it.

Most scholars assume that ActThom was originally written in Syriac and then translated into Greek. In a bilingual milieu, however (see below), we cannot completely rule out the possibility of an original Greek version, or of a more or less contemporaneous conception of the work in both languages. We come closest to the earliest form of ActThom—to the extent that one can use such an expression in relation to a text that was continually changing—via the Syriac and the Greek textual traditions. Six or eight manuscripts of the Syriac version are known up to now (two of which are inaccessible); but this version displays large-scale traces of a secondary revision which seeks to assimilate the contents to the norms of Catholic orthodoxy. In many cases, it is the Greek text that makes the impression of greater antiquity. Bonnet based his edition on twenty-one Greek manuscripts; by now, approximately eighty are known. Since, however, many textual witnesses contain only excerpts from the lengthy text, two principal manuscripts are particularly important: a complete Vatican codex from the eleventh century (U) and a tenth- or eleventh-century codex from Paris (P) in which only the Song of the Pearl is missing.

The Song of the Pearl is in a special category, since it is transmitted only in one Syriac and one Greek manuscript. This may indicate that it was inserted only at a later stage into an already complete narrative—into which, however, it fits perfectly—by a Manichaean reviser (see below). It is sometimes suggested that the same is true of the Song of the Bride (§§6–7), but here the text-critical situation is better.

We also have translations—often very free, so that it would be better to speak of adaptations—into Latin, Armenian, Coptic, Ethiopic, Georgian, Arabic, and Old Slavonic. The martyrdom of the apostle, which forms the close of ActThom, and his final prayer in §§144–48 were also transmitted separately in some witnesses. Later Greek paraphrases were made by Simeon Metaphrastes in the tenth century and Nicetas of Maroneia in the eleventh.

Structure and Unity of the Work

Bibliography: Y. Tissot, "Les Actes apocryphes de Thomas: exemple de recueil composite." Pages 223–32 in *Les Actes apocryphes des Apôtres*. Edited by F. Bovon et al.

In some manuscripts and in our editions, ActThom is structured in thirteen Acts and the Martyrdom, and a clear sequence can be discerned. The first six Acts (§§1–61) are written in an episodic style. After an initial exposition, individual adventures, experiences, and miracles are loosely strung together. The seventh and eighth Acts (§§61–81), which are closely connected, form the transition. They still have the episodic style, with the exorcism which Thomas performs and the appearance of the wild asses, but new characters are introduced (Siphor and his family) who will play a minor role until the close of the work. The second part (§§82–169) begins with the ninth Act, the longest of all, in which we meet one of the main future protagonists, Mygdonia, the wife of Charisius. She is soon joined by Tertia, the wife of King Misdaeus, and the attentive reader at once knows what will happen in the second part of the work: the apostle will convert these two women to sexual continence, thus kindling the anger of their highly placed husbands, and this will ultimately lead to his death.

This narrative structure is filled out with other passages in which direct speech predominates: short and long prayers, discourses, sermons, catecheses, dialogues and monologues, epicleses, and hymns. These passages are important because they interpret the events in the narrative and make it possible to understand them symbolically. Interpretative help is also provided by the frequent descriptions of the Christian ritual of initiation, which consists of an anointing with oil (recalling the anointing as king, priest, and Messiah), a baptism in water followed by the proleptic clothing in a new "garment" (a symbol of the body), and the celebration of the Eucharist, where the emphasis clearly lies on the breaking of the bread; if anything is drunk in this rite, it is water. The Eucharist establishes table fellowship with the Lord and with the Spirit.

It is striking that a number of motifs occur twice. There are two epicleses of the Spirit (in §27 and §50), and in the present form of the book there are two poems, the Song of the Bride and the Song of the Pearl. The initiation is twice described in detail,

in the case of Mygdonia and in the case of Tertia (together with
Vazan and his wife), and on both occasions the apostle leaves the
prison into which he is thrown. There are also parallels between
the jealous dragon in the third Act and the jealous young man in
the sixth Act, both of whom commit a murder; between the foal of
an ass in the fourth Act and the wild asses in the eighth Act; and
between the exorcisms that the apostle performs in the fifth and in
the eighth Acts.

It is certainly correct to infer from this that the composition of
the narrative draws on a variety of source materials, but at some
point an individual hand was needed to arrange and shape the
highly skillful narrative upon which all the later versions and elaborations are based. And it is certainly possible that the author of
ActThom intends the doublets to draw the reader's attention,
through the narrative structure itself, to the ambivalence of the
entire work. The motif of twins—Jesus and Thomas as *doppelgänger*—also makes sense in this context. Ultimately, we can see
that everything is a variation on a few basic themes, which include
the apostle's fight against evil and the persistent insistence on
purity or holiness. More specifically, this means sexual continence,
since only this makes possible the reunification of the human soul
with the heavenly Spirit.

Thomas and India

Bibliography: A. Dihle, "Neues zur Thomas-Tradition." *JAC* 6 (1963):
54–70; also pages 61–77 in idem, *Antike und Orient. Gesammelte Aufsätze*
(SHAW.PH.S 2). Heidelberg: 1984. – Idem, "Indien." *RAC* 18 (1998):
1–56. – **A. von Gutschmid**, "Königsnamen." 332–64. – **C. Dognini and
I. Ramelli**, *Gli apostoli in India: nella patristica e nella litteratura sanscrita*
(Collana La zattera 5). Milan: 2001. – **G. Huxley**, "Geography in the
Acts of Thomas." *GRBS* 24 (1983): 71–80. – **L. P. van den Bosch**, "India
and the Apostolate of St. Thomas." Pages 125–48 in *The Apocryphal Acts
of Thomas*. Edited by J. N. Bremmer. – **H. Waldmann**, *Das Christentum
in Indien und der Königsweg der Apostel in Edessa, Indien und Rom*.
Tübingen: 1996. (Too uncritical.)

Before we look more closely at the anonymous author, we must
briefly investigate the link between the apostle Thomas and India
that is established in ActThom. The Thomas Christians of India
venerate him to this very day as the herald of the faith who was the

first to bring them the gospel, and they believe that they possess his grave. The first point competes with another tradition from the early church, which relates that Bartholomew was the apostle of India and that the missionary work started from Alexandria (Eusebius, *Hist. eccl.* 5.10.1–4). Thomas' grave is localized in the East Syrian city of Edessa no later than the fourth century, by Ephrem the Syrian and the pilgrim Egeria; this is reflected in the passage in ActThom 170 about the clandestine translation of the apostle's bones to the West.

According to Eusebius, who appeals to Origen as his authority, Thomas was responsible for the missionary work in Parthia, that is, the Persian kingdom (*Hist. eccl.* 3.1.1). Parthia borders Syria on the west and northwest India on the east, and there were many contacts, both for reasons of geography and through power politics. Some of the personal names in ActThom have a Persian (and Roman) origin rather than an Indian origin. King Gundaphorus in the second Act is a historical figure, attested by coins. He reigned over an Irano-Indian kingdom in the first century BCE or CE (the proposed dates are 30–10 BCE or 20–46 CE: cf. van den Bosch, 132f.), and lives on in Christian legend as Caspar, one of the Three Wise Men. As a "daughter of Parthia," Edessa also had Indian connections. The philosopher and theologian Bardaisan (154–222 CE), who lived in Edessa, spoke with Indian emissaries who were passing through on their way to Emperor Heliogabalus (218–222 CE); he also wrote about India (FGH 919 F 1–2).

We have no truly guaranteed historical information about the beginnings of Christianity in India. It is possible that missionary activity began along the maritime trade routes, starting from Egypt down the Red Sea and that later, when this was no longer possible, the links to the Syrian-Persian sphere were strengthened (cf. Dihle). This may be reflected in the competing traditions about Bartholomew and Thomas.

These considerations mean that Thomas' visit to India is a construction of the gifted author of ActThom, who has put together individual pieces of historical information and the general cultural knowledge that people in his milieu had about India to form a rather vague picture. It is possible that he wanted to suggest to his readers that they themselves should see to the spreading of missionary work as far as India (van den Bosch 143f.).

Another fact that increases skepticism about the historical value of ActThom is that Clement of Alexandria knew that Thomas had not died as a martyr (*Strom.* 4.71.1–4).

Author, Place, and Time of Composition

Bibliography: J. M. Bremmer, "The Acts of Thomas: Place, Date and Women." Pages 74–90 in idem, *The Apocryphal Acts of Thomas*. – **H. J. W. Drijvers**, *East of Antioch. Studies in Early Syrian Christianity*. London: 1984. Vol. 1: 1–27. – **S. E. Meyers**, "Revisiting Preliminary Issues in the Acts of Thomas." *Apocrypha* 17 (2006): 95–112.

All the clues that we have encountered up to now point to Syria and Edessa, and it is plausible to suppose that an early version of ActThom was written in Edessa. The city had long been hellenized and was bilingual; for a time, it was also romanized (cf. the Roman names Tertia and Marcia in the text). Scholars generally date it to the first half of the third century; we can narrow this down to the years between 220 and 240 CE (cf. Bremmer, 74–78, with the discussion of very specific details).

Some scholars have suggested that the author was Bardaisan— a fascinating figure, a man of great culture who wrote in Syriac but also read Greek—or one of his pupils. His works were suspected of heresy, and therefore very little has survived. This means that we unfortunately know too little about him to be able to say anything with certainty on this point. In terms of concepts, some points of contact have been identified with Tatian, who returned from Rome to his Syrian home in 172 (Drijvers). Although we should be on our guard against exaggerating the similarities, this is a correct description of the author's general milieu.

In addition to individual narratives, traditions about persons, and liturgical material, the author has also made extensive use of the Bible, especially the gospels, which he may have known in the form of the Diatessaron, Tatian's harmony of the four gospels. He has made less use of the Acts of the Apostles because he draws parallels, not between his protagonist and Peter or Paul, but between Thomas and Jesus.

Of the other ancient apocryphal Acts, the author most likely knew ActJoh (it suffices here to compare ActJoh 48 with ActThom 29f.) and ActAndr (for detailed evidence, cf. J. M. Prieur, CChrSA 5, 392f.). He may also have known ActPaul (Mygdonia and Tertia play a similar role in ActThom to Eubula and Artemilla in ActPaul). Despite parallel motifs (the dog and the wild asses as speaking messengers of the apostles), it is better to leave open the question of the relationship between ActThom and ActPet.

A Thomas School?

Bibliography: P. J. Hartin, "The Role and Significance of the Character of Thomas in the Acts of Thomas." Pages 239–53 in *Thomasine Traditions in Antiquity: The Social and Cultural World of the Gospel of Thomas* (NHMS 59). Edited by J. M. Asgeirsson, A. D. Deconick, and R. Udo. Leiden: 2006. – **B. Layton**, "The School of St. Thomas." *The Gnostic Scriptures*. Garden City, N.Y.: 1903. 357–409. – **P.-H. Poirier**, "The Writings Ascribed to Thomas and the Thomas Tradition." Pages 295–307 in *The Nag Hammadi Library after Fifty Years* (NHMS 44). Edited by J. D. Turner and A. McGuire. Leiden: 1997. – **G. J. Riley**, "Thomas Tradition and the Acts of Thomas." *SBLSP* (1991): 533–42. – Idem, *Resurrection Reconsidered: Thomas and John in Controversy*. Minneapolis: 1995. 157–75. – **P. Sellew**, "Thomas Christianity: Scholars in Quest of a Community." Pages 11–35 in *The Apocryphal Acts of Thomas*. Edited by J. N. Bremmer.

The author of ActThom had also read and used the Gospel of Thomas (NHC II.2). The full form of his name, "Didymus Judas Thomas" from the prologue to the Coptic EvThom (the Greek version in P.Oxy 654 has: "Judas, also [called] Thomas"), is also found with a slight alteration in ActThom 1: "Judas Thomas, also [called] Twin." Thomas knows the hidden, deeper meaning of the words of Jesus but cannot express this completely in human language (compare EvThom 13 with ActThom 47 and, on the drinking from the "living spring," also with ActThom 147). The exchange between left and right (ActThom 92) and between inside and outside (ActThom 147), which amounts to a reversal of all innerworldly criteria, like the crucifixion head-downward in ActPet, has a parallel in EvThom 22. When Jesus teaches his own teachers (ActThom 79), this recalls not only Luke 2:41-59, but also several scenes from the Infancy Gospel of Thomas. ActThom shares the motifs of the secret words and of the brotherhood of twins with the "Book of Thomas" (LibThom: NHC II.7).

These and other observations have led scholars to postulate the existence of a "Thomas school," that is, a community or group of communities that venerated Thomas as their founder and employed the writings transmitted under his name (with the exception of the Infancy Gospel) as their canon. Characteristic elements would be the negative attitude to the material world, the rejection of sexuality and of bodily resurrection (since only the soul returns to heaven), and a thinking structured by means of sharp antitheses. The most consistent representatives of this position (cf. Riley) project the beginnings of the Thomas school back into the first century and date it even earlier than the Gospel of John with its pericope about Thomas (John 20:24-29), which is understood as a polemic against the "Thomasine" Christianity. However, one cannot infer societal structures so easily from texts; here, much more nuanced methods of gathering information are needed (cf. Sellew). Most of the undisputed parallels can be explained as literary dependence (cf. Poirier, arguing that LibThom is later than ActThom). Even when one takes this more skeptical view, however, it is clear that the creation of Thomas literature in the East went hand in hand with a high esteem for the apostle, who did not enjoy anything like the same veneration in the West.

The Relationship to Manichaeism

Bibliography: W. Bousset, "Manichäisches in den Thomasakten." *ZNW* 18 (1917–1918): 1–39. – **P. Nagel**, "Die apokryphen Apostelakten." 171–73, 178–81. – **P.-H. Poirier**, "Les Actes de Thomas et le Manichéisme." *Apocrypha* 9 (1998): 263–87.

We shall return at the end of this chapter to the question of the place occupied by the author of ActThom in the history of religion; here, we shall look only at his relationship to Manichaeism, since this also affects the question of what belongs to the original text. Mani (216–76/77), the founder of a new religion, who himself also carried out missionary work in India, came from the same region as ActThom (Mesopotamia, Parthia) and the same century. Simple reasons of chronology mean that ActThom cannot be the work of Manichaean circles; it is only in the case of the Song of the Pearl that this possibility continues to find support (the king's son in the hymn would then a priori be Mani himself). It remains an open question whether the text went through a Manichaean redaction and therefore contains interpolations from a Manichaean hand. Relevant passages here (cf. Bousset) would be the mention of a mother deity in hymns (§7) and doxologies (§39); the signifi-

cance in ActThom of the anointing with oil; the five members of
the intellect in the epiclesis in §27 and the five dark rooms in the
description of hell in §§55–57; the fasting of the apostle on a
Sunday in §29; insertions into the Song of the Pearl, especially
toward the close; and the striking points of contact between the
Song of the Pearl and the newly discovered Cologne Mani codex.

Improved knowledge of the theological milieu, thanks not least
to the Nag Hammadi discoveries, has now led to a more cautious
evaluation of these parallels (cf. Poirier). Most of them can be traced
to a background of traditions that were shared both by the milieu
from which ActThom comes and by Manichaeism at a somewhat
later date. Irrespective of how we judge this issue, however, the fact
remains that, of the five ancient apocryphal Acts, it was ActThom
that the Manichaeans found particularly congenial, and they made
extensive use of it. The asceticism and dualism that are fundamental elements in ActThom and its symbolic ambivalence predestined
it for a Manichaean reading; it is even possible that the figure of the
apostle in ActThom had a significant influence on Mani's own self-
understanding as the "apostle of light" and the earthly representative of his heavenly twin, the "Paraclete" (cf. Nagel). In that case,
ActThom would have made an enormous historical impact, surpass-
ing the expectations even of its learned author.

B. Contents

1. Act 1: Departure and Wedding Feast

Bibliography: E. Junod, "Origène, Eusèbe et la tradition sur la réparti-
tion des champs de mission des apôtres (Eusèbe, HE III 1,1-3)." Pages
233–48 in *Les Actes apocryphes des Apôtres*. Edited by F. Bovon et al. – J.-
D. Kaestli, "Les scènes d'attribution des champs de mission et de départ
de l'apôtre dans les Actes apocryphes." Ibid., 249–64. – J. J. Gunther,
"The Meaning and Origin of the Name 'Judas Thomas.'" *Muséon* 93
(1980): 113–48. – J. M. LaFargue, *Language and Gnosis*. – R.
Reitzenstein, *Hellenistische Wundererzählungen*. 3rd ed. Darmstadt:
1974. 134–50.

The narrative begins in the second person plural: "We apostles" (a
list of eleven names follows) were assembled in Jerusalem and cast
lots to divide the regions of the earth as mission territories (1).
This introductory scene has a parallel in Eusebius (*Hist. eccl.*

3.1.1–3), who appeals to Origen's lost commentary on Genesis as his authority. It has often been assumed that other apocryphal Acts began in a similar fashion, but since this is the only beginning that has survived, we cannot check this hypothesis.

The protagonist is introduced as "Judas Thomas, also called Didymus." A part of the Syriac tradition reads the double name "Judas Thomas" at John 14:23, instead of "Judas (not Iscariot)." In Aramaic, the nickname "Thomas" means "twin," and this is the meaning of the Greek addition *Didumos* (cf. John 11:16, etc.). In Mark 6:3, one of the brothers of Jesus is called "Judas." All this helps to explain why the apostle Thomas could be regarded as the twin brother of Jesus, as his earthly *doppelgänger* and representative (cf. Gunther, who also assumes a confusion between Judas Thaddeus, as the apostle of Syria, and Didymus Thomas, as the apostle of Parthia).

Thomas' lot is to go to India, but he refuses to do so. Not even an apparition of the Lord by night persuades him to change his mind. He insists, "Wherever you wish to send me, send me, but elsewhere. For I am not going to the Indians." Accordingly, the Lord takes drastic measures in §2. An Indian merchant named Abban is in the city, charged to hire a carpenter for his king, Gundaphorus. The Lord sells him Thomas for three pounds of silver (the Syriac version has "twenty pieces of silver": cf. Gen 37:28), and writes the following bill of sale: "I, Jesus, son of the carpenter Joseph, declare that I have sold my slave [cf. Phil 2:7], Judas by name, to you, Abban, a merchant of Gundaphorus, king of the Indians." It is only now that Thomas accepts his fate, and the Lord gives him the money he has received for the sale. This means that ultimately, Thomas sets out on the journey as a free man. When the merchant asks him what is his craft (3), he says that he is a worker:

> . . . in wood, ploughs and yokes and balances and ships and boats' oars and masts and small blocks; in stone, pillars and temples and royal palaces.

The first station on their journey is Andropolis (the "city of human beings"; the Syriac text calls it "Sandaruk"), where a great feast is being held to mark the wedding of the only daughter of the king (§4; cf. the marriage scene in Chariton I: 1.11-13). Everyone is invited, "rich and poor, bond and free, strangers and citizens" (cf. Matt 22:3-14; Gal 3:28), and Abban and Thomas also enter the festal hall. All eyes are drawn to Thomas, especially because he neither eats nor drinks (5); but when ointment is offered, he anoints his head, nose, ears, mouth, and breast (a model for the later sacramental anointings in the ritual of initiation?). He puts on a garland and takes a branch of reed in his hand. A Hebrew flute girl remains standing beside him; a cupbearer strikes him, thus completing Thomas' imitation of the mockery of Jesus. The apostle threatens a speedy punishment: The hand that struck him will be carried off by a dog. He then begins to sing a song.

The Song of the Bride

Bibliography: J. M. LaFargue, *Language and Gnosis.* 91–129. – **H. Kruse**, "Das Brautlied der syrischen Thomas-Akten." *OCP* 50 (1984): 291–330. – **M. Marcovich**, "The Wedding Hymn of Acta Thomae." Pages 156–73 in idem., *Studies in Graeco-Roman Religions and Gnosticism* (SGRR 4). Leiden: 1988. – **R. Murray**, *Symbols of Church and Kingdom: A Study in Early Syriac Tradition.* Cambridge: 1975. 131–58.

The exuberance of its many metaphors makes the Song of the Bride in §§6–7 hard to understand, as we see from its first lines (the English translation follows the reconstruction in Kruse, 326):

> The maiden is a figure of light;
> the splendor of kings is in her eyes.
> Exalted and delightful is the sight of her,
> beautiful and adorned with the good.
> Her garments are like flowers,
> for they smell fragrant and sweet.
> As her head, the king is on his throne;
> from there, he feeds his subjects.
> Her head is crowned with truth,
> joy sets her feet in motion.

We can identify some principles that help us to understand the text. In the first line, the Syriac version reads "the church" instead of "the maiden." This is probably a secondary clarification, but it correctly interprets the meaning of the poem as a whole, which employs the characteristic means of Syriac theology to depict the intimate relationship between the fellowship of believers and Christ, the heavenly bridegroom. Inspiration came from the figure of Lady Wisdom (in Proverbs, Sirach, and Wisdom), the description of the bride in the Song of Songs, which was understood allegorically (cf. Cant 4:1–5; 7:1–10), and the metaphors associated with the eschatological wedding feast or joyful meal.

This explains the apparently strange idea in our text that the king sits on his throne "as her head" or (in another translation) "on the parting of her hair." Here, the model of Christ as the "head" of the church (from Col 1:18 and Eph 5:23) is translated into a somewhat different image (for "he feeds his subjects," cf. Eph 4:16). The girl's feet, "set in motion by joy," recall the "feet" of the messenger who brings joyful news in Isaiah 52:7 (cf. Rom 10:15). Astrology may be involved here too: The seven bridesmaids and the twelve servants at a later point in the poem can be taken as a symbol of the seven planets and the twelve constellations, as well as of the seven archangels (cf. Tob 12:15) and the twelve tribes of Israel or the twelve apostles.

Since Thomas speaks his poem in Hebrew, the flute girl is the only one of those present who understands him. She gazes at him and falls in love with his youthful, handsome appearance (8). The evil cupbearer goes out to draw water and is torn asunder by a lion. A black dog brings his right hand into the festal hall, and the flute girl recognizes that this is the fulfillment of the apostle's prediction. Her reaction is to break her flute (implying the renunciation of her way of life hitherto, which may have included prostitution) and to declare: "This man is either God or God's apostle." The king then leads the apostle into the bridal chamber, so that he may pray for the newly wedded couple (9).

The Apostle and the Bridal Couple

The apostle begins his first prayer in §10 with words from John 20:28, as if he were quoting himself: "My Lord and my God" (cf. also §81, where he rehabilitates himself: "My Lord and my God, I *doubt not* in you . . ."). The address is continued with nouns coupled with genitive plurals, for example, "deliverer of the captives" and "physician of the souls laid low by disease," and frequent relative clauses with participles, for example, "you, Lord, who reveal hidden mysteries and declare secret words" (cf. Sir 42:18f.; Dan 2:28f.), before the prayer takes the form of a request that the Lord may do for the young people "what helps, benefits, and is profitable for them."

All leave the room, including the apostle; but when the bridegroom draws back the curtain of the bedroom, he sees Jesus in the form of Thomas, and is astonished (11). Jesus presents himself as the brother of Thomas and exhorts the bridal couple to abstain from "filthy" sexual intercourse. In a lengthy catalogue of vices, he says that it is a great torment to have many children. For the sake of their children, parents "become grasping and avaricious, plundering orphans and deceiving widows," while most children are "unprofitable, being possessed by demons. . . . For they become either lunatics or half-withered or crippled or dumb or paralytics or idiots" (12). And if, contrary to expectation, they are healthy, they will turn out to be adulterers, murderers, and thieves. As the reward for childlessness and the renunciation of marriage, the Lord promises the bridal couple a life free of care and the right to enter the heavenly bridal chamber.

The young couple follow this advice to the letter (13). On the next morning, the royal parents find the bride unveiled, sitting opposite the "very cheerful" bridegroom. The mother finds this behavior appalling, but the king says, "Is it because of your great love to your husband that you are unveiled?" The bride's reply in §14 is initially ambiguous, but she goes on to speak of another marriage, and of her renunciation of intercourse with a mortal man (cf. Charicleia in Heliodorus 2.33, who initially wants to spend her life as a virgin in the service of Artemis). In §15, the bridegroom addresses a prayer of thanks to the Lord, which includes the main theme of gnosis (according to Clement of Alexandria, *Exc.* 78.2): "You have shown me how to seek myself, and to know who I was and who and how I now am, that I may become again what I was."

When the king realizes what is going on, he falls into a rage (16) and sends his servants to look for the apostle, "the sorcerer" who is responsible for all these events. However, Thomas has already boarded a ship. The flute girl joins the young couple, and a kind of community comes into existence.

2. Act 2: The Palace in Heaven

Bibliography: A. Hilhorst, "The Heavenly Palace in the Acts of Thomas." Pages 53–64 in *The Apocryphal Acts of Thomas*. Edited by J. N. Bremmer. – **H.-J. Klauck**, "Himmlisches Haus und irdische Bleibe.

Eschatologische Metaphorik in Antike und Christentum." *NTS* 50 (2004): 5–35. – **R. Schöter**, "Gedicht des Jakob von Sarug über den Palast den der Apostel Thomas in Indien baute." *ZDMG* 25 (1871): 321–77.

The second Act, which almost has the character of a comedy, illustrates the logia of Jesus about the "treasure in heaven" (Matt 6:20) and the "many dwellings" (John 14:2). Abban presents Thomas to King Gundaphorus as a "carpenter and house-builder" (§17). The king brings him to the place where he wishes a palace to be built, and Thomas sketches with a reed on the earth the outline of the planned building, to the complete satisfaction of the king (§18), who comments: "You are truly a craftsman, and it is fitting that you should serve kings." (The reader grasps the double meaning in these words.) He gives the apostle a large sum of money, and sends more money periodically. Thomas, however, distributes everything to the poor in the surrounding towns (§19). After much time has passed, the king's friends tell him what has happened, and give a comprehensive description of the apostle which reflects the ambivalence in their evaluation of him (§20):

> He has neither built a palace, nor did he do anything of that which he promised to do, but he goes about in the cities and villages, and if he has anything he gives it to the poor, and teaches a new God, heals the sick, drives out demons, and performs many miracles. And we believe that he is a magician. But his acts of compassion and the cures done by him as a free gift, still more his simplicity and gentleness and fidelity, show that he is a just man, or an apostle of the new God, whom he preaches. . . .

The king does not accept Thomas' declaration that he will see the palace when he departs from this life. He throws the merchant and the apostle into prison and considers how he may torture them most terribly to death. His brother Gad is so distressed by this affair that he dies of grief (§21). Angels accompany his soul to the heavenly dwellings, and Gad expresses the desire to live in one of the lower chambers of a particularly splendid building. The angels tell him that this is impossible, because the apostle has erected this palace for his brother, the king (§22). Gad proposes that he be allowed to return to the earth, in order that he may purchase the palace from his brother, who knows nothing of all this.

Gad's soul returns into its body. The king is both surprised and delighted, and Gad asks him—first in cryptic words, then openly—to sell him the palace in heaven (§23). The king now grasps what the apostle had meant when he spoke of the palace as a *future* possession. At once, he liberates Thomas and Abban from the prison. The king and his brother (who apparently is allowed to remain alive on earth) fall at the apostle's feet and ask for his prayer. They also declare themselves willing to accept his teaching (§24). This presupposes that they receive the sacraments of initiation, baptism and the anointing, which are also called "the seal" (§26). There are considerable divergences here between the Syriac and the Greek texts, especially as regards the sequence of the anointing with oil and baptism. In the Syriac church, an anointing precedes baptism, but the opposite sequence is followed in the West, and this is reflected in the texts. (Besides this, only the Syriac version tells us that the bath house is closed for seven days so that the baptism can take place on the eighth day.)

The First Epiclesis of the Spirit

Bibliography: C. Johnson, "Ritual Epicleses in the Greek Acts of Thomas." Pages 171–204 in *The Apocryphal Acts of the Apostles*. Edited by F. Bovon et al. – **H. Kruse**, "Zwei Geistepiklesen in den syrischen Thomasakten." *OrChr* 69 (1985): 33–53. – **G. Winkler**, "Weitere Beobachtungen zur frühen Epiklese (den Doxologien und dem Sanctus)." *OrChr* 80 (1996): 177–200.

Among the prayers of the apostle on this occasion, the epiclesis of the Spirit is particularly striking. It has a close parallel in §50, but here it is related to the anointing with oil, and this is more original (cf. also "Let your power come" at the anointing in §121 and §157); in §50, it leads into the Lord's Supper (cf. "Let the power of blessing rest upon the bread" in §133). Nine petitions are introduced with the urgent imperative "Come!" (§27). I quote some examples:

> Come, holy name of Christ . . .
> Come, power of the Most High!
> Come, compassionate mother!
> Come, fellowship of the male!
> Come, revealer [feminine] of secret mysteries!
> Come, mother of the seven houses . . .

> Come, elder of the five members: intelligence, thought,
> prudence, reflection, reasoning!

Some of this may be derived from the language of the Bible. For example, we read at Ezekiel 37:9, "Come from the four winds, O Spirit!" The "mother of the seven houses" recalls Wisdom in Proverbs 9:1, and the "power of the Most High" recalls Luke 1:35; we should certainly also bear in mind Didache 10.6, "Let grace come . . . May our Lord come (*maranatha*)." There are also numerous parallels in magical texts to the summoning of a deity, introduced by "Come!" (cf. Johnson).

After the king and his brother are sealed at night, a young man with a brilliantly shining light (probably Christ himself) appears for a short time. The Eucharist follows in the early morning; it seems to consist only of the breaking of bread. The apostle holds another sermon in which he attacks the three main vices of "fornication, covetousness, and gluttony" (28) without this time mentioning marital intercourse. In view of their earthly needs, he allows his companions to take their fill at a meal of bread, oil, vegetables, and salt (29), but he himself remains fasting, although the day of the Lord is dawning, when fasting is not allowed (the Syriac accordingly alters the text). An apparition of the Lord by night prepares the next Act: "Thomas, arise up early . . . and go along the eastern road two miles, and there I will show my glory in you."

3. Act 3: The Dragon that Fell in Love

Bibliography: T. Adamik, "The Serpent in the Acts of Thomas." Pages 115–24 in *The Apocryphal Acts of Thomas*. Edited by J. N. Bremmer. – **H. Conzelmann**, "Zu Mythos, Mythologie und Formgeschichte, geprüft an der dritten Praxis der Thomasakten." *ZNW* 67 (1976): 111–22.

Two miles outside the city, the corpse of a handsome young man lies by the wayside (§30). Thomas at once declares that this is the work of the evil adversary acting in a form that is peculiarly his own. A huge dragon (in the Syriac: a black serpent) comes out of its cave and confesses that it had fallen in love with a beautiful woman in the neighborhood and had followed her secretly (§31; on the motif of the jealous dragon, on which this passage is a variation, cf. Tob 3:8 and so forth). It spied on the young man as he made love with the woman, but out of consideration for her it did not intervene at once; however, when the young man passed by its cave in the evening, it killed him—*a fortiori* because this sin had been committed on the Lord's day. (G. Bornkamm, *Mythos*, 24, observes that the dragon "thus assumes the role of guardian of morals and judge—a role for which it is ill suited.") The dragon correctly identifies the apostle as "the twin brother of Christ."

When the apostle asks the dragon where it comes from, the reply is a brief outline of the history of sin: It is the offspring of the ruler of this world and is a relative of the world-serpent that girdles the earth, "whose tail lies in his mouth." It seduced Eve in paradise, incited Cain to murder his brother, provoked the fall of the angels (cf. Gen 6:1-4), hardened Pharaoh's heart, and led astray the people in the wilderness so that they worshiped the golden calf (§32). It moved Judas to betray Jesus and staged Jesus' trial before Pilate. The one who will come from the East and rule over the earth (i.e., the Antichrist) likewise belongs to its family.

The apostle rebukes its impertinence and commands it to suck its poison out of the young man. After some resistance, the dragon does so. The "color of the young man, which was like purple, grew white," but the serpent swells up and explodes (§33). A huge chasm is the result of this explosion. The apostle orders that it be filled up so that houses for foreigners may be built there (cf. Matt 27:7).

This is basically the end of the story. The rest of this Act consists of speeches by the young man (in §34, much amplified in the Syriac), who addresses Thomas as "a man having two forms," and by Thomas himself. The Act closes in §38 with the repentance of the onlookers. In his discourse in §36, the apostle formulates a fundamental hermeneutical principle: "For it is not concerning these visible things that God preaches the gospel to us, but greater things than these he promises us." Because of the inherent limitations of human language, we find it difficult to speak of these greater things, but the apostle must attempt to do so: "We speak about the world above, about God and angels, about watchmen and saints. . . ." This is the basic reason why all his words and deeds have a second, symbolic dimension, as we see, for example, in §37, where Thomas offers an interpretation of the fact that people seek elevated places in order to see him better. This is not due simply to his small stature; rather, if one wishes to come closer to God, one must raise oneself up from the earth and from all that is earthly.

4. Act 4: The Foal of an Ass

Bibliography: G. Bornkamm, *Mythos und Legende*. 33–38. – **C. R. Matthews**, "Articulate Animals." 223–25. – **J. E. Spittler**, *Wild Kingdom*. Chap. 6.

The positive counterfoil to the dragon is presented by the foal of an ass, which also addresses the apostle in human speech as "Twin brother of Christ . . . initiated into the hidden word of Christ . . . who, though free, has been a servant, and being sold, has brought many to freedom . . ." (§39). The colt can point to a nobler ancestry than the dragon: One member of its family served Balaam (cf. Num 22:21-33), while another bore Jesus when he entered Jerusalem (§40). The colt insists that Thomas ride upon it, and now he enters the city in the same way as Jesus, accompanied by the crowd. After its task is done, the foal dies; despite the plea of the onlookers, it is not raised to life again (§41).

The key to a symbolic reading of this episode is supplied by some words in the prayer of thanksgiving that Thomas addresses to the Lord in §39: "Savior and nourisher, keeping us and making us rest on strange bodies." The apostle's body too can be understood as a "strange body" that transports his soul to its goal here on earth. In that case, the foal's death would function as a proleptic narrative anticipating the apostle's death in the closing paragraphs of the work.

5. Act 5: The Demon Who Fell in Love

Bibliography: I. Czachesz, "The Bride of the Demon: Narrative Strategies of Self-definition in the Acts of Thomas." Pages 36–52 in *The Apocryphal Acts of Thomas*. Edited by J. N. Bremmer. – **H. Kruse**, "Zwei Geistepiklesen."

In the city, a very beautiful woman appeals to the apostle for help. She begins by describing how things once were: "As a woman I formerly had rest, surrounded everywhere by peace" (§42). This can be interpreted as a metaphor of the state of the soul that is in the longed-for condition of rest (as we are told in §43, this is the soul's "original nature"). When she left the bath house (a priori a suspicious place), she met a man who made an immoral proposition, but she repulsed him indignantly: She had not even once slept with her fiancé, since she rejected marriage (§43). She herself saw a young man, but her maid saw an old man. This appearance "in two forms" immediately alerts the reader to the hidden dimension of the story. At night, the man came to her "and made me share in his foul intercourse." This has by now been going on for five years.

The apostle utters a lamentation over the work of the evil adversary, whom he apostrophizes as "polymorphous" and as the "wickedness that creeps like a serpent" (§44, establishing a link to the third Act). The adversary, that is, the demon who torments the woman, now appears in person, but although everyone hears what he says in a loud voice, only the apostle and the woman see him. He repeats several times: "What have we to do with you?" (§45; cf. Mark 1:24; 5:7) and accuses the apostle of transgressing a boundary, since the demonic powers are still authorized to work in their own sphere. The demon admits that they did not recognize Jesus when he came into the world (cf. 1 Cor 1:28) and that they therefore underestimated him. He then begins to weep, since he must leave his beloved "consort" (§46). He will go to a place where no one has ever heard of the apostle and look for a replacement for the woman. But he also threatens to return as soon as the apostle has departed (cf. Luke 11:24-26). He disappears, leaving behind fire and smoke.

The apostle now addresses another lengthy prayer to Jesus, in which he cites logion 13 from the Gospel of Thomas: "You are he . . . who separated me from all my companions and told me three words with which I am inflamed, but which I cannot communicate to others" (§47). He also calls Jesus "polymorphous" (§48). The woman asks for the seal, which the apostle imparts to her and to many others through the laying-on of hands (in the Syriac text, through baptism in the nearby river). A Eucharist with bread is prepared and begins with a second epiclesis. I quote only four of the nine lines of what is probably the oldest version, which is already expanded by later glosses in both the Greek and the Syriac (§50):

Come, she who knows the mysteries of the Chosen One!
Come, she who partakes in the combats of the noble combatant!
Come, O silence that reveals!
Come, holy dove that bears twins!

Thomas calls Jesus the "invincible champion" in §39. The dove is a symbol both of the bride (Song 5:2, etc.) and of the Spirit

(Mark 1:11). This may perhaps mean that the "twins" are the church as the daughter of the Spirit and the bride of Christ, formed out of Israel and the Gentiles (Kruse, 39), unless this is an allusion to Jesus and Thomas.

6. Act 6: The Young Man Who Committed Murder

Bibliography: M. Himmelfarb, *Tours of Hell: An Apocalyptic Form in Jewish and Christian Literature*. Philadelphia: 1983. 11–13, 86–89, 132–34.

During the celebration of the Eucharist that has just been prepared, a young man comes forward to receive the sacrament, but both his hands wither (§51). He is convicted in this manner of a grave crime and admits that he had loved a beautiful young woman. Under the impression of the apostle's exhortations, he wanted to convince her to live together with him in sexual continence, in a spiritual marriage. When she completely refused to do so, he killed her with the sword, both because he saw this as a good deed and because he could not endure the thought that she might enter a relationship with another man.

After duly lamenting the "insane" sexual instinct and its effects, the apostle invokes the Spirit of the Lord upon a vessel filled with water. When the young man washes his hands in this water, they are restored to health (§52). The whole company goes to an inn outside the city, where the above-mentioned woman had lived (this may imply that she worked as a prostitute there). Her corpse lies on a bier in the middle of the courtyard (§53), and the young man himself is allowed to raise her through prayer and the laying-on of hands. The woman at once throws herself at the apostle's feet and asks him where the other man—Christ—is, who has rescued her with Thomas from a terrible place together (§54). She then relates her experiences in the underworld. This description of hell in §§55–57 is parallel to the Apocalypse of Peter and may be dependent on it (cf. ApocPetr 21–24; for other contemporary examples, cf. Lucian, *Ver.* 2.30f.; Plutarch, *Sera* 566E–567D).

Some details: An ugly, black, dirty man receives the woman and shows her five different places where the souls of the evildoers are tormented. They are hung upon fiery wheels, they writhe in mud and worms, they are hung up by the tongue, the hair, the hands, and the feet and must endure a foul stench. Among their misdeeds, sins of impurity take a prominent place, but we also hear of slander, theft, and other crimes. The woman is only just rescued by being handed over to the apostle, "for she is one of the sheep which have wandered away" (§57). The apostle takes the opportunity to hold a moral sermon that contains an unambiguous evaluation: "For with God adultery (or fornication) is an evil exceedingly wicked above all other evils" (§58).

The result of this encounter is very positive: A large sum of money is donated, which Thomas gives to the widows. He preaches and heals many persons (§59). In his concluding prayer, Thomas recalls how he and his fellow apostles abandoned houses, possessions, wife and children, for the sake of the intimate fellowship with the exalted Lord (§61).

7. Act 7: The Royal Officer and His Family

The seventh Act helps set the scene for a new chain of events. A high commander in the army of the Indian King Misdaeus, whose name Siphor we learn only much later on in §100, brings a request to the apostle (§62). As his wife and his daughter were returning one evening from a wedding feast (§63), they were attacked on the way by two demons who presented themselves as father and son. Both demons were ugly; the woman saw them "with teeth like milk and lips like soot" (§64). This happened three years previously, and since then Siphor's wife and daughter can no longer leave the house, because the demons at once throw them to the ground and tear off their clothes.

Thomas asks: "Do you believe that Jesus can heal?" The officer declares himself willing to believe in Jesus (§65). Thomas now addresses the crowd, whom his deacon Xenophon has called together, and he announces for the first time: "I am about to go from you, and it is uncertain whether I shall see you again in my body" (§66). Xenophon will take his place, but it is only the Lord who can "heal the wounds" of his people and "keep them from the grievous wolves" (§67).

8. Act 8: The Wild Asses

Bibliography: J. E. Spittler, *Wild Kingdom*. Chap. 6.

Thomas takes his place in the officer's chariot and departs (§68). It is extremely hot, and after some time the beasts tire and remain standing (§69). A herd of wild asses is grazing nearby, and at the apostle's direction, the officer commands four of them to take the place of the horses. The whole herd hastens to meet him, and all the asses fall on their knees before Thomas, vying with one another to serve him. Only the four strongest asses are yoked (§70). They find by themselves the path to the officer's house, where they remain standing outside the gate (§71). The apostle commands one of the asses on the right side of the chariot to go into the courtyard and summon the demons, father and son, to meet it there (§73). The ass holds a discourse in which it not only carries out the commission it has received, but also reviles the demons at length and asks them where they come from (§74).

The officer's wife and daughter come out of the house. When the apostle commands the demons to leave them (§75), the two women fall down dead (or as if dead?). The older of the two demons protests, and we learn that this is the same demon who was driven out of a woman in Act 5. He then switches from protests to pleas: He too must render an account to his father (i.e., the devil), just as Thomas must render an account to Jesus. He draws further parallels: "And as you enjoy your prayer and good works and spiritual hymns, so I enjoy murders and adulteries and the sacrifices offered with wine upon the altars" (§76). Finally, however, the two demons disappear, while the women remain lying speechless on the ground (§77).

In §78, the wild ass which has received the gift of speech reproaches the apostle and says that he must do something about the two women: "Why do you stand idle . . . ? Why do you delay? For your teacher wishes to show his great deeds by your hands." It then repeatedly exhorts the crowd to believe and announces that false apostles and prophets will appear, who themselves practice all the vices against which they admonish, for example, the fornication in which they themselves indulge with many women (§79). This inspires the apostle to utter a long doxological prayer in which he repeats the word "glory" (*doxa*) ten times (§80). The raising up of the two women now seems a mere formality; but there is a deeper meaning in his words: "I beseech you, let these women rise up healed, and become again as they were before the demons struck them" (§81). The apostle sends the wild asses back in peace to their grazing grounds.

Why does the author introduce wild asses? There may be a special reason for this (cf. Spittler). In his *De natura animalium*, Aelian describes the Indian ass as an almost mythical being with enormous strength and speed (4.52). It is alleged to have a highly pronounced sexuality as well as a remarkable custom: According to Pliny the Elder in his *Natural History* (8.108) and other ancient authors, the male alpha animal in a herd of asses castrates all the new born male foals with one single bite in order to eliminate unwished-for competition. In the Christian *Physiologus*, the core of which goes back to the second century CE, this provides a model from nature for sexual continence and the striving for spiritual progeny (§9): Wild sexuality can be tamed with drastic means. It may seem strange to a modern reader, but from this perspective a herd of male wild asses can illustrate the possibility of a life without marriage and sexual intercourse—precisely the life to which the apostle attaches such importance.

9. Act 9: The Wife of Charisius

Bibliography: P. Germond, "A Rhetoric of Gender in Early Christianity: Sex and Salvation in the Acts of Thomas." Pages 350–68 in *Rhetoric, Scripture and Theology* (JSNT.S 131). Edited by S. E. Porter and T. H. Olbricht. Sheffield: 1996.

The ninth Act is by far the longest and plays a central role in the main plot of the narrative. Mygdonia, the wife of Charisius, a close relative of King Misdaeus, is borne by her slaves to the apostle (§82). Thomas applies to the slaves the logion in Matthew 11:28, "Come to me, all you that are weary and are carrying heavy burdens. . . ." In §83, he quotes the Golden Rule (Matt 7:12, etc.). This leads into an admonition (§§84–86) in which he summons his hearers above all to "holiness," that is, sexual continence. In a vivid comparison, he calls sexual intercourse ("uncleanliness") the "metropolis" of all evils (§84). Mygdonia is deeply impressed and throws herself at his feet, expressing the wish that she herself may become a holy temple of the Lord (§87). Thomas warns her inter alia against intercourse with her husband and the procreation of children (§88).

When she arrives home, Mygdonia declines to eat supper with her husband Charisius, under the pretext that she feels unwell (89); she also declines to sleep with him (§90). Charisius spends the night alone, and has an eloquent dream (§91): while he is eating with the king, an eagle swoops down from the sky, steals two partridges from the table, and bears them off to its nest (cf. Achilles Tatius 2.12). An arrow pierces it, but with no effect: it flies down a second time and bears off a dove and a pigeon from the table. When Charisius dresses in the morning, in order to wait on the king, he puts his left shoe on his right foot—another portent of evil, although Mygdonia denies this (§92). She herself visits the house of the officer Siphor a second time in order to see Thomas (§93). The apostle intones a *catena* of eleven beatitudes on those who are holy and meek (§94), and this confirms Mygdonia in the faith.

In the evening, Charisius asks his wife where she has been (§95), and she replies, "To the physician." When he asks whether the foreigner is a doctor, she replies more specifically: "Yes, a physician of souls." The scene from the previous evening is repeated: Mygdonia declines to eat and to sleep with Charisius, who fears the worst (§96):

> I am more suspicious, for I heard that this sorcerer and deceiver teaches that no man should cohabit with his wife, and he reverses what nature demands and the deity has ordered. . . . Be not led astray by deceitful and foolish words, nor by the works of sorcery.

When Charisius brushes aside his wife's resistance and attempts to have intercourse with her, she cries out, asks the Lord for help, and flees to her nurse, tearing down the bedroom curtain to cover her nakedness (§98). Charisius spends an unhappy night and then breaks out in lamentations (§100). We learn that the couple have been married for less than a year and that they have no children.

Charisius seeks to avenge himself on the foreigner and on Siphor, who has brought him to the city. He tells the king about the "Hebrew magician" and the events concerning his wife (§101). Siphor is the first to be summoned before the king (§102), so that the apostle has time to learn from Mygdonia what is going on, and to console her: "Believe in Jesus, and he will destroy Charisius' wrath and madness and passion, and he will be your companion on the dangerous road and guide you into his kingdom" (§103).

Siphor speaks in defense of the apostle before the king and describes his ascetic way of life and his message (§104). Nevertheless, the king sends a troop of soldiers to arrest him. When they return empty-handed, Charisius himself seizes him. At the king's orders, Thomas is flogged, receiving 128 lashes, and thrown into prison (§106). The apostle thanks the Lord that he is allowed to resemble him in so many things (§107).

The Song of the Pearl

Bibliography: K. Beyer, "Das syrische Perlenlied. Ein Erlösungs-mythos als Märchengedicht." *ZDMG* 140 (1990): 234–59. – **P.-H. Poirier**, '*L'Hymne de la perle des Actes de Thomas*': *Introduction, texte, traduction, commentaire* (HoRe 8). Louvain-la-Neuve: 1981. – **H. Jonas**, *Gnosis. Die Botschaft des fremden Gottes*. Frankfurt am Main: 1999. 144–63. – **H. Kruse**, "The Return of the Prodigal. Fortunes of a Parable on Its Way to the Far East." *Orientalia* 47 (1978): 163–214. – **G. P. Luttikhuizen**, "The Hymn of Jude Thomas, the Apostle, in the Country of the Indians." Pages 101–14 in *The Apocryphal Acts of Thomas*. Edited by J. N. Bremmer.

In the prison, the apostle declaims the so-called Song of the Pearl (§§108–13), which deals, strictly speaking, with the king's son and his garment of light more than with the pearl, and with an imprisonment of a particular kind (which presents an analogy to the speaker's own situation). Despite uncertain points in the reconstruction of the text—due partly to corruption (especially in the Greek) and partly to a revision which inserts glosses (especially in the Syriac, which has the more reliable version here)—the basic structure is still recognizable. It appears to be borrowed from folktales, where innumerable young men go out into the world to seek their luck in dangerous far-off places and return home laden with treasures.

A king's son, who relates his experiences in the first person singular (lines 1f.: "When I was a little child, in my father's palace . . ."), is sent out by his parents from his home in the East. He must go to Egypt and fetch a pearl that is guarded by a serpent or a dragon in the sea there. He is given food, gold, silver, and jewels for his journey, but he must leave behind the radiant garment that exactly fits his size. When he returns from his journey, he will be allowed to put on this garment once more and will exercise a high office in the state, together with his brother.

Initially, two companions accompany him on the journey to Egypt, which proves long and difficult. When he at last reaches the country, he lodges in the vicinity of the serpent in the hope that it will fall asleep and that he will thus be able to take the pearl from it without being noticed. He finds a companion there, a man of his own age from the East, who warns him against having dealings with the Egyptians (this is in fact the only function of this figure). Although he has clothed himself in local garments, the Egyptians realize that the king's son is a foreigner. They give him some of their own food to eat, with the result that he forgets his mission and falls into a deep sleep (lines 32–35):

> I tasted their food.
> I no longer recognized that I was a king's son,
> and I served their king.
> I forgot the pearl for which my parents had sent me.
> And I fell into a deep sleep
> because of the heaviness of their food.

When news of this reaches the East, his parents, his brother, and all the courtiers write him a letter that begins: "Awake, and rise from your sleep. Listen to the words in this letter; remember you are the son of kings. You have fallen beneath the yoke of slavery . . ." (cf. Eph 5:14). The letter flies like an eagle through the air to Egypt, where it lands beside the king's son and is transformed into speech. The king's son is awakened by this noise and opens the letter. As he reads it, he remembers his mission and succeeds in casting a spell on the dragon so that it falls asleep. He then steals the pearl from it. Leaving behind the filthy Egyptian garments, he sets out on his return journey. The letter goes ahead of him, lighting up the path with its radiance.

Two treasurers, who have the same form, bring him his garment of light, which resembles him like his mirror image. The poem describes its splendid embroidery, but even more importantly, "I saw that motions of knowledge were stirring throughout it," and it begins to speak (following Bayer, 249): "It is I who belong to the one who works eagerly [i.e., the king's son], for whom I was brought up in the presence of my father. And I

observe that my form grew with me in keeping with his development." The king's son is united to his garment and is welcomed
back into his father's court. What is probably the older version
ends with music from a hydraulic organ (in line 103).

This colorful story recalls not only motifs from folktales, but
also biblical motifs such as the parable of the prodigal son (Luke
15), the parable of the precious pearl (Matt 13:45f.), the theme of
the exodus (liberation from slavery in Egypt), and the splendid
vestment of the high priest. It is nevertheless too simple to interpret the narrative as a whole only as Christian allegory of the fall
and redemption of the human person (as Kruse does). It is difficult
to deny the presence of elements found in the gnostic systems.
Bayer lists the following items: "the heavenly world of light as one's
home; the doubling of the brothers and of the prince with his garment of light; Egypt and the serpent in the sea as images of the evil
earthly world; descent and ascent; messengers who accompany him
on the journey; the change of clothing as an image of the change of
bodies; life as a foreigner and loneliness; the overwhelming of the
heavenly messenger; sleep and the wakening call; forgetting one's
origin and then remembering it" (240). On the other hand, it is
better not to interpret the king's son as a gnostic redeemer and the
pearl as the spark in the soul that must be set free. Rather, the king's
son is the soul for which a heavenly body (the garment of light) is
already prepared, but which threatens to sink down in the earthly
body (the Egyptian garment). To some extent, there is a parallel in
books 3–6 of Apuleius' *Metamorphoses*, where the fable of Amor and
Psyche is inserted into the already finished narrative. The theme of
this fable is precisely the uniting of the human soul with its heavenly counterpart. (Only the Syriac tradition inserts after §113 a
lengthy prayer of praise, running to forty-two doxologies and five
macarisms; translation in Klijn, 195–98.)

Charisius' Lament

Charisius thinks that his marriage is now once again intact, but
when he comes home, he finds his wife with her garments rent.
She rejects him even more strictly than before (§114), and he
laments in moving words, asking how he has sinned, that the gods
should punish him in this way. What is he to do? "Shall I keep
silence and endure? Who can bear it when his treasure is taken

from him?" (§115). He reminds Mygdonia of how persistently he had wooed her (§116), but her only reply (§117) is:

> He whom I love is better than you and your possessions . . . do not remind me of your actions to me. For I pray to the Lord that you would forget and think no more of the former pleasures and the bodily intercourse, which shall pass like a shadow. Jesus alone remains forever.

Uttering a final threat, Charisius goes off to sleep, and Mygdonia hastens to the prison. On the way, she meets the apostle but does not recognize him because "a great light went before him," and she thinks he is one of the archons, that is, one of the rulers in the heavenly sphere. Her soul, which has not yet received the seal, cannot endure his presence, so she runs away and hides.

10. Act 10: The Baptism of Mygdonia and Siphor

The apostle visits Mygdonia in her hiding place. In her fear, she falls down as if dead, but Thomas raises her to her feet (this too is a kind of resurrection) and says: "Arise from the ground, since you are raised above it" (§119; cf. 37). Mygdonia's soul has already detached itself from earthly things and set out on the upward path.

Mygdonia asks her nurse, Marcia, for help in the preparation and administration of her baptism. She must procure bread, oil, and a mixture of water (§120; despite this expression, the original reference was probably only to water; as usual, the Syriac text changes this to "wine"). First, the apostle anoints Mygdonia's head with oil. For reasons of propriety, he leaves it to the nurse to remove Mygdonia's clothes (the Syriac also gives the nurse the task of anointing her; cf. 157) and to clothe her in a garment of linen (§121). He baptizes Mygdonia in a spring of water. Once she has put on her clothes again, he gives the Eucharist, which consists of bread and water. A voice from above says: "Yes, Amen!" This voice so frightens Marcia that she too asks to be allowed to receive the seal.

When the apostle returns to the prison, the doors are opened by a miracle (§122; cf. Acts 12:6-10, but with the difference that in ActThom all the doors are open, and the sentries are sleeping). In the morning, Charisius finds Mygdonia and Marcia praying to their "new God" that he may deflect from them "the madness of Charisius" (§123). Charisius asks Mygdonia to believe him, to endure his words, and to "be toward me as before"—a highly ironic play on words that is repeated several times. Charisius has sexual intercourse in mind, but the reader knows that Mygdonia believes the word of the Lord and that her soul is returning into its state of purity. Charisius reminds Mygdonia of their former married life and asks where he was not more handsome in her eyes *then* than Jesus is *now*. Mygdonia's reply adopts the structure of his question, with twelve contrasts between the former state and the present state of things: "You have seen the wedding which passed over and remains here. This wedding remains in eternity. That communion was of destruction, this is of eternal life . . ." (§124).

Charisius' final hope is that the apostle can get Mygdonia to change her mind (§125), so Thomas is brought once more before the king. When he is asked why he teaches doctrines that bring him into such difficulties, the apostle replies with a simile: "Are you not indignant when your soldiers accompany you in filthy garments?" (§126). In exactly the same way, "Those who serve my king must be holy and pure and free from grief." This refers not only to the concern for children, but also to riches, restlessness, and vices such as theft and gluttony. The king nevertheless commands him to restore peace and harmony to the marriage of Charisius, and once again (as so often) we find the accusation of magic: Since the apostle has employed magical means, he can now deprive these of their effectiveness (§127). Charisius supports this royal command in the form of a petition with arguments that cannot simply be dismissed (§128):

> I never did anything wrong to you or anybody else or against the gods—why have you brought such great misery upon me? Why have you incited such sedition in my house? And what profit do you have from it? But if you think to profit from it, tell me what kind of profit it is, and I will obtain it for you without trouble. . . . Persuade Mygdonia to behave toward me as she did before she saw you.

Should this not happen, he threatens to kill both the apostle and himself. He even adds an eschatological prospect to lend a special point to his plea: if there is a judgment, he is perfectly willing to appear with the apostle before the judge, for a just God will necessarily declare that Charisius has been wronged: "If God, whom you preach, is just and judges justly, I know that I shall be vindicated" (§128).

In the meantime, Mygdonia has prayed that she may depart from this life as soon as possible (§129). The apostle does in fact say to her: "My daughter Mygdonia, obey what brother Charisius says" (§130), but presumably this is only in order to put her to the test. Mygdonia refuses to do so, and reminds the apostle of what he himself has taught her earlier. Charisius imprisons her in his house, while the apostle goes to Siphor.

Siphor has resolved from now on to live together with his wife and his daughter in holiness and purity. He therefore asks that his whole family may receive the seal, and this seems to touch on a central issue, for the apostle reacts in a strange way, by recalling the limits of what can be put into words (cf. §36): "I fear to say what I think. I know something, and what I know I cannot express" (§131). Despite this, he goes on to speak of the mystery of baptism (§132). The ritual of initiation takes the same form as in the case of Mygdonia: an anointing with oil, baptism in water, and the celebration of the Eucharist with bread (§133).

11. Act 11: The Wife of the King

The king relates all these events to his wife, Tertia, asking her to go to Mygdonia and get her friend to see reason (§134). One piece of advice that she gives Mygdonia is highly ambiguous: "Know yourself and return to your own ways" (§135). Mygdonia holds a brief discourse, part of which is a repetition of the apostle's ideas from §§35–36, and she succeeds surprisingly quickly in convincing Tertia of her own point of view. Eager to learn more, Tertia goes quickly to the house of Siphor in order to see and hear the apostle in person (§136). Here too, no great work of persuasion is needed in order to bring about her inner repentance. The first part of the prophetic dream in §91 is now fulfilled: the eagle has carried off the two partridges, and Charisius and Misdaeus are left empty-handed.

When she arrives home, Tertia wishes to convert her husband, the king, who at once knows what is in store for him (§137). He blames this development on Charisius and falls into a furious rage; when he meets Charisius in the market place, the king demands, "Why did you not allow me to kill the sorcerer before he destroyed my house by his sorcery?" (§138). They both enter Siphor's house, where the king seizes with both hands the chair on which the apostle is sitting and strikes him on the head with it, wounding him. The king then orders his soldiers to drag him off to the place of judgment.

12. Act 12: The Son of the King

Bibliography: H. W. Attridge, "Intertextuality in the Acts of Thomas." *Semeia* 80 (1997): 87–124.

Vazan, Misdaeus' son, takes Thomas aside and proposes a bargain: If the apostle teaches Vazan his magical arts, Vazan will persuade his father to set Thomas free. In his reply, Thomas demonstrates in many ways the superiority of his own "eternal king" to every earthly king. He contrasts two different ways of life and forms of fellowship, when he tells Vazan: "You glory in possessions, slaves, garments, revelry, and unclean beds; but I glory in poverty, love of wisdom, humility, fasting, and prayer, and communion with the Holy Spirit and with my brethren" (§139). This suffices to convince Vazan. He wants to help the apostle flee, but at this moment, the king enters and summons Thomas to appear before him. His answers displease the king, who orders iron plates to be heated and the apostle to be put barefoot on them (§140). They obey his command, but water gushes forth from the earth—so much water that a flood threatens, and the king becomes afraid. The apostle asks his Lord to "calm" the water, because "there are some here among those present who shall live, because they have believed in you" (§141; cf. Mark 9:1).

Thomas is brought back into the prison, accompanied by Vazan on his right hand and Siphor on his left. Siphor's wife and daughter are also present (§142). The rest of this Act consists of discourses and prayers by the apostle. In the first prayer, thirteen sentences (in the Greek) or fifteen (in the Syriac) begin with "Behold. . . ." He understands his death as setting him free for eternal life, using the following image: "Behold, I sleep and wake up and shall not sleep again." His words: "Behold, I undress myself and I dress myself, and I shall not again be undressed" refer to the earthly and the heavenly body and form a link to the Song of the Pearl. He exhorts those present to believe in Jesus, the physician of souls, and alludes to various New Testament episodes, for example, to the transfiguration of Jesus (§143).

A particularly lengthy prayer begins in §144 with the words of the Lord's Prayer. This continues to §148. (Our most important textual witnesses diverge here both in the wording and in the sequence: P, which has the better text, brings the prayer only after §167.) In a manner typical of farewell discourses, the apostle gives an account of the life he has led: "I was never joined to a wife, that the temple worthy of you might not be found in pollution" (§144). He describes himself as "poor and needy and a stranger and a bondman and set at naught and a prisoner and hungry and thirsty and naked and unshod" (§145). There are many striking reminiscences of New Testament traditions, above all the parables of Jesus. Some examples (§146f.):

> With your one mina I have traded and have made ten [Luke 19:16]; you have added more to me beside that which I had, as you covenanted. . . . I was bidden to the supper, and I came; and I refused the land and the yoke of oxen and the wife [Luke 14:16-20]. . . . I was bidden to the wedding, and I put on white raiment, that I might be worthy of it and not be bound hand and foot and cast into the outer darkness [Matt 22:11-13]. . . . My hands I have put to the yoked plough and have not turned back, lest my furrows go crooked [Luke 9:62]. The plough-land is white and the harvest is come [John 4:35], that I may receive my wages . . . I have kept the first watch and the second and the third [Luke 12:38], that I may behold your face . . . The inward I have made the outward and the outward the inward [Gos. Thom. 22].

In §148 the apostle speaks of the ascent of his soul. When it is borne aloft, the powers and officers in the lower heavens, who are metaphorically called "publicans and tax gatherers," will seek to hold it back and block its path. The true nature of a human being will then be revealed, and the "children of the evil one" will be convicted and will not get any further. But the light of Christ, which dwells in the apostle, dazzles the eyes of the slanderer. Thomas will "pass by in quietness and joy and peace, and pass over and stand before the judge."

13. Act 13: In the Prison and in Vazan's House

Vazan wishes to bring the apostle secretly to his own house, where his wife Mnesara lies chronically ill in bed. Although he is only twenty-one years old, he has already lived with her for seven years, at his father's command; but he adds that they have lived together in chastity (§150). In the meantime, Tertia and Mygdonia, who had been shut up together in a room by their husbands, come to the prison so that Tertia may at least receive protection through the sacrament of initiation with "oil, water, and bread," which her husband regards as highly dangerous (§152). When the apostle asks how they were able to come to him, Tertia declares that he himself was with them the whole time, and that it was he who opened all the doors for them (§151). Clearly, this was the work of Jesus, in the form of Thomas, and this leads the apostle to begin his short prayer of thanksgiving with the words: "Glory to you, polymorphous Jesus!" (§153). The prison guards insist that all the lamps be extinguished. While they and the other prisoners sleep, the prison becomes "as light as the day" for the believers.

The apostle and his companions make their way to Vazan's house, led by Vazan himself. He meets his wife Mnesara, who is going in the opposite direction, to the prison. He asks her how she is able to stand up, and she points to a young man who leads her by the right hand, but is invisible to others (§154). When she sees the apostle, she falls to her knees before him and declares that it was he who entrusted her to the young man—once again, we have the *doppelgänger* motif. The young man, apparently some kind of angel, suddenly disappears, and Mnesara is no longer able to see him, but Thomas consoles her: "Jesus shall lead you" (§155).

When they enter the house, Thomas prays over Vazan, Mnesara, and Tertia, who have not yet received baptism: "Be the physician of their bodies and souls, make them your holy temples, and let your Holy Spirit dwell in them!" (§156). He asks Mygdonia to undress the two women and to clothe them in the baptismal garment. He anoints the women on the head, but Mygdonia anoints them on the body, while Thomas anoints Vazan's body (§157). After they are baptized by descending into the water, the Eucharist is celebrated with bread and a cup. The apostle recalls here the passion of the Lord: gall and vinegar, the spittle, the reed and the crown of thorns (the crown has already been mentioned in the prayer over the oil), the linen cloth in which the body of Jesus was laid, and the resurrection (§158), because these events become effective in the Eucharist, which is here (as in §49) called a participation in the body and blood of the Lord. With the baptism of Vazan and Mnesara, the second part of the dream in §91 is fulfilled: The eagle has carried off the dove and the pigeon.

14. The Death of the Apostle

On the way to the prison, the apostle speaks to the women who accompany him and interprets his death as an act of liberation (§159). He emphasizes that, despite all evidence to the contrary, he is not identical to the Lord: "I am not Jesus, but I am his servant. I am not Christ, but I am his minister. I am not the Son of God, but I pray to become worthy of God" (§160; there is some tension between the two motifs of Thomas as Jesus' twin brother and Thomas as his slave, but these could be harmonized by means of Philippians 2:7, "he emptied himself, taking the form of a slave, being born in human likeness"). The apostle goes alone into the prison (§161). The guards are irritated by all these comings and goings, and they complain to the king—but when he inspects the seals, he finds them intact (§162).

The king interrogates the apostle one last time. He is accused of being a runaway slave and of practicing sorcery (§163). The king is afraid of the crowd, who sympathize with the apostle, so he takes him outside the city and hands him over to four soldiers and an officer, ordering them to kill him with spears on the mountain (§164). Here too, Thomas discerns a symbolic dimension: "Four are they that cast me down, for of four am I made; and one is he who draws me, for of one I am, and to him I go" (§165; cf. the puzzling expression "the four standing brothers" in §32). A long prayer (in manuscript U) speaks once more of the ascent of the soul which at last is set free: "Let not the publicans see me, and let not the tax gatherers accuse me falsely. Let not the serpent see me, and let not the children of the dragon hiss at me" (§167). He urges the soldiers to carry out the command they have received, and all four pierce him simultaneously with their lances. The brethren bury his body in a royal tomb (§168).

Siphor and Vazan spend the night by the grave, but Thomas appears to them and declares that this is pointless, since he is no longer there. He also appears to Tertia and Mygdonia and strengthens their resolve to resist the attempts of their husbands to win them over; and the two men finally give up and allow their wives to live as they wish. Siphor and Vazan have the pastoral care of the young community as presbyter and deacon (§169; cf. the withering comment by E. Preuschen, HNTA 601: "The ordination that Siphor and Vazan have received is the unintelligent invention of a know-all who cannot imagine assemblies without ministers set over the community").

The last paragraph, which is probably a later addition, even makes Misdaeus a member of the Christian community. We learn that one of his sons was possessed by an obstinate demon and that the king planned to take one of the bones of the apostle from his grave and heal his son by touching him with this relic. When the grave is opened, they discover that brethren have secretly translated the bones to the West (i.e., to Edessa; see above). But dust from the grave suffices to restore the king's son to health—and Misdaeus becomes a Christian.

15. The Legend Is Elaborated

Bibliography: M. Bonnet, AAAp II: 1. 128–50: *Passio Bartholomaei.* – **M. R. James**, *Apocrypha anecdota*, Vol. 2 (TS 5.1). Cambridge: 1897. 27–63. – **R. A. Lipsius**, *Die apokryphen Apostelgeschichten*, Vol. 1: 273–77. – **A. de Santos Otero**, NTApo 6th ed. II: 408–14. – **K. Zelzer**, "Zu den lateinischen Fassungen der Thomasakten." *WSt* 84 (1971): 161–79; 85 (1972): 185–212. – Idem, *Die alten lateinischen Thomasakten* (TU 122). Berlin: 1977.

As ActThom 170 shows, the elaboration of the legendary stories about the apostle Thomas began as early as the manuscript transmission of the primary textual witnesses. The *Acta Thomae minora* are a new recension in Greek, which was translated into oriental Christian languages (Greek text and a translation from the Ethiopic in James). In the city where Thomas is charged to build the palace, he causes all the statues of the gods in the temples to fall to the ground. As a punishment for this and other crimes, he is flayed alive, but the Lord appears to him and heals his wounds. From then on, the apostle carries his flayed skin around with him. With its aid, he performs great miracles, including several raisings of the dead. Sexual continence in marriage and the renunciation of marriage continue to be an important theme, illustrated in two episodes. When the priest of Apollo in another city incites the people to try to stone him, the hands of all those who reach for stones wither. Later, the flesh of the apostle is covered with a new skin, and he himself is borne off on a cloud.

There are two Latin elaborations, the fifth- or sixth-century book *De miraculis beati Thomae apostoli*, which forms chapter 9 of Pseudo-Abdias' collection, and a fourth- or fifth-century *Passio sancti Thomae apostoli*. The *Miracula* stick more closely to the original version of ActThom, although they abbreviate. In their additional material, they agree with the *Passio* in a scene set in the temple of the sun god.

The *Passio* introduces a number of new elements into the story. The bridegroom from Act 2 of ActThom now holds in his hand a branch of a date tree with lovely fruits, from which the bridal couple eat (11 in Zelzer's enumeration). The Lord, in a royal garment, and their guardian angels appear to them (14). The bridegroom subsequently becomes a bishop, while the bride remains a virgin and dies a martyr (15). In a long homily, the apostle emphatically teaches the orthodox, anti-Arian doctrine of the Trinity (26–29). After delivering an exhortation to chastity, he baptizes nine thousand men, not counting women and children (30f.). Syntyche, who has been healed after being blind for many years, brings Mygdonia to the apostle (33). The healing of a leper is narrated in 44–47. Charisius suggests to the king that he compel the apostle to offer a sacrifice to the invincible sun god, who is portrayed in his temple in a golden chariot drawn by four horses (55–60). The apostle compels the demon who lives in this cultic image (and with whom he speaks in Hebrew) to destroy the statue, which then melts like wax. The priest of the sun god is furious and kills the apostle with a sword.

It is possible that some elements from the Latin *Passio Bartholomaei* (chap. 8 in Pseudo-Abdias) have penetrated the Thomas tradition here: Bartholomew too carries out missionary work in India, fights with demons, and destroys idols (and according to another tradition, he was flayed alive). This would then be a new instrumentalization of the "competition" between the two missionaries to India.

C. Evaluation

Bibliography: P. Brown, *The Body and Society: Men, Women, and Sexual Renunciation in Early Christianity*. New York: 1988. 83–102. – **H. J. W.**

Drijvers, *History and Religion in Late Antique Syria*. Aldershot: 1984. – **M. Elze**, *Tatian und seine Theologie* (FKDG 9). Göttingen: 1960. – **K. L. Gaca**, "Driving Aphrodite from the World: Tatian's Encratitic Principles of Sexual Renunciation." *JTS* 53 (2002): 28–52; also pages 221–46 in idem., *The Making of Fornication*. – **E. J. Hunt**, *Christianity in the Second Century: The Case of Tatian*. London: 2003. 155–63. – **Y. Tissot**, "L'encratisme des Actes de Thomas." *ANRW* II/25.6 (1988): 4415–30. – **A. Vööbus**, *Celibacy, a Requirement for Admission to Baptism in the Early Syrian Church* (PETSE 1). Stockholm: 1951.

Older scholarship took it for granted that the theology of ActThom had its provenance in the gnosis that was particularly prominent in Syria. More recently, a significant closeness has been noted to Tatian, who had a decisive influence on the formation of Syriac theology and piety ca. 200 CE (Drijvers), and the similarities are undeniable. Tatian upheld a strict encratism: Baptism presupposes the renunciation of marriage, and married persons who receive baptism are obliged to live in sexual continence, since it is only in this way (according to Tatian) that the human soul can succeed in being reunited with its counterpart, the heavenly spirit. Through the fall, the soul has separated from the spirit, but it still bears within itself one last spark of the spirit's being (*Or. Graec.* 7.3; 12.1; 13.2). Another element in Tatian's "Address to the Greeks" is the rejection of the pagan religiosity that had created in Aphrodite a goddess of sexual intercourse (cf. Gaca). ActThom also includes more general warnings against fornication and adultery, and the pains of hell in §§55–57 are inflicted because of such sins; although marriage is not mentioned in the list of transgressions here, there can be no doubt that the author or redactor proclaims a strictly encratite message especially in the second part of the work, when Mygdonia and Tertia boycott their marriages and Siphor and Vazan ultimately live together with their wives in chastity. In baptism, one is transposed into a pre-sexual paradisiacal state that knows no shame (like the bride in §14). And when one is united to Christ, the heavenly bridegroom (cf. §124), it is no longer possible to consummate an earthly marriage.

In Tatian, the strict sexual continence is linked to the renunciation of wine and meat and to a very simple lifestyle: "I do not wish to be a king; I am not anxious to be rich; I decline military command; I detest fornication; I am not impelled by an insatiable love of gain to go to sea. . . . I despise death; I am superior to every kind of disease. . . . Am I a slave, I endure servitude . . ." (*Or. Graec.* 11; English translation by J. E. Ryland, *Ante-Nicene Fathers*, Vol. 2. Grand Rapids: 1975). The apostle Thomas could have made these words his own, since he is the embodiment of one who leads a poor life and does good to others (§100: ". . . he teaches a new doctrine by saying that none can live unless he free himself from all his possessions and, like himself, become an abstainer"). In ActThom 76f., wine (and by association, perhaps meat too) is infected by demons and is mentioned in the context of pagan sacrificial rites and feasts. The believers eat their fill of bread, oil, vegetables, and salt (29). This is also the reason why the Eucharist is celebrated only with bread and water. Both writers, Tatian and the author of ActThom, present a complex demonology.

Tatian affirms the resurrection of the body more clearly than ActThom (*Or. Graec.* 6.1; 13.1). ActThom speaks only once, in §158, of the "renewal of soul and body," in a passage which otherwise seems to have been revised in keeping with doctrinal orthodoxy. Otherwise, the emphasis lies entirely on the liberation of the soul from the body and from the world. It suffices to quote §30: "Father not of the souls that are still in bodies, but of those who have left them" (cf. §§117, 160). Neither Tatian nor ActThom knows the evil demiurge who is responsible in gnosis for the creation of the world.

There are virtually no christological affirmations in Tatian. In ActThom, we can discern at most a slight tendency toward docetism (cf. the statement in §165 that Thomas consists of four elements, but the Lord was "of one"). ActThom speaks impressively of the human aspect of Jesus, his life and his death (cf. §§47, 59 [in fulfillment of Scripture], 72, and 80; with reservations, 158) and says that the disciples could touch his human body with their hands (§143; cf. 1 John 1:1). In ActThom (unlike ActJoh and ActPet), the polymorphy is strictly reserved to the appearances of the risen Lord, who manifests himself in an overwhelmingly radiant light (27, 35). During his time on earth, only the transfiguration gave a foretaste of this; §143, which speaks of touching the human body of Jesus, notes: "we could not see his heavenly form on the mountain." But a post-Easter polymorphy corresponds exactly to the idea of a liberation of the soul from death that ignores the body; and this seems to apply to Jesus too.

In a standard monograph on Tatian, M. Elze writes that his basic conception is "a consistent application of Middle Platonic positions to Christianity." On questions of practical conduct, he "comes dangerously close to the gnostic answers" (Elze, 120, 128). These two points are connected because Middle Platonic dualism not only made an important contribution to the genesis of the gnostic systems, but also influenced the average Christian anthropology. Both these verdicts can be applied to ActThom as well. The boundaries were fluid in Syria in the early third century, and the distinctions were both very fine and very fragile, as we see in the reception of this work: ActThom was accepted both in the mainstream church and in gnosis (Manichaeism), although the catholicizing tendencies in the Syriac version show that the mainstream church felt obliged to undertake larger-scale revisions than the gnostics.

Chapter 6

The Acts of Peter and the Twelve Apostles

Edition: R. McL. Wilson and D. M. Parrott, Pages 197–229 in *Nag Hammadi Codices V.2–5 and VI with Papyrus Berolinensis 8502.1 and 4* (NHS 11). Edited by D. M. Parrott. Leiden: 1979. (With English translation.)

Translations: H. M. Schenke, NTApo 6th ed. II: 368–80. – Idem, *Nag Hammadi Deutsch*. 2 Vols.: *NHC V.2-XIII.1, BG 1 und 4* (GCS n.s. 12). Berlin: 2003. 443–53.

Bibliography: I. Czachesz, "The Identity of Lithargoel in the Acts of Peter and the Twelve." Pages 485–502 in *The Wisdom of Egypt: Jewish, Early Christian, and Gnostic Essays in Honour of Gerard P. Luttikhuizen* (Ancient Judaism and Early Christianity 59). Edited by A. Hilhorst and G. H. van Kooten. Leiden: 2005. – **A. L. Molinari**, *The Acts of Peter and the Twelve Apostles (NHC 6.1): Allegory, Ascent, and Ministry in the Wake of the Decian Persecution* (SBLDS 174). Atlanta: 2000. – **M. J. Smith**, "Understand Ye a Parable! The Acts of Peter and the Twelve Apostles as Parable Narrative." *Apocrypha* 11 (2000): 29–52. – **J. Tubach**, "Reisewege der Apostel in den Acta Petri aus Nag Hammadi." Pages 461–83 in *The Wisdom of Egypt: Jewish, Early Christian, and Gnostic Essays in Honour of Gerard P. Luttikhuizen* (Ancient Judaism and Early Christianity 59). Edited by A. Hilhorst and G. H. van Kooten.

A. Context

Title and Genre

Bibliography: A. Guillaumont, "De nouveaux actes apocryphes: les Actes de Pierre et des Douze Apôtres." *RHR* 196 (1979): 141–52. – **M. Krause**, "Die Petrusakten in Codex VI von Nag Hammadi." Pages

36–38 in *Essays on the Nag Hammadi Texts in Honour of Alexander Böhlig* (NHS 3). Leiden: 1972.

The first work in the sixth of the thirteen codices which were discovered at Nag Hammadi in Upper Egypt in 1945 is a brief text which bears the title, as a *subscriptio*: "The Acts [*praxis*, with the article in the plural] of Peter and the Twelve Apostles" (NHC VI:1 1.1–12.22). The fact that the text itself speaks of eleven apostles (9.21) indicates that this title, which was translated from Greek into Coptic, was given to the text only at a secondary stage. The mention of eleven apostles suggests that the work is situated shortly after Easter, before the ascension of Jesus (cf. Acts 1:26).

Even as an addition, the title shows that this enigmatic narrative reminded a later reader of the Lukan Acts of the Apostles. Although there are a few points in the Acts of Peter and the Twelve (ActPet12) which may lend plausibility to the title (Guillaumont, 142, compares motifs from the hellenistic novels: a sea voyage, a strong wind, a lonely island, adventures, a mysterious stranger . . .), it does not really identify the genre to which the text belongs (despite the claim by Parrott, 202, that ActPet12 "almost certainly is to be grouped with the apocryphal Acts of the second and third centuries"), since the protagonist is not an apostle, nor even a group of apostles, but ultimately the risen and polymorphous Lord.

This means that Krause's attempt, via the Act of Peter in BG 4, to identify ActPet12 as a part of the lost beginning of the ancient Acts of Peter, is unsuccessful; in fact, no other scholar has followed him here. The text as a whole is best understood as an allegory with visionary elements, or as an allegorical description of a vision that returns to earth at the close.

Literary Character and Composition

Bibliography: I. Czachesz, *Commission Narratives*. 162–63. – **A. L. Molinari**, "The Acts of Peter and the Twelve Apostles: a Reconsideration of the Source Question." Pages 461–83 in *The Nag Hammadi Library after Fifty Years* (NHMS 41). Edited by J. D. Turner and A. McGuire. Leiden: 1997. – **S. J. Patterson**, "Sources, Redaction, and Tendenz in the Acts of Peter and the Twelve Apostles (NH VI, 1)." *VC* 45 (1991): 1–17. – **M. J. Smith**, "Understand Ye a Parable!"

The strangely oscillating character of this text can be seen in the repeated change of narrative perspective and the integration of different sorts of texts. "We sailed" at page 1.6 comes in a section written in the first-person plural, which is typical in accounts of journeys and sea voyages, but only a little later, at page 1.30, the first-person singular of Peter takes center stage and remains there until page 3.11. From then onward, the authorial third person dominates, but it is interrupted by another passage in the first-person singular (6.9–7.22), a passage by the travelers in the first-person plural (7.23–8.20), and a passage by the apostles in the first-person plural (9.15–29). In addition to the travel narrative, which turns out to be a journey outside this world, we can discern elements of a vision, of an Easter apparition, of a revelatory dialogue, and of a church order. One passage mentions a parable that seems important (10.24).

Such a state of affairs presents a clear invitation to disentangle and identify the sources of the text, but this proves difficult, since the changes of perspective and the combination of typical genres are insufficient as criteria. Several scholars have explained the present text as a redactional composition that draws on two, three, or four sources (for an overview, see Molinari). Patterson distinguishes a "Petrine source" in the first-person singular from a first-person plural source and a third-person source. Molinari himself identifies the narrative of the merchant of pearls (1.1–9.1) and the apparition of the risen Jesus (9.1-29) as source passages (with redactional additions) and attributes the entire conclusion (9.30–12.19) to the redactor or author. Czachesz postulates as the oldest source passage a text closely related to the Song of the Pearl in ActThom, which spoke of a man looking for pearls, who was not yet identified with Christ. The identification with Christ and his commissioning of the apostles would be the result of a later revision in several stages. This revision also involved a shortening of the narrative, which originally was longer.

There can be no doubt that a complicated history of tradition lies behind ActPet12, and it is not improbable that the motif of the pearl was the starting point for the entire development. In the present context, however, our task is to understand the final product, which now lies before us, as a linguistic production that makes at least some sense; Smith sees this task as particularly important.

Place and Date

Bibliography: I. Czachesz, *Commission Narratives.* 162–83. – **F. Lapham,** *Peter: the Myth, the Man and the Writings. A Study of the Early Petrine Text and Tradition* (JSNTS 239). Sheffield: 2003. 71–82. – **A. L. Molinari,** *Allegory, Ascent, and Ministry.* – **H. M. Schenke,** NTApo 6th ed. II: 368–80.

In view of the singular character of ActPet12, it is impossible to say much more about the place and date of its composition than that the Coptic text was written no later than 350 CE, as we see from the dated contracts and receipts that were used to strengthen the bindings of the codex. This does not help us to date the Greek original. Scholars have suggested the second or third century, and the "usual suspects" have been proposed: Asia Minor, Syria, and Alexandria. Schenke finds that the strict asceticism prescribed with regard to possessions and food is reminiscent of itinerant Syrian monasticism; but one can also very well envisage the use of ActPet12 in a Coptic monastery of monks as an introduction to the contemplative life, which brings healing for body and soul (Czachesz).

Molinari gives an unusually precise date, 252–256 CE. This is connected with a very thorough localization of the text as a whole, and we shall return to this question at the close of the present chapter. There are no convincing reasons to accept the early dating to the reign of Trajan (i.e., 90–110 CE) by Lapham, who simply passes over Molinari in silence. Czachesz has recently proposed a dating between 347 and 357, but this seems to me almost too late. As our reading of the text will show, the final redactor is very well acquainted with New Testament traditions, in whatever form these may have reached him.

B. Contents

Bibliography: C.-A. Keller, "De la foi à la connaissance: les sens des 'Actes de Pierre et des Douze Apôtres.'" *RTP* 110 (1979): 131–37. – **A. L. Molinari,** *Allegory, Ascent, and Ministry.*

Since the first pages are very badly damaged at the upper margin, it is no longer possible to reconstruct the beginning of the narrative with adequate certainty; the first person plural (1.4: "us"), the word "apostles," the expression "we sailed," and "of the body" (*sôma*) are still legible. One plausible suggestion is that here, the preexistent souls of the apostles enter their bodies and begin the journey to the world (Molinari, 96).

A sea voyage is now described. The apostles are of one mind and are ready to carry out the service that the Lord has enjoined on them. They go to the shore of the sea, where a ship lies anchored and seems to be waiting for them. The sailors treat them with great kindness and take them on board. After a day and a night, a wind springs up and drives the ship to a city in the midst of the sea. (Allegorically, the city represents the world; Keller, 135, interprets it less plausibly to mean the church.)

All the apostles go on shore (2.7), but it is Peter who now takes the role of narrator and speaker. He seems to be acting alone in the next scene, when he asks the curious onlookers who stand on the quay what the city is called. Their answer links the concepts "habitation," "foundation," and "endurance" in a manner that is difficult to grasp. The meaning may be: "Dwell here. The requirement is: establish yourself on endurance" (2.3f.). It is also unclear whether the leader who is then mentioned, who emerges with a palm branch in his hand, still forms part of the direct speech (and thus describes the far-off ruler of this city) or belongs rather to the narrative (so that this person would be one of the people who form the reception committee on the quay). The general meaning seems to be that those who live in this city must have patience, but they will receive the prize of victory if they endure.

The Merchant of Pearls

Bibliography: I. **Czachesz**, *Commission Narratives*. 162–83. – **A. L. Molinari**, *Allegory, Ascent, and Ministry*. – **J. Sell**, "Jesus the 'Fellow-Stranger': A Study of CG VI: 2.35-3.11." *NovT* 23 (1981): 173–92.

Peter goes ahead on his own to look for lodgings, and it is only he who meets a man who is "beautiful in his form and stature" (2.18f.) and wears a linen cloth (*lention*, cf. John 13:14) with a golden girdle (cf. Rev 1:13) about his body, while his head, hands, shoulders, and breast are covered with a napkin (soudarion, cf. John 20:7). Peter sees four parts of his body: the soles of his feet, a part of his breast, the palms of his hands, and his face (2.19-24). The allusions to the marks of the wounds of the risen Jesus in John 20:27 are unmistakable; at most, one can debate whether polemical reasons mean that they are not mentioned explicitly (in other words, this silence would be intended to support a docetic Christology) or whether the author simply assumes that his readers will themselves draw the correct inferences and understand the hidden reference (on this point, I do not entirely agree with Molinari, 165). The stranger also carries a book cover in his left hand (cf. perhaps Ezek 9:2; Rev 5:1) and a wanderer's staff in his right hand. This is made of styrax wood, which exudes a fragrant resin with healing properties. (Here, an association with Asclepius, the god of healing, may be intended.)

Slowly, in an echoing voice, the stranger calls out: "Pearls (for sale)! Pearls (for sale)!" (2.32; repeated at 3.13). Who would not be reminded of the pearl of great price in the parable at Matt 13:45f. (also in EvThom 76; cf. PsClem R 3.62.2, where Peter cites this parable in a homily)? Likewise, the Song of the Pearl in ActThom has more than one point of contact with this narrative. By now, the reader certainly knows something that Peter, strangely enough, does not yet perceive, that the merchant of pearls is the risen Lord. Peter thinks at first that he is a local resident and addresses him in polite and friendly words: "[My brother and] my friend" (2.35). He asks about a lodging place. The stranger says that Peter is right to address him as "my brother and my friend" but tells him that he too is only a foreigner in this city. In this sense, they are companions.

He cries out again: "Pearls! Pearls!" At first, it is only the rich people in the city who react. They emerge from their hidden storerooms, but when they see that he has no pouch or bundle that might contain treasures, they turn away in disdain. The merchant of pearls does not reveal his identity to them. Then the poor appear on the scene. Their only wish is to look at a pearl so that they can tell their friends that they have seen something so precious at least once in their lives (3.32–4.10). The merchant invites them to come to his city, where he will give them the pearl without requiring any payment. The poor, who describe themselves as beggars, object that they do not want anything more than bread and a little money; they are content just to look at the pearl. The merchant repeats his offer, and this time the poor rejoice (4.15–5.1), although they do not actually go to this city in the further course of the narrative. At the moment, the mere promise of a future transformation of their lot is enough.

Lithargoel and His City

Bibliography: I. Czachesz, *Commission Narratives*. 162–83. – **J. Sell**, "A Note on a Striking Johannine Motive Found at CG VI:6.19." *NovT* 20 (1978): 232–40.

After a transitional passage about the hardships of the way, where it is difficult to reconstruct the text, we return to the conversation between Peter and the merchant of pearls. Peter asks the stranger about his name and about the dangers on the way to his city. He defines his own group as "servants of God" who must bear his Word to every city (5.8-14; here, the mission still has a universal scope, but it is later limited to the ecclesiastical sphere; see below). The merchant of pearls presents himself as follows: "Lithargoel is my name, the interpretation of which is, the light, gazelle-like stone" (5.6-18). The comparison with the gazelle refers to its shining eyes; this is transferred metaphorically to the radiance of the pearl. It is not by chance that the ending of the name in -el recalls the names of archangels such as Michael or Gabriel. The later Coptic church knows an angel called Litharkūēl, a healer who bears a medicine chest (cf. H. M. Schenke, NTApo 6th ed. II: 374). The other components of his name are *lithos* ("stone") and *argos* ("shining"); this means that the translation offered in the text is accurate, but does not take account of the *-el*. The full form is: "the radiant stone of God" or "God is a radiant stone." This establishes a direct link between the merchant and the precious pearl. In a lengthy list of metaphors in ActPet 20, Jesus is called inter alia "pearl" and "treasure" (cf. Rev 2:17). Czachesz opts for a different etymology: His starting point is the Greek word *lêthargos* (from which *lethargic* is derived), which means "forgetful." The name Lithargoel would then indicate that the one who bears it has forgotten God, like the king's son in the Song of the Pearl in ActThom.

The next subject is the dangers on the way to that city. Only one who abandons all his possessions (cf. the regulations when the disciples are sent out, Luke 9:3 par.) and fasts between one night lodging and the next can survive these dangers (5.21–6.8):

> For many are the robbers and wild beasts on that road. The one who carries bread with him on the road, the black dogs kill because of the bread. The one who carries a costly garment of the world with him,

the robbers kill [because of the] garment. [The one who carries] water [with him, the wolves kill because of the water], since they were thirsty [for] it. [The one who] is anxious about [meat] and green vegetables, the lions eat because of the meat. [If] he evades the lions, the bulls devour him because of the green vegetables.

Peter sighs and says within himself: "If only Jesus would give us power to walk" on this path (6.11f.). The merchant of pearls assures him that Jesus has the power to do so and that he himself believes in the Father who sent Jesus (6.14-19). When Peter repeats his question, the merchant says: "This is the name of my city, 'Nine Gates'" in which God is praised, with a tenth principal gate (6.23-26). It becomes ever clearer that this city is in heaven, comparable to the heavenly Jerusalem in the Book of Revelation (although that city has twelve gates, cf. Rev 21:12). The number ten may be related to the fact that the highest number of heavens known from other texts is ten. In this case, we should interpret the robbers and wild beasts as demonic powers that block the path of the soul on its ascent to the heavenly city.

As he returns to his companions, Peter sees that the city in the midst of the sea (where the narrative is still set) is surrounded on every side by walls of water, as high as a tower. An old man explains this with a reference to the name of the city, "Habitation": "we [inhabit] here because [we] endure" (6.27–7.5). Peter meditates on this in a little discourse in which he praises the virtue of patience, which allows one to hold firm in all trials and tribulations (cf. Jas 1:2f., 12).

An Encounter with the Risen Lord

Bibliography: J. Sell, "Simon Peter's 'Confession' and The Acts of Peter and the Twelve Apostles." *NovT* 21 (1979): 344–56.

The apostles abandon everything and set out on the way to Lithargoel's city. This is why they evade the robbers, wolves, lions, and bulls (the black dogs are not mentioned, unless this happened in a portion of the text that has not survived). When they reach their goal, they rest full of joy and in peace before the gates of the city and speak with one another about the faith and about the dangers they have overcome (7.23–8.13).

Lithargoel comes out of the city, but the apostles do not recognize him: He now looks like a physician, with an "unguent box" under his arm, and a disciple follows him with a pouch full of medicine. Peter asks him where Lithargoel's house is, since they want to reach it before evening falls. The stranger declares himself astonished that they know Lithargoel, since "he has not revealed himself to every man, because he himself is the son of a great king" (8.18-32). He tells them to rest for a little while, because he must go quickly to heal someone (8.33–9.1).

The next episode has traits of an Easter apparition. When he returns, the physician—whom the narrator now (but only this once) calls "Savior" (9.5: *sôtêr*)—addresses Peter by his name. Peter reacts with fear, "for how did he know that his name was Peter?" Lithargoel asks him who it was that gave him the name "Peter," and when Peter replies, "It was Jesus Christ, the son of the living God" (cf. Matt 16:16), the stranger finally discloses his identity: "It is I! Recognize me, Peter" (9.14f.). He then takes off his garment (his earthly body?), which had prevented them from recognizing him. The eleven know the risen Lord and prostrate themselves on the ground before him (9.15-21). The equation of garment and body is so widespread that we may presuppose it here; but this prompts the question whether this Christology is docetic. What becomes visible, once the earthly body is laid aside? A purely spiritual being? Since, however, it is also possible that what is involved is the transformation of the earthly, "fleshly" body into the spiritual body of the resurrection, one should not be too quick to draw conclusions here.

The Commissioning of the Disciples

Bibliography: M. Dörnemann, *Krankheit und Heilung in der Theologie der frühen Kirchenväter* (Studien und Texte zu Antike und Christentum 20). Tübingen: 2003. – **H. M. Schenke**, NTApo 6th ed. II: 379. – **M. J. Smith**, "Understand Ye a Parable!"

The disciples ask the Lord what commission he has for them. He gives them the box of unguent and the pouch with medicines and sends them back to the island city, that is, to the world. (In an older version of this journey into the heavenly realm, he may have sent them with the commission to show other people the way to the "nine gates.") They are to be patient and to teach the believers (10.1-6; here follows the restriction of their proclamation to Christians) and to see that the poor get "what they need in order to live," until he himself gives them "what is better," that is, the pearl from the earlier passage in the story. Peter objects that they have done as they were told and have abandoned everything in the world (cf. Mark 10:28). They now have food only for a single day (cf. Matt 6:11)—how then are they to help the poor (10.15-21)? The Lord's reply is very enigmatic: "O Peter, it was necessary that you understand the parable that I told you!" (10.23-25). The text continues, somewhat more clearly: The name of Jesus, which they teach, and the wisdom of God are more valuable than gold, silver, and jewels. It remains unclear to what the "parable" refers—to an earlier event about which we know nothing, since it is not recorded in the present text (thus Schenke), or to the symbolic action which the merchant of pearls has performed in the island city (thus Smith)? The latter option has the advantage that it does not require a further unknown quantity.

The next commission to the disciples, which gives the final section something of the character of a church order, is connected to the pouch with medicines, which they are to use to heal those sick persons who believe in the name of Jesus (10.31-34). Peter is afraid to ask yet another question, so he signals to John: "You talk this time" (cf. John 13:24). John declares that they have not been trained as physicians. How then are they to heal human bodies (11.6-13?) In his reply, Jesus interprets the miracles of healing that the disciples will also perform as signs of the healing of human hearts, which is a task for the physicians of souls (11.14-26). However, the disciples are not to be concerned about the rich. They must not become their friends or eat in their houses, as other persons (office bearers?) in the communities (12.4: *ekklêsia*, with the article in the plural) all too often do (cf. Jas 2:5-10; 5:1-6). Rather, the disciples are to judge such persons "so that your ministry may be glorified, and (so that) I too, and my name, may be glorified in the churches" (12.8-13). The disciples accept their tasks and prostrate themselves on the ground a second time. The Lord raises them up, and they part from one another in peace (12.13-19).

C. Evaluation

Bibliography: I. Czachesz, *Commission Narratives.* 162–83. – **A. L. Molinari,** *Allegory, Ascent, and Ministry.* 173–236.

ActPet12 is a short but very rich and beautiful text. In some parts, there are palpable affinities to the gnostic myth. We find parallels in gnostic texts to the following elements: preexistent souls find their way into the body and the world; they remain foreigners there, like the Redeemer himself; the return to the highest heaven requires one to overcome the demonic powers in the intermediate sphere; in order to attain this goal, it is best to renounce all that is material and even to lay aside the body like a garment; that masses of water separate this world from the other; human beings are divided into three classes (here, the rich, the poor, and the disciples, which may correspond to the *khoïkoi*, beings completely bound to matter, the *psukhikoi*, "human beings with a soul," and the *pneumatikoi*, "spiritual persons"). These parallels make it possible to read ActPet12 from a gnostic perspective; however, one is not obliged to do so, since these components, which derive from one of the preliminary stages of the present text, no longer determine the character of the final version, in which the foreground is occupied by a different, more specifically ecclesial interest in the apostles as models for the office-bearers in the Christian communities.

It is clear from our text that much in the Christian communities is not as it should be and that the church which the author has in mind has gone through difficult times. How precise may we be in our interpretation? Andrea Lorenzo Molinari has made a suggestion that deserves to be presented here. His starting point is the persecution of Christians under Emperor Decius (249–251), which is generally considered to have been the severest of all the persecutions in the early church and the one with the gravest consequences. Since exile or condemnation to death also entailed the confiscation of all one's property, wealthy Christians were particularly at risk, and large numbers apostatized. There were admirable examples of church leaders who were ready to suffer martyrdom, but there were also many who failed the test. It was very difficult for the communities to work through these experiences in the following years, to which Molinari dates ActPet12. Another factor was a severe plague in North Africa and Egypt in the summer of 250, where the Christian love of neighbor proved its worth and many Christians took on the function of physicians, although they did not have the necessary training. When we read the present text in the light of these events, many individual points take on contemporary relevance: the renunciation of material goods, which reduces the risk of persecution; the warning against making any concessions vis-à-vis the rich; an implicitly critical attitude toward the lapsi, those who fell away under persecution; the criticism of many office bearers; the activity of lay doctors, encompassing both the body and the soul; the dangers encountered on the way to the heavenly city, which must now be related concretely to the persecution by the Roman authorities and by the military (cf. Ignatius' description of the soldiers who guarded him as "leopards," Rom 5.1); and not least the lions and bulls who were let loose in the arena upon men and women Christians (cf. Thecla) who professed their faith.

Czachesz proposes a different model that, like Molinari's, is complete in itself. He identifies Pachomian monasticism as the home of the text in its final form. The journey is a description of the spiritual development of a monk. As in the vita of Antony, the dangers from wild animals represent the temptations to which the monk is exposed. The labors of the journey remind him of his own hard life, his continuous fasting, and his renunciation of meat. The warning not to compromise with the rich was necessary because monasteries also were tempted to secure the patronage of influential and wealthy citizens and to give preferential treatment to such persons. Monasteries were also places of healing in a comprehensive sense: they undertook the healing of the body and the healing of the soul. Several healing miracles by the monastic founder Pachomius himself are recorded. These considerations mean that the final text was written only after the death of Pachomius in 346 or 347. The Nag Hammadi codices, which include ActPet12, were probably written in a Pachomian monastery; this would lend further support to Czachesz' hypothesis.

We must wait and see which of these two hypotheses gains acceptance in scholarly circles. I believe that they both provide help for a better understanding of the text, but this does not mean that one must accept every detail that they propose. At the very least, they confirm that ActPet12 is a very compact and rich narrative, which can be interpreted in widely divergent ways.

Chapter 7

The Pseudo-Clementines

Editions: B. Rehm, *Die Pseudoklementinen*. Vol. 1: *Homilien* (GCS 42). 3rd ed. Edited by G. Strecker. Berlin: 1992. – Idem, *Die Pseudoklementinen*. Vol. 2: *Rekognitionen in Rufins Übersetzung* (GCS 51). 2nd ed. Edited by G. Strecker. Berlin: 1994. – **W. Frankenberg**, *Die syrischen Clementinen mit griechischem Paralleltext. Eine Vorarbeit zu dem literargeschichtlichen Problem der Sammlung* (TU 48.3). Leipzig: 1937.

Translations: J. Irmscher and G. Strecker, NTApo 6th ed. II: 439–88. (A very limited selection.) – **T. Smith**, *Pseudo-Clementine Literature* (ANF 8; 1886. Repr. 1995): 73–346. (Complete English translation; quoted in this chapter.) – **H. J. Meyboom**, *De Clemens-Roman. Eerste Deel: Synoptische Vertaling van den Tekst; Tweede Deel: Wetenschappelijke Behandeling*. Groningen: 1902/1904. – **A. Schneider and L. Cirillo**, *Les Reconaissances du pseudo Clément. Roman chrétien des premiers siècles* (Apocryphes 10). Turnhout: 1999. (French translation of the Recognitions.) – **P. Geoltrain and J.-D. Kaestli**, eds. *Écrits apocryphes chrétiens*. Vol. 2 (Bibliothèque de la Pléïade 516). Paris: 2005. 1173–2003. (Complete French translation of the Homilies and the Recognitions.)

Bibliography: **O. Cullmann**, *Le problème littéraire et historique du roman pseudo-clémentin. Étude sur le rapport entre le gnosticisme et le judéo-christianisme* (EHPhR 23). Paris: 1930. – **J. Rius-Camps**, "Las Pseudoclementinas. Bases filológicas para una nueva interpretación." *Revista Catalan de Teologia* 1 (1976): 79–158. – **C. Schmidt**, *Studien zu den Pseudo-Clementinen. Nebst einem Anhange: Die älteste römische Bischofsliste und die Pseudo-Clementinen* (TU 46.1). Leipzig: 1929. – **H. J. Schoeps**, *Theologie und Geschichte des Judenchristentums* (1949; Gesammelte Schriften 1.2). Hildesheim: 1998. – **G. Strecker**, *Das Judenchristentum in den Pseudoklementinen* (TU 70). 2nd ed. Berlin: 1981. – **M. Vielberg**, *Klemens in den pseudoklementinischen Rekognitionen. Studien zur literarischen Form des spätantiken Romans* (TU 145). Berlin: 2000. – **H. Waitz**, *Die*

Pseudoklementinen. Homilien und Rekognitionen: Eine quellenkritische Untersuchung (TU 25.4). Leipzig: 1904.

A. Context

The literary and historical analysis of the Pseudo-Clementines (PsClem) faces problems of an exceptional character, and this may be one reason why scholars have tended to neglect them (for example, there is still no complete translation into German, although there is reason to hope that this situation will change). The PsClem, or the texts on which they are based, are attested at a relatively early date in antiquity. The authenticity of a quotation by Origen is disputed; it is possible that this may have been inserted by the compilers of the *Philokalia*, a florilegium of excerpts from his works. If it is genuine, it would establish the *terminus ad quem* at ca. 230 CE. Eusebius knew "other wordy and lengthy treatises" that had been "brought forward just recently . . . containing dialogues of Peter, forsooth, and Apion" but "do not preserve the stamp of apostolic orthodoxy intact" (*Hist. eccl.* 3.3.5, translated by H. J. Lawlor and J. E. L. Oulton, London: 1927). In his presentation of Jewish Christianity, Epiphanius appeals inter alia to "Travels of Peter, written down by Clement" (*Pan.* 30.15.1).

The Name "Clement"

Bibliography: B. Pouderon, "Flavius Clemens et le proto-Clémens juif du roman pseudo-clémentin." *Apocrypha* 7 (1996): 63–79.

The "Pseudo-Clementines" ("Clementines" would in fact suffice as a title) bear their modern name thanks to the first-person narrator, who introduces himself in the first words of his work as follows: "I, Clement, who was born in the city of Rome. . . ." Various historical and legendary data come together in this figure. In the list of Roman bishops given by Irenaeus, *Haer.* 3.3.3, Clement is listed as the third successor to Peter, after Linus and Anacletus (in other lists, he is the first or second successor). He is regarded as the authentic author of 1 Clement (ca. 96 CE) and as the pseudepigraphical author of 2 Clement and of two treatises on virginity and several church orders. Philippians 4:3 mentions one of Paul's

fellow workers named Clement. It was thus easy to infer the identification that is made for example by Eusebius, *Hist. eccl.* 3.15–16.
From Roman history, we know of a senator and consul named
Titus Flavius Clemens, a cousin of Domitian, who was married to
Flavia Domitilla, who was likewise related on the maternal side to
the imperial house. Domitian had this senator executed in 95 CE
(cf. Suetonius, *Dom.* 15.1) because of "godlessness" (*asebeia*). This
could imply sympathies with Judaism, perhaps on the part of
Clemens' wife, who was sent into exile; this, at any rate, is how Dio
Cassius interprets these events (47.14.1f.). Some scholars believe
that the historical Christian Clemens was a freedman of this family. The PsClem propose a simple identification: Both Clement
himself, who was later to become bishop of Rome, and his parents
are descended from the imperial lineage.

Other names in PsClem establish a pseudohistorical link to the
Roman imperial house. Clemens' mother is called Matthidia, as
were a niece and a great-niece of Trajan. The consort of
Antoninus Pius was called Faustina, and this may be reflected in
the names of Clemens' father and brothers: Faustus, Faustinus,
and Faustinianus.

The Two Versions and Their Text

Bibliography: V. Calzolari, "La tradition arménienne des Pseudo-
Clémetines: état de la question." *Apocrypha* 4 (1993): 263–93. – **F. S.
Jones**, "Evaluating the Latin and Syriac Translations of the Pseudo-
Clementine Recognitions." *Apocrypha* 3 (1992): 237–57. – **F. Paschke**,
*Die beiden griechischen Klementinen-Epitomen und ihre Anhänge. Überliefer-
ungsgeschichtliche Vorarbeiten zu einer Neuausgabe der Texte* (TU 90).
Berlin: 1966. – **R. Riedinger**, "Die Parallelen des Pseudo-Kaisarios zu
den pseudoklementinischen Rekognitionen. Neue Parallelen aus
Basileios προσέχε σεαυτῷ." *ByzZ* 62 (1969): 243–59.

We speak of Pseudo-Clementines in the plural because we have
two versions of this work, the *Homilies* (H) and the *Recognitions* (R).
The title of H already draws attention to the numerous discourses
of Peter, which occupy a considerable portion of both texts; we
also find philosophical dialogues and scholastic controversies. The
title of R refers to the narrative framework, the plot into which the
passages of direct speech are integrated.

Unfortunately, H survives in Greek, the original language, only in two manuscripts, a codex in Paris (P, 11/12 c., which ends at 19.14) and a codex in the Vatican (O, 14 c.). The original Greek version of H and R seems to have been supplanted by two epitomes that shorten the text by omitting problematic passages and add an account of the martyrdom of Clement. These were used in the liturgy and, therefore, were often copied; according to Paschke, almost two hundred copies are known. Both epitomes are important for purposes of textual criticism. In terms of contents, H often seems more archaic. The Christology is Arian, and there is no lack of affirmations that sound heterodox when judged by the criteria of the mainstream church.

R survives to a large extent only in the Latin translation made by Rufinus ca. 406 CE, in more than one hundred manuscripts. A Syriac translation that was made at an early date (411 CE) covers parts of R and H. Together with an Armenian translation, which is likewise independent (cf. Calzolari), and some quotations from the original in other authors (cf. Riedinger), the Syriac translation allows us to check Rufinus' translation at a number of places. The Latin translation has something of a bad reputation, but this is undeserved (cf. Jones), for here—unlike in his translation of Origen's *De principiis*—Rufinus decided on a simple, literal rendering and basically kept to this plan with the exception of a few theologically explosive parts, which he neutralized. However, the Greek version on which he worked was itself already somewhat "tamer" than H; and R seems to have preserved the thread of the narrative better than H.

Possible Earlier Stages in the Composition of PsClem

Bibliography: F. S. Jones, "The Pseudo-Clementines. A History of Research." *SecCent* 2 (1982): 1–33, 63–96. – **B. Rehm**, "Zur Entstehung der pseudoclementinischen Schriften." *ZNW* 37 (1938): 77–184. – **E. Schwartz**, "Unzeitgemäße Beobachtungen zu den Clementinen." *ZNW* 31 (1932): 151–99. – **H. Waitz**, *Pseudoklementinen*. 2–77. – **J. Wehnert**, "Literarkritik und Sprachanalyse. Kritische Anmerkungen zum gegenwärtigen Stand der Pseudoklementinen-Forschung." *ZNW* 74 (1983): 268–301.

The narrative plot in H and R is identical: On his search for the meaning of life, the Roman Clemens, an *anima naturaliter*

Christiana, puts himself into the hands of Peter. On his travels with the apostle, he not only experiences the bitter clashes between Peter and Simon Magus, but also rediscovers his relatives, whom he had lost when he was young: his mother, his two brothers, and finally his father.

There are passages where the vocabulary in H and R agrees in detail, and other extensive passages are at least thematically related. Besides this, however, there is a considerable amount of material found only either in H or in R, and there are significant differences in the sequence of the material.

The literary-critical problem of PsClem, to which no universally agreed solution has been found even after 150 years of research, is how this ambivalent state of affairs is to be explained. All that can be said with some degree of probability is that simple theories of literary dependency (i.e., that R copied H, or vice versa) have proved unsatisfactory; rather, H and R go back, independently of each other, to a common basic document (*Grundschrift* in German; hence, G), the outlines of which can still be discerned (see below; the studies of Waitz pioneered new developments here). Rehm postulated that R drew on both G and H, but this is an unnecessary complication. (Rehm's teacher, Schwartz, was very skeptical about the very possibility of reconstructing G.)

The real difficulties begin when we seek to reconstruct the sources and materials on which G drew, for this brings us into the sphere of hypotheses of the third and sometimes even the fourth degree. Some scholars have very confidently identified the *Kerygmata Petrou*, "The Preachings of Peter" (which must be distinguished from the *Kerygma Petrou*, "The Preaching of Peter," which Clement of Alexandria quotes), as one of G's sources, but recent research tends increasingly to call into question the existence of this document; even within this compilation, some want to distinguish between older and newer components. It has been argued that the ancient Acts of Peter were a second source, especially for the conflict between Peter and Simon, but here we should note that the miracles of the two men are mentioned in a rather summary fashion and that the real competition is fought with words, that is, by means of arguments. A sufficient explanation would be that the author of G knew relevant traditions about Peter and that he was familiar with Acts 8:4-25 and with the affirmations by the writers against heresies that Simon was the progenitor of gnosis.

This is not to call into question the possibility in individual instances of identifying passages from older sources that existed before G; for one example, see the discussion of R 1.27–71 below. In general, however, one must be extremely cautious when working with so many unknown quantities.

The Form of the Narrative

Bibliography: M. J. Edwards, "The Clementina: A Christian Response to the Pagan Novel." *CQ* 42 (1992): 459–74. – **D. U. Hansen**, "Die Metamorphose des Heiligen: Clemens und die Clementina." *Groningen Colloquia on the Novel*, Vol. 8. Groningen: 1997. 119–29. – **B. E. Perry**, *The Ancient Romances*. 285–93. – **B. Pouderon**, "Aux origines du roman clémentin: Prototype païen, refonte judéo-hellénistique, remaniement chrétien." Pages 231–56 in *Le Judéo-christianisme dans tous ses états* (LD). Edited by S. C. Mimouni and F. S. Jones. Paris: 2001. – Idem, "Dédoublement et création romanesque dans le roman pseudo-clémentin." Pages 269–83 in *Les personnages du roman grec* (Collection de la Maison de l'Orient Méditerranéen 29). Edited by idem. Lyons: 2001. – **M. Vielberg**, *Klemens*.

The same applies to another "source," a pagan novel about a family that is separated by an unlucky fate and is reunited thanks to the favor of the gods. There can be no doubt that such a plot underlies PsClem (or G). In terms of its predominant genre, G is a Christian *Bildungsroman* and family novel with a gradual recognition as its center. In his *Poetica*, Aristotle defined *peripeteia* ("reversal of circumstances") and *anagnôrismos* ("recognition") as the most important elements in a plot (1452a: 31f.), and a combination of *peripeteia* and *anagnôrismos* as the most effective technique of a writer, especially when the recognition was the result of the actions in the story themselves and did not need external signs such as scars (as with Odysseus), jewels (as in Longus, *Daphnis and Chloe* 4.31.2, etc.), or letters (1455a: 16f.). Many individual motifs in G are well known from the novels: escape, shipwreck, pirates, being sold into slavery, the intention to commit suicide, twin brothers, a fruitless search, and the villainous brother (about whose punishment we hear nothing in PsClem, surprisingly enough); *The Wonders beyond Thule* by Antonius Diogenes is framed by two letters at the start and two at the close.

G is particularly close to the *Historia Apollonii regis Tyri*, which was very widely diffused in its Latin, slightly Christianized, form.

Its oldest version is dated to ca. 200 CE or slightly later. The list of parallels is impressive (cf. Vielberg, 139–44): Antioch as the starting point (1), a rich young man from a royal family as hero (4), a secret escape by ship with plentiful stores (6), the encounter with a poor old man (8), storm and shipwreck (11; repeated later), help from a fisherman (12), lovesickness (18), the separation of family members (25), kidnapping and being sold by pirates on the slave market (32f.), the preservation of chastity under extremely difficult circumstances (34) (also as a married woman [48]), a competition in riddles (42f.), instructions given in a dream (48), recounting one's own fate—in one case, in a temple—as a path to a solution (44f.; 48f.).

The question is what is meant by a "source." One simple solution would be that the author of G knew an early version of the *Historia*, and possibly other stories of the same type (on points of contact with the vita of Apollonius of Tyana, which Flavius Philostratus completed ca. 220 CE, cf. Vielberg 152–64; Hansen compares the *Aethiopica* of Heliodorus). He has employed this well-tried structure as a framework that was sure to please his readers and into which he could insert the less exciting discourses. (We should also note Pouderon's suggestion. Like Bousset, he assumes that the earliest stage in the history of the composition of PsClem, or an intermediary stage, was a Jewish novel about conversion.)

Place and Time

Bibliography: J. Chapman, "On the Date of the Clementines." *ZNW* 9 (1908): 21–34, 147–59. – **A. Salles**, "La diatribe anti-paulinienne dans le 'Roman pseudo-clémentin' et l'origine des 'Kérygmes de Pierre.'" *RB* 64 (1957): 516–51. – Idem, "Simon le Magicien ou Marcion?" *VC* 12 (1958): 197–224.

The pendulum of scholarship has swung very widely on the question of the dating of PsClem, which depends largely on how the history of its composition is evaluated. The Tübingen School, which followed its master Ferdinand Christian Baur in detecting ancient Petrine Jewish Christianity in PsClem, dated it as early as the first or second century CE (cf. Salles, who still dates the *Kerygmata Petrou* to the late first century and G to the period before 150, though without offering convincing reasons). The other extreme is the dating of all the versions to the decades between 320 and 400, which goes hand in hand with a general refusal to see Jewish Christian and anti-Pauline tendencies in PsClem (cf. Chapman).

The Christology of the work, which survives in H, is pre-Nicene. We can assume that H was composed between 300 and 320; R is probably somewhat later, around the middle of the fourth century. Since G probably quotes Bardaisan (died 222), a date between 220 and 250 seems likely. Theoretically, material that is included in G could be decades older, going back to the second century, but it is only in exceptional cases that one can bring evidence to support this.

The Tübingen School favored Rome as the place of composition of G, but one of the few points on which more recent scholars agree is that all the versions of PsClem were written in Syria (with Palestine and Transjordania as the adjacent territories). There are many arguments in favor of Syria, such as the prominent role played by Antioch and other Syrian cities in the narrative, the orientation to Jerusalem and to James, the strong influence of Marcion (against whom there is already polemic in G) on Syrian Christianity, and the fact that communities of strict Jewish Christians survived longer in Syria than elsewhere.

B. Contents

1. The Greek Homilies (H)

The Prooemium of the Work

Bibliography: B. Pouderon, "L'attribution de l'Epistula Petri et la genèse du roman clémentin." Pages 259–78 in *Epistulae Antiquae*, Vol. 2. Edited by L. Nadjo and É. Gavoille. Louvain: 2002. – **H.-J. Klauck**, "Epistolographie und frühchristliche Literatur: Briefliche Rahmung und Briefeinlage in den Pseudoclementinen." Chap. 6 in idem, *Die apokryphe Bibel*. – **W. Pratscher**, *Der Herrenbruder Jakobus und die Jakobustradition* (FRLANT 139). Göttingen: 1987. 121–50. – **C. Schmidt**, *Studien*. 91–124. – **G. Strecker**, *Judenchristentum*. 97–116, 137–45. – **W. Ullmann**, "The Significance of the Epistola Clementis in the Pseudo-Clementines." *JTS* 11 (1960): 295–317.

Only H has an "overture," which consists of three parts: a letter from Peter to James, an "Adjuration concerning the receivers of the book" (also known as the *Contestatio*), and a letter from Clement to James (Rufinus translated only this last text into Latin but published it separately). In the first letter, Peter addresses James, the brother of the Lord and bishop of the community in Jerusalem, requesting him to give his sermons, which are written down in the accompanying text, only to brethren whom he is to select after a strict scrutiny. This is because Peter's preaching, which adheres strictly to the Law, has been rejected and replaced by the lawless teaching of "the man who is my enemy" (2.3; cf. Matt 13:28; this is a reference to Paul). The situation is made even worse by the following consideration (and here the pseudepigraphical character of the text becomes visible): "But if, while I am still alive, they dare thus to misrepresent me, how much more will those who shall come after me dare to do so!" (2.7). One specific task will be the resolution of contradictions in the sacred Scriptures (1.4).

Following the pattern of Moses, James now summons the seventy elders and issues regulations about how one is to deal with the writings of Peter. After a period of six years' probation, the one who receives them is to stand beside flowing water and call upon heaven, earth, water, and air (swearing is forbidden: cf. Matt 5:34; Jas 5:12) to witness his promise that he will not under any circumstances give these books to inappropriate persons, not even if he himself should fall away from the faith: "But even if I should come to the acknowledgment of another god, I now swear by him also, be he or be he not, that I shall not do otherwise. And in addition to all these things, if I lie, I shall be accursed living and dying, and shall be punished with everlasting punishment" (4.3).

In his letter, Clement informs James that in the meantime, Peter has died in Rome. Before his death, Peter had appointed Clement bishop, despite much resistance on Clement's part. In a discourse, which Clement reports, Peter sets out the obligations of the bishop, presbyters, deacons, and "laity" (this word is used in the Greek and the Latin at 5.5). He recommends marriage and warns against adultery and fornication. In a beautiful and elaborate image, he compares the church to a great ship in which all have their own appointed places and tasks. Christ the helmsman will steer it on its dangerous course through the storms of the age (14.1–15.3):

For the whole business of the church is like unto a great ship, bearing through a violent storm men who are of many places, and who desire to inhabit the city of the good kingdom. Let, therefore, God be your shipmaster; and let the pilot be likened to Christ, the mate to the bishop, and the sailors to the deacons, the midshipmen to the catechists, the multitude of the brethren to the passengers, the world to the sea; the foul winds to persecutions, temptations, and dangers. . . . Let therefore the passengers remain quiet, sitting in their own places, lest by disorder they occasion rolling or careening. Let the midshipmen give heed to the fare. Let the deacons neglect nothing with which they are entrusted; let the presbyters, like sailors, studiously arrange what is needful for each one. Let the bishop, as the mate, wakefully ponder the words of the pilot alone. Let Christ, even the Savior, be loved as the pilot, and alone believed in the matters of which he speaks; and let all pray to God for a prosperous voyage.

This lengthy letter closes with Peter's commission to Clement to write down their shared experiences and his doctrinal discourses, and to send the document to James. The title of this work, which is appended to Clement's letter to James as a kind of oversized accompanying letter, is: "Clement's Epitome of the Popular Sermons of Peter" (19.2). This means that it is given a fictitious location in Rome and dated shortly after Peter's death. The narrative itself, which now begins, is set either immediately (H) or seven years (R) after Jesus' death and resurrection, that is, in the period from Acts 9:32 onward, in which Peter is traveling in the coastal regions of Palestine and Syria.

In these introductory documents, it is impossible to overlook the church-political preeminence of James the brother of the Lord, to whom even Peter is happy to report back. James has this role in the body of the Pseudo-Clementines too, with a varying intensity that is ultimately linked to the use of various traditions and sources (cf. Pratscher). It is a reflection both of the Jewish Christian inheritance and of the attempt at self-assertion on the part of a community that remained faithful to the Law vis-à-vis the dominance of the (Petrine) mainstream church.

Clement Becomes the Disciple of Peter

Bibliography: F. Boll, "Das Eingangsstück der Ps.-Klementinen." *ZNW* 16 (1917): 139–48. – **C. Grappe**, *Images de Pierre aux deux premiers siècles* (EHPhR 75). Paris: 1995. (See the detailed Index of passages.)

From his earliest youth, Clement has pondered the riddles of existence and has therefore consistently led a chaste life. Above all, he is concerned about the immortality of the soul. He seeks answers in philosophy but is soon disappointed and turns his back on the philosophical schools (1.3f.). He plans a journey to Egypt, where a magician will summon a soul up from the underworld to speak to him, but a friend advises him against this (1.5). At this point, news reaches Rome of a worker of miracles in Judea, a man who raises the dead and promises eternal life (1.6). Clement at once sets sail, but unfavorable winds blow him off course, and he lands in Alexandria, where he meets Barnabas (1.9), whom he defends against the mockery of the philosophers. He has long conversations with Barnabas until the latter returns to Judea (1.14). A few days later, Clement follows him. In Caesarea, Barnabas introduces him to Peter, who accepts him as his pupil and companion. Peter begins by teaching him about the true prophet who alone shows the path to salvation (1.19). Initially, since Clement is not yet baptized, he must eat on his own (1.22). The fellowship meal, which is mentioned frequently in the course of the narrative and sometimes has slightly sacramental overtones, usually consists of bread, water, and salt.

The instruction continues on the next day. In a text found only in H, Clement is taught about the corresponding or contrasting "pairs" (the technical term is *syzygies*): Cain and Abel, the false and the true prophet, Simon Magus and Simon Peter, the antichrist and the Christ (2.15-18), and above all a negative female principle and a positive male principle. In Peter's entourage, Clement meets the twin brothers Nicetas and Aquila, who had been sold as slaves in their youth and purchased by Justa, the Syro-Phoenician woman from Mark 7:24-30; in the meantime, she has become a Jewish proselyte and has therefore separated from her husband (2.19f.). For a time, Nicetas and Aquila had been disciples of Simon Magus, with whom they had grown up, and now—before the duel between Simon and Peter begins—they tell Clement the story of his life.

The Earlier History of Simon Magus and the First Discussion

Bibliography: **D. Côté**, *Le thème de l'opposition entre Pierre et Simon dans les Pseudo-Clémentines* (Collection des Études Augustiniennes. Série Antiquité 167). Paris: 2001. – **S. Haar**, *Simon Magus: The First Gnostic?*

(BZNW 119). Berlin: 2003. esp. 109–12. – **G. Strecker**, *Judenchristen-tum*. 166–87. (On the false pericopes.)

Simon came originally from Samaria. He learned the tricks of the magician's trade in Alexandria and calls himself both Christ and "the one who stands" (a divine predicate based on Exod 3:14 [LXX]; 17:6, etc.). As John the Baptist's disciple and successor, he chooses a wife to accompany him and presents her as the Helena of Greek tradition and the heavenly Sophia (2.25). He obtains the soul of a murdered child as his demonic helper. He forms a copy of the child's body out of air and then transforms it back into air (in order to outdo the creation of the human being from the dust of the earth in Genesis 2; the souls of those who had departed prematurely from this life by a violent death were considered particularly available for magical purposes). This is why Simon is able to perform the magical illusions that are summarized briefly (2.32):

> And they told me that he makes statues walk, and that he rolls himself on the fire, and is not burnt; and sometimes he flies; and he makes loaves of stones [cf. Matt 4:3]; he becomes a serpent. . . . He opens lockfast gates; he melts iron. . . . In his house he makes dishes be seen as borne of themselves to wait upon him, no bearers being seen.

By comparison, the miracles of Jesus are characterized by *phil-anthrôpia*, love of the human race (2.34.2). Clement is disappointed that the duel is postponed; but Peter has spies in the enemy camp, who keep him informed of Simon's doings. In this context, the explosive theory of the false pericopes in the Old Testament, which was hinted at in the introductory letter, turns up again: There are affirmations in Scripture which the Adversary has smuggled in, in order to lead the credulous astray. Examples are the statement at Genesis 9:21 that Noah was drunk, as well as passages about the sacrificial cult, the temple, and the kingdom, and the entire written prophecy, which forms the counterpart to the true prophecy. Simon will appeal to such passages. For example, he will maintain that there exists a highest, unknown, ineffable God who sent out two other, lesser gods. One of these gods created the world, while the other gave the law (3.2.2). This doctrine presents no danger to believers with a Jewish background, who are convinced of the "monarchy" of God, but it certainly presents a

danger to Gentiles whose background means that they are accustomed to a polytheistic worldview (3.4). Peter comments on this
by quoting the agraphon, "Be good money-changers!" He interprets this as a reference to the gift of discernment, which must be
used when expounding the Scriptures (2.51; cf. 3.50).

Three days later, the first debate between Simon and Peter is
held before a large audience. Simon wishes to demonstrate that
the biblical God is neither the highest God nor omnipotent. For
example, Genesis 6:6, "The Lord was sorry that he had made
humankind on the earth," implies for Simon that this creator God
did not know from the outset what he was doing and that he vac-
illates in his decisions (3.39.4). Peter's reply affirms that Jesus has
taught the correct discernment of the Scriptures, since he is the
definitive incarnation of the true prophet who had earlier been
present in figures of the First Covenant such as Adam and Moses
(3.49; cf. Deut 18:15f.). The words of Jesus that have been handed
down offer an answer to all such questions (3.55).

The first act ends after three days. Simon escapes to Tyre, and
Peter must follow him to that city. At the installation of Zacchaeus
(cf. Luke 19:1-8) as his representative and bishop in Caesarea, we
find a number of elements that we already know from the account
in the prooemium of the installation of Clement as bishop in
Rome, which will take place at a later date.

An Intermezzo: Clement and Apion

Bibliography: W. Adler, "Apion's 'Encomium of Adultery': A Jewish
Satire of Greek Paideia in the Pseudo-Clementine Homilies." HUCA 64
(1993): 15–49. – J. van Amersfoort, "Traces of an Alexandrian Orphic
Theogony in the Pseudo-Clementines." Pages 13–30 in Studies in
Gnosticism and Hellenistic Religions (EPRO 91). Edited by R. van Broek
and M. J. Vermarsen. Leiden: 1981. – J. N. Bremmer, "Foolish
Egyptians: Apion and Anoubion in the Pseudo-Clementines." Pages
311–29 in The Wisdom of Egypt: Jewish, Early Christian, and Gnostic Essays
in Honour of Gerard P. Luttikhuizen (Ancient Judaism and Early
Christianity 59). Edited by A. Hilhorst and G. H. van Kooten. Leiden:
2005. – D. Côté, "Une critique de la mythologie grecque d'après
L'Homélie pseudo-clémentine IV." Apocrypha 11 (2000): 37–57. – B.
Pouderon, "La literature pseudo-épistolaire dans les milieux juifs et
chrétiens des premiers siècles: l'exemple des pseudo-Clémentines."
Pages 223–41 in Epistulae Antiquae, Vol. 1. Edited by L. Nadjo and É.
Gavoille. 2nd ed. Louvain: 2002. – P. W. van der Horst, "Who Was

Apion?" Pages 207–21 in idem, *Japheth in the Tents of Shem: Studies on Jewish Hellenism in Antiquity* (Contributions to Biblical Exegesis & Theology 23). Louvain: 2002.

When the advance party of Peter's companions (consisting of Clement, Nicetas, and Aquila) reaches Tyre, they lodge with Berenice, the daughter of the above-mentioned Justa. Simon has already left for Sidon, but three of his friends are still in Tyre: the grammarian Apion from Alexandria, the astrologer Annubion, and the Epicurean philosopher Athenodorus. It is Apion who now takes center stage (only in H, not in R; but the contents of this passage occur at another position in R). We know Apion from Flavius Josephus' *Contra Apionem* as an enemy of Judaism. Apion is presented here as a friend of Clement's father and seeks to persuade Clement to abandon his leanings towards the "barbarian" Jewish doctrine, since one must always keep to the customs of one's ancestors (4.8).

A discussion begins in an idyllic garden (4.10: the classical commonplace of the *locus amoenus*). Clement attacks the amoral quality of the Greek sagas about the gods and the concept of *genesis*, which means fate, destiny, determination, and the horoscope at one's birth (4.12f.). He speaks in detail of Zeus and his amorous adventures. All this has evil consequences for those "who from their childhood learn letters by means of such fables" (4.18.2). The *ethos* in which they are trained, which is at least as powerful as their natural dispositions, engenders almost by necessity an immoral way of life. Apion promises that he will reply on the following day (4.24).

When he fails to appear at the appointed hour, Clement takes the opportunity to tell about a trick he played on Apion as a young man. His fruitless search for the truth had so weakened him that he lay sick in bed. Apion, a fatherly counselor with knowledge of medicine, diagnosed lovesickness (5.2f.), and offered to use magic to bring Clement's far-off lover to him. However, Clement declared himself unwilling to force her by magical means to come. He wanted to persuade her with words, all the more so since she had philosophical leanings (5.8). Apion therefore wrote a letter praising free love and adultery, declaring that Eros was the most powerful god and giving an exact list of the numerous romantic affairs of Zeus. He also quoted philosophers who had given free rein to their lust (5.10-19). Clement then wrote a letter, in the

name of his fictitious lover, in which he demolished Apion's arguments one by one. Towards the close, this letter praises enthusias-
tically the ideal of monogamous marriage, saying that she (i.e., the
fictitious lover) has learned this "from a certain Jew" (5.25f.)—and
Clement also praises the doctrine of the Jews when he tells Apion
about the trick he has played on him. This only serves to reinforce
Apion in his well known hatred of Judaism.

H presents here a literary elaboration of a novelistic motif that
usually takes the following form: The family doctor tells the father
that the grave illness of his son is due to his unfulfilled love for the
second, young wife of the father (cf., e.g., Appian, *Syr.* 59–61). In
terms of contents, this passage evokes the conflict over the valid-
ity of the sacred ancestral customs and the fascination that pagan
culture continued to hold for young people who were inclined
toward Judaism or Christianity. The answer in PsClem is that for
the sake of the higher truth, one must accept and endure the conflict with one's own family and cultural origins (cf. Adler).

On the third day, Apion finally presents his truth: One must
not take the myths literally, since the people of old intentionally
concealed the real message in (or better, behind) stories with "a
peculiar and philosophical meaning, which can be allegorically set
forth" (6.2.12). In his sketch of cosmology, Apion follows
Orphism, which thought of the initial chaos out of which the
world emerged as a huge egg (6.3-6). For the Orphics, Zeus represents fire, Hera air, Apollo the sun, and so forth (6.7-10).
Clement has heard all this so often that he can repeat it in his own
words and even make his own additions, for example, the psycho-
logical explanation that Heracles embodies "the true philosophical
reason" (6.16.1); but he is no longer convinced by the thesis that
the myths are only veils for such ideas, since this could have been
done in a more worthy manner. He now believes that the gods of
the myths were the people of former times—not dead kings (as
was suggested by Euhemerus, from whose name this interpretative
principle is called *euhemerism*), but evil magicians (6.20f.). This
intermezzo is ended by Peter's arrival in Tyre.

Four days in Tripolis

Bibliography: E. **Molland**, "La circoncision, le baptême et l'autorité du
décret apostolique (Actes XV, 28 sq.) dans les milieux judéo-chrétiens des
Pseudo-Clémentines." *ST* 9 (1955): 1–39. – **H. J. Schoeps**, "Die

Dämonologie der Pseudoklementinen." Pages 38–81 in idem, *Aus frühchristlicher Zeit. Religionsgeschichtliche Untersuchungen* (1950; Gesammelte Schriften 1.3). Hildesheim: 1998.

Peter follows Simon from Tyre via Sidon, Beirut, and Byblos to Tripolis, and everywhere a "mopping-up operation" is necessary. By means of the meat sacrificed to demons, which he served at the banquets he organized, Simon had subjected many persons to the demons by a kind of infection, causing them to fall ill. Peter heals, consoles, and instructs. He quotes the Golden Rule (7.4.3), the doctrine of the Two Ways (7.7), and the Apostolic Decree (7.8.1f.). Before continuing on his journey, he installs office-bearers in each city who are charged with the continuing pastoral care of the believers there.

Peter makes a pause in Tripolis. Each morning, he bathes in the sea or in a reservoir that is continuously supplied with water (cf. the description of John the Baptist as a man who bathed every day: 2.23.1). On the first day, he explains in a discourse that there is a general divine law that is able to save those who keep it and put it into practice, even outside of Genesis 6:1-4; these angels were the originators of magic and astronomy, and it was thanks to them that precious metals and gems and other luxuries were discovered (8.12-14). The flood came because of the crimes committed by their descendants, the giants. They live on as demons and penetrate human beings who eat sacrificial meat, the meat of strangled animals, and blood (8.19f.; cf. Acts 15:20).

On the second day, Peter presents a review of the history of religion. He mentions the magus Zoroaster and the worship of fire by the Persians (9.4-6). He explains why the demons want to penetrate human beings by means of impure food: Since they are spiritual beings, they lack the necessary organs for the lusts of the senses, which they can satisfy only by using a human being (9.10). Demons also appear in dreams; it is they who answer when one consults oracles; and they even perform healings. But all this is merely outward appearance (9.15-18). The bath of immersion in a river, a spring, or a lake drives them away (9.19).

Peter's sermon on the third day is a collection of the commonplaces of the polemic against idols found in biblical (cf. Isa 44:9-20; Ps 115:3-8), Jewish (cf. Wis 13:1-19; 15:7-17), and philosophical writers (cf. Seneca, *Ep.* 95.47-50 with H 10.23.4;

Lucian, *Gallus* 24 with H 10.22.2). Gold and silver images of the gods must be guarded by soldiers and dogs because they cannot protect themselves, and no one attempts to steal idols of wood or clay (10.8). The ancient serpent, whose promises "creep from the brain to your spinal marrow," bears the guilt for all this (10.10). The utter absurdity of it all can be seen most clearly in Egypt, where even cats, serpents, fish, the rumblings of the stomach, and the act of urination are worshiped. The hearers laugh at these words (10.16f.). Nor do allegorical explanations help here (10.18). The basic error consists in setting created things in the place of the Creator (10.20). As on the other evenings, Peter closes by healing sick and possessed persons. He begins the common meal with a blessing and thanksgiving "according to the accustomed faith of the Hebrews" (10.26.3).

On the fourth day, Peter defends human free will (11.8) and the immortality of the soul, which in the case of evildoers means "endless torture under unquenchable fire," with no longer any prospect of a death to put an end to the suffering (11.11). Pagan orgies, with their wild revelry, are depicted with particular intensity: "cutting of hands, and emasculations, and fury and mania, and disheveling of hair, and shoutings and enthusiasms and howlings ..." (11.14f.). There is a great deal of repetition; we may interpret this either as lending a necessary intensification to Peter's message or as a sign that nothing new occurred to the author. Peter's stay in Tripolis is prolonged; when it ends, Clement's period of probation is ended. After fasting for several days, he is baptized in a spring close to the sea and experiences his rebirth (11.35.1f.).

The Unhappy Story of a Family

Bibliography: P. **Boulhol**, Άναγνωρισμός. *La scène de la reconnaissance dans l'hagiographie antique et médiévale.* Aix-en-Provence: 1996. esp. 63–70. – W. **Bousset**, "Die Wiedererkennungs-Fabel in den pseudoklementinischen Schriften, den Menächmen des Plautus und Shakespeares Komödie der Irrungen." *ZNW* 5 (1904): 18–27. – Idem, "Die Geschichte eines Wiedererkennungsmärchens." *NAWG* (1916): 469–551, esp. 529–43.

The next stop is Antioch in Syria. Nicetas and Aquila are sent separately to other towns, where they are to prepare for the arrival of Peter (as we shall see, the next development in the story requires them to be temporarily absent). Clement rejoices that he is allowed to remain with Peter, who has taken on for him the position of "father, mother, brothers, relatives" (12.5.2; cf. the logion that Jesus addresses to Peter at Mark 10:29f.). Peter relates that he and his brother Andrew grew up as orphans in great poverty (12.6.7).

This sets the scene for an account of the story of Clement's family, told from his own perspective (12.8-10). His father, Faustus, and his mother, Matthidia, both belonged to the imperial family. They had twins, Faustinus and Faustinianus (R has the names Faustus and Faustinianus), and then a third son, Clement. He has only a vague memory of his mother and his brothers. His father later told him that shortly after Clement's birth, his mother had a vision in which she was told to leave Rome with the twins for ten (according to another reading, twelve) years, for otherwise they would die. The father was deeply concerned and sent her with enough money and an escort of men and women slaves to Athens, where the twins were to be brought up; but they never arrived there, and all investigations into their whereabouts proved fruitless. When Clement was twelve years old, his father also went off to look for his family, and Clement has never heard any more news of him. In the meantime, twenty years have passed (in other words, Clement is thirty-two years old at the time when this story takes place).

On the following day, the group undertake a pleasure trip to the island of Arados, where the attractions include the pillars of a temple, covered with vine-leaves (or fashioned from the wood of vine stocks), and sculptures by Pheidias (cf. Chariton's novel *Callirhoë* VII.5, where two lovers rediscover each other on Arados). While the others wander around looking at the sights, Peter remains beside a beggar woman and asks why she is begging instead of working with her hands. The woman answers that she has bitten her hands so severely in her despair that they are no longer good for anything. She would have committed suicide long ago, but she lacks the courage. Peter promises to give her a drug (*pharmakon*), "that you may live and die without torment," if she tells him her story (12.12-14).

She does so in 12.15-18. The beggar woman had three children, first twins and then a third son. Her brother-in-law had fallen in love with her and tried by every means at his disposal to seduce her. In order to avoid a scandal, she resorted to a ruse: She pretended that someone had ordered her in a dream to leave Rome at once with the twins for a time, in order to avoid a great disaster. Her husband sent her to Athens, but their ship encountered a violent storm and capsized. She herself was washed ashore on the island, but there was no trace of the twins. A poor woman who had lost her husband, a sailor, many years ago in a shipwreck and had not remarried took her into her hut. In the meantime, this woman became bedridden and cannot leave the house. She begs for both of them so that their modest needs may be met.

Peter begins to suspect something that the readers have long guessed, but the woman initially evades the issue by giving false names (12.19). But when Peter tells her what he has heard from Clement, she almost faints and tells him the truth (12.20-21). When Clement returns from his little excursion, she embraces him and kisses him. He reacts by "shaking her off as a madwoman." It is only when Peter tells him what has happened that the beggar suddenly reminds him of his mother, and there is no longer any obstacle to their recognition (the term *anagnôrismos* occurs at 12.23.8). The poor woman who had received Matthidia into her hut is carried out, and Peter heals her. When he departs, Clement leaves a thousand drachmas for her and takes his mother with him to Antioch (12.24).

Up to this point, the wording of the family story is almost identical in H and R, but the rest of this book (12.25-33) is found only in H. Peter explains to Clement the difference between philanthropy, mercy, and friendship. He promotes philanthropy as the highest value; this is possible only because he somewhat artificially equates it with love of one's neighbor and one's enemy, a love that seeks nothing for itself, while there remain elements of self-interest in friendship and even in mercy.

The Family Grows

The family history and the history of faith intertwine ever more. On the further journey from Antioch to Laodicea, we meet for the first time the wife of Peter (cf. 1 Cor 9:5), who is now needed to assist Matthidia (13.1; cf. C. Schmidt, *Studien*, 48: "It seems that it was necessary to give a female companion, especially in view of the night quarters, to Matthidia, since it was regarded as indecorous for a woman to travel on her own in a group of men"). In Laodicea, Nicetas and Aquila are already waiting for Peter and his companions. They inquire about the identity of the unknown woman who has entered the lodgings with Peter's wife and is now sleeping. Peter gives a résumé of the events of the past two days, and now the reader's expectation is fulfilled: Nicetas and Aquila disclose that they are in reality Faustinus and Faustinianus (13.2f.).

Peter does not allow them to reveal themselves to their mother at once. When she awakens, he first tells her why she may not yet eat together with Clement. The baptized do not eat together with the unbaptized, not even with "our father, or mother, or wife, or child, or brother" (13.4). Matthidia expresses the wish to be baptized that very day; but first, it is time for the second act of recognition. After Matthidia's emotions, which have brought her to the brink of death, have calmed down to some extent, Nicetas alias Faustinus relates how they both fell into the hands of pirates on the night of the shipwreck and were then sold as slaves in Caesarea (13.6f.). They had the good fortune to be purchased and adopted by Justa (see above). They studied the pagan philosophers in order to be able to defend the Jewish faith better. They survived unharmed their acquaintance with Simon Magus, who had grown up together with them (13.7f.).

Matthidia once again asks that she may receive baptism, together with the woman who had given her a home on the island and who is to be brought to Laodicea. This is a strong argument in her favor, for it seems to be a genuine problem (which Peter laments) that the baptized often neglect to concern themselves about the conversion of their closest relatives (13.10). But one must fast for at least one day before baptism. On this point, Peter is immovable and is not to be swayed by the fact that Matthidia has fasted involuntarily during the past two days (13.11f.). In the evening, he praises the marital chastity that Matthidia has preserved in an exemplary manner; this is why God has rescued her (13.13-21). This form of chastity does not exclude marriage, parenthood, and children but explicitly includes them (13.18.1).

On the following morning, Peter baptized Matthidia at a lonely place near the sea. The other men in the group withdraw to pray, at another hidden place, out of consideration for the women (14.1). Peter returns to their lodgings alone, after several hours have passed. He tells them that he met an old man by the sea, who followed them in secret and then began a discussion with him. The stranger declared that he did not believe in God or in providence, but only in the blind fate that is written unalterably in the stars.

When Peter argues against this position, the old man relates a personal experience (14.6f.). He is an astrologer and once drew up a horoscope for a friend in Rome that predicted that his wife would fall in love with one of her slaves, would run off with the slave, and would perish at sea. The woman did in fact leave Rome with two sons, allegedly because of a dream; but the brother of the astrologer's friend revealed the true reason. She had made immoral advances to him, but as a man of honor, he had rejected her. Her shame at this rejection was so great that she fled. After a long time had elapsed and no news reached Rome, the friend himself set out with the astrologer to look for his wife. He died of a broken heart in Seleucia.

Peter passes on this news to Clement and his relatives, who grieve profoundly, because they inevitably assume that the father of their family is dead. But Peter has summoned the old man to the lodgings, and when the old man enters, he and Matthidia look questioningly at each other—and recognize each other. The old man is none other than Faustus himself, who had assumed a false identity in his conversation with Peter, and still wishes to remain incognito. Annubion, who has already been mentioned in the text, had given him the astrological interpretation of the dramatic events in his family story (14.11f.).

The last task to be accomplished is the conversion of Faustus, so that the family may also be united in the faith, now in life and later after death (15.1). Peter attempts to convince Faustus of the workings of divine providence in the path taken by his family (15.4), but Faustus' faith in the stars remains an obstacle. In H, the long-overdue confrontation with Simon Magus now takes center stage, and Faustus, too, will play a role in this encounter.

The Four-day Disputation with Simon in Laodicea

Bibliography: L. L. Kline, *The Sayings of Jesus in the Pseudo-Clementine Homilies* (SBLDS 14). Missoula, Mt.: 1975. – **H. J. Schoeps**, "Der Ursprung des Bösen und das Problem der Theodizee im pseudoklementinischen Roman." *RSR* 60 (1972): 129–41. – **J. Wehnert**, "Petrus versus Paulus in den pseudoclementinischen Homilien 17." Pages 175–85 in *Christians as a Religious Minority in a Multicultural City: Modes of*

Interaction and Identity Formation in Early Imperial Rome (JSNTSup 243). Edited by J. Zangenberg and M. Labahn. London: 2004.

Peter has promised Faustus that he will demonstrate the uniqueness of God. Simon, who comes with the Epicurean Athenodorus from Antioch to Laodicea, now intervenes in this discussion. Faustus ensures that the debate will be carried out in an orderly fashion, according to the rules of the Greek *paideia*, with each speaker delivering a discourse in turn.

Simon quotes a long list of Old Testament passages that speak of "God" in the plural, for example, Psalm 82:1, "God stands up in the assembly of the gods; in the midst of the gods he holds judgment" (16.6.12). This list culminates in the words of God in Genesis 1:26, "Let us make humankind in our image, according to our likeness" (16.11). Peter's reply cites texts such as Isaiah 45:22, "I am God, and there is no other" (16.17.6), and explains the plural in Genesis 1:26 as a reference to God and his Wisdom (16.12).

Simon now enters the field of Christology. Peter draws a distinction between "God" and "Son of God," which he associates with the technical terms "unbegotten" and "begotten" (16.15f.). The begotten Son is not consubstantial (*ousia* in 16.16.3) with the Father (here, Peter argues against a dogmatic formulation). Peter himself senses that this does not clear up all the difficulties and goes to bed that evening a careworn man.

After some preliminary skirmishes on the second day, a new main topic emerges: Is revelation communicated via the natural sensuous experience of the human person (his hearing, sight, and thinking) or via visions with a supernatural origin? Simon is a proponent of the theory of visions, but Peter is skeptical (this is probably a further criticism of Paul, who based his position as apostle on a vision; cf. Wehnert). In principle, God never shows himself, since he is pure light and it is completely impossible for human beings to perceive him. When he sends angels, they assume a human form out of consideration for us. Peter sees the devil as the author of other apparitions (17.16). His own confession, "You are the Son of the living God" (Matt 16:16), was directly inspired in his heart by God, without the medium of visions and dreams (17.18).

At the beginning of the third day, Simon returns to his earlier thesis, which he supports with biblical quotations: The highest God, who alone is good (cf. Mark 10:18) and is unknown up to now (cf. Acts 17:23), is not the demiurge and law-giver. Nor can this God be both good and righteous, since as the righteous judge, he would have to punish without mercy those who transgress the law—and that is incompatible with goodness (18.1). The spotlight now turns to the logion of Jesus, "No one knows the Father except the Son and anyone to whom the Son chooses to reveal him" (Matt 11:27), which Simon understands as supporting his own position. Once again, one cannot resist the impression that Peter has difficulties in refuting this. Finally, he offers an explanation linked to the concrete situation: the Jewish contemporaries of Jesus thought that David was the ancestor of the Messiah (and Joseph the father of Jesus); only Jesus knew that God was his true Father (18.13).

On the final day, the discussion concerns the figure of the devil, the personification of evil. Peter accepts the reality of his existence on the basis of logia of Jesus such as Luke 10:18. Was he too created by the creator God, or not? If yes, does this make this God responsible for all the evil in the world? And if no, are there then limits to his omnipotence? Because Scripture gives no clear information about this question, Peter agrees to discuss it only with reservations (19.8). Evil too has a task to fulfill in God's saving plan and is connected in general with sin, which in turn is derived from the free will of the human person (19.15). Emotions such as sensual lust and anger can lead to sin, but they can also be harnessed correctly; for example, lust can be employed in marriage to secure the continued existence of the human race. Peter attaches great weight to the observance of the times in which the Law permits marital intercourse (19.21f.). Through rebirth in baptism and a life in accordance with the Law, a human being can change his *genesis*—that is, the burden of his provenance and the horoscope of his birth, which many persons regard as blind fate— for the better (19.23.6).

Genuine theological problems are involved here, as we see from the fact that Peter's disciples continue the discussion with him that evening. Peter hints that at the end, perhaps even the evil can cross over to the good through a change in the ordering of the elements of which it is composed (20.9.6f.); but he also underlines that such doctrines are not contained in scripture and are based only on our "conjecture" (20.8.4). Accordingly, one ought not to speak of them "as if you were accurately acquainted with the discovery of secret truths, but you ought simply to reflect over them in silence" (20.8.6).

An Incomplete Postlude

In the meantime, Apion and Annubion, old friends of Faustus, have arrived from Antioch and meet Simon. Peter allows Faustus to visit them. On his return, Faustus has assumed the outward appearance of Simon in the eyes of everyone except Peter, who sees through the magical transformation; but his family hears him speaking with the voice of Faustus. This new narrative thread is gradually disentangled in flashbacks. Peter's followers in Simon's entourage had succeeded in spreading the news, first in Antioch and finally also in Laodicea, that the emperor had ordered that Simon be hunted down in order to condemn him as a magician and execute him; this was why Simon had fled to Judea. The astrologer Annubion, who had already parted company with Simon in his heart and remained behind, relates what had happened earlier: By means of a specially prepared ointment, Simon transformed Faustus, who was taking part in a meal with his friends, into his own form, so that Faustus would be arrested instead of himself. Besides this, he wanted to take vengeance on Nicetas and Aquila (alias Faustinus and Faustinianus), who had abandoned him (20.12-17).

The family and the group of friends are greatly disturbed, but Peter promises that Faustus will regain his own external form once he has performed a certain task: He is to go as Simon to Antioch, where Simon had stirred up the populace against Peter, and bring about a change of mood. He is to proclaim publicly: "I Simon proclaim this to you: I confess that all my statements in regard to Peter are utterly false. . . . I counsel you to believe what he preaches. . . . I confess to you that I am a magician, I am a deceiver" (20.19). At this point, H abruptly breaks off, and we must wait until the end of R before we get a genuine closing scene.

2. The Latin Recognitions (R)

The Beginnings in Rome and Caesarea

Bibliography: F. S. Jones, *An Ancient Jewish Christian Source on the History of Christianity: Pseudo-Clementine Recognitions 1.27–71* (SBLTT

37). Atlanta: 1995. – **N. Kelley**, "Problems of Knowledge and Authority in the Pseudo-Clementine Romance of Recognitions." *JECS* 13 (2005): 315–48. – **J. L. Martyn**, "Clementine Recognitions I.33–71, Jewish Christianity, and the Fourth Gospel." Pages 265–95 in *God's Christ and His People* (Festschrift for N.A. Dahl). Oslo: 1977. – **A. Stötzel**, "Die Darstellung der ältesten Kirchengeschichte nach den Pseudo-Clementinen." *VC* 36 (1982): 24–37. – **F. Tosolini**, "Paolo in Atti e nelle Pseudoclementine (*Recognitiones* I.33–71)." *Aug* 26 (1986): 369–400. – **R. E. van Voorst**, *The Ascents of James: History and Theology of a Jewish-Christian Community* (SBLDS 112). Atlanta: 1989.

The main difference between R and H in the exposition of the narrative is that the detour via Alexandria is not found in R. Barnabas proclaims the Gospel in Rome (1.7), and Clement follows him directly to Caesarea (1.12), where his initial instruction by Peter about the true prophet and the Law occupies more space. Clement displays his good memory by repeating what he has learned (1.25). R says nothing about the false pericopes in Scripture; the reviser found this subject too explosive.

It is only in R that we find a lengthy section in which Peter gives an outline of salvation history from a Jewish Christian perspective, beginning with the creation and continuing to the earliest community. We learn inter alia that a bloody sacrifice was offered for the first time in the fourteenth generation, on an altar that was erected for demons (1.30.4), and that Moses allowed the sacrificial cult only as a temporary solution (1.36.1) that would later be replaced by baptism (1.39.1). In the description of Jewish groups in the period of transition from the old covenant to the new, Peter declares that the disciples of the Baptist regarded their master as the Messiah (1.54.8). Rabbi Gamaliel is a "crypto-Christian" (on this group in the Gospel of John, cf. Martyn) who defends the standpoint of the apostles in the Sanhedrin to the best of his ability. Toward the end, Saul makes his appearance as the persecutor of the community, which flees to Jericho. He seizes James, the brother of the Lord, in the temple and throws him down a flight of stairs so that he lies there as if dead (1.70.8). (This passage is a good example of the complex stratification of the material in PsClem. According to Jones, the basis is a Jewish Christian source composed ca. 200 CE, which was integrated into G and was expanded by means of 1.44.4–52.6 and some smaller corrections. This source ended originally with the death of James as a result of his fall. However, this has no connection to the *Anabathmoi Jakobou* that Epiphanius mentions [*Pan.* 30.16.6-9]. R has preserved this source, but H has eliminated it.)

Zacchaeus writes from Caesarea, urging Peter to challenge Simon (1.72). Twelve disciples follow Peter to Caesarea (cf. 3.68); Clement joins them as the thirteenth (2.1). This group includes Nicetas and Aquila, who describe Simon not only as a magician, but also as an eloquent rhetorician (2.5). In R, his companion is called "Luna" (possibly because of the verbal closeness in Greek between "Helena" and *selênê*, "moon"). Among his disciples, Simon presents himself as God and asserts that his mother Rachel conceived him while still a virgin (2.14.2)—a transparent imitation of the virginal conception of Jesus. His teachings also seem to include the concept of an "alien" god (2.18.8), which recalls Marcion.

The Three-Day Debate with Simon in Caesarea

Bibliography: H.-J. Klauck, "Simon Petrus und Simon Magus: Ihr Zweikampf in den Pseudoclementinen." Chap. 5 in idem, *Die apokryphe Bibel.*

R, unlike H, now presents the debate with Simon, which takes place in Caesarea. On the first day, before they begin discussing substantial matters, they negotiate in great detail questions of procedure (the influence of ancient rhetoric and of the discussion culture can be clearly felt). Peter pleads for a peaceful disputation and quotes Matthew 5:9; Simon counters with Matthew 10:34 (2.26f.). The central theme is the question of God. Peter's creed runs as follows: "There is one God; and he is the creator of the world, a righteous judge, rendering to every one at some time or other according to his deeds" (2.36.5). Simon's highest god, with many other gods under him, is unknown and is not identical to the Creator. In this context, writings by Simon are mentioned (2.28.5; this may perhaps be an allusion to Marcion's *Antitheses*). R alone contains statements about the guardian angels of the nations (2.42) and about daydreams that Peter had while fishing in Capernaum. This provides the occasion to demonstrate how dangerous such daydreams are (2.62–65; cf. the criticism of visions in H 17.13–19). We are given a detailed explanation at 2.71 of why Clement must eat alone: Pagans who worship foreign gods absorb a demonic, impure spirit when they eat meat that has been sacrificed, and this spirit can be expelled only through baptism.

The central topic on the second day is not the evil one (as in H) but evil itself, and we immediately note the more philosophical tone in Peter's question: "What is evil—a substance, an accident, or an act?" (3.17.3). Peter defends the freedom of the will, but Simon objects that fate holds sway in human affairs (3.22.1). Peter quotes eschatological doctrines that the true prophet has taught: Only when the number of souls is full will this visible sky be rolled up like a book, and the great separation of good persons from evil persons begin (3.26). (Chaps. 2–11 in this section, which are missing in numerous Latin manuscripts because Rufinus did not translate them but survive in the Syriac version, come from the milieu around Eunomius, an Arian bishop in the second half of the fourth century. They were subsequently interpolated into Rufinus' version of R.)

Apart from the usual "sideshows" such as the esoteric instruction of the disciples and the discussion of procedural questions, the third day is devoted to two closely linked problems. Can God be simultaneously just and good (3.37)? Is the soul immortal (3.39)? Apparent injustice in this life will find compensation in the future life (3.41). Simon does not admit that Peter's arguments have got the better of him, but Peter unmasks him as a magician who makes use of the soul of a young murdered boy (3.45). Simon feigns conversion (cf. Acts 8:13), but Peter is not fooled by this. Simon is so enraged that he openly declares himself to be the Son of God and boasts of his miracles (cf., e.g., 3.47.2: "I have flown from mountain to mountain; I have moved from place to place, upheld by angels' hands"; on this, cf. Matt 4:5-8). At the close, the hearers turn against him and drive him away.

In the absence of Simon, who has departed for Rome (cf. ActPet!), the fourth day is devoted to the instruction of the disciples and preaching to the people. Peter compares his struggle against Simon with Moses' struggle against the magicians of Pharaoh (3.55f.). He sends twelve disciples out into the Gentile world (3.70) on the tracks of Simon (3.73), while he himself remains for three months in Caesarea. Clement notes at 3.75 that he has written down these events in ten books, which he has sent to James in Jerusalem. This work (if it ever existed) must be distinguished from R; at most, these remarks may refer to a source on which R draws. But it is more probable that this is a narrative fiction of the author or reviser of R (cf. the further reference to "the books" at 5.36.5).

Three Days and Three Months in Tripolis

Peter and his group arrive in Tripolis after stopping in a number of places, which are described in greater detail in H 4–7. There is a parallel in H to most of what is said in the sermons and catecheses that Peter now holds (cf. H 8–11). The account in H is usually more colorful, while R is better ordered and more logical. In view of the ever-present danger that false apostles and prophets may make their appearance, Peter warns on the first day (4.35.1f.; cf. H 11.35.3f.):

> Believe no teacher, unless he brings from Jerusalem the testimonial of James the Lord's brother, or of whosoever may come after him. For no one, unless he has gone up thither, and there has been approved as a fit and faithful teacher for preaching the word of Christ . . . is to be received.

This may be directed against Paul, who (according to the Letter to the Galatians) explicitly refrained from seeking any such accreditation. As an example of the preaching on the second day, I quote a passage from a christological summary (5.10.1-3):

> He, therefore, is the true prophet, who appeared to us, as you have heard, in Judea, who, standing [*stans*, an attribute of Simon] in public places, by a simple command made the blind see, the deaf hear, cast out demons, restored health to the sick, and life to the dead; and since nothing was impossible to him, he even perceived the thoughts of men, which is possible for none but God only. He proclaimed the kingdom of God; and we believed him as a true prophet in all that he spoke.

On the third day, Peter defines the purpose of sexuality even more clearly than in H: "But this kind of chastity is to be observed, that sexual intercourse must not take place heedlessly and for the sake of mere pleasure, but for the sake of begetting children" (6.12.1). When the three months have passed, Clement is finally baptized, as in H (6.15.2f.).

The Family History

In the seventh book, during and after the voyage from Tripolis to Laodicea, we read the account of the "recognitions" (in the plural) that gave the work its title. This book could be printed in parallel columns to H 12–13, since the two texts are extremely similar, down to points of vocabulary. R lacks the instruction about *philanthrôpia* in H 12.25–33; the recapitulation of the day's events by Peter is more detailed in R 7.26f. than in H 13.2 and is a good summary of the plot of the novel. At the mother's baptism (R 7.38; cf. H 14.1), the whole family is reunited with the exception of the father.

It is not on this occasion (as in H) but on the following morning, when Peter, with Clement and his brothers, withdraws to pray, that a poor old man engages them in a conversation that leads into discussions with him which extend in R to the end of the text and include in book 10 much of the material of the controversy with Apion in H. The fact that this old man is Clement's father is revealed only later on, but it is clearly signaled to the reader as soon as the old man appears. Peter admits that he is behaving toward them "like a father anxious on behalf of his children" (8.1.5). Clement feels his heart beating strongly, because he sees familiar traits in the old man (8.2.4). The old man addresses Nicetas as "my son," and the young man calls him "my father" (8.5.2f.); and the problematic aspect of this address is pointed out in 8.8 with reference to Matthew 23:9.

Philosophical Debates

The old man's creed, which prompts the debate, runs as follows: "There is neither any God, nor any worship, neither is there any providence in the world, but all things are done by fortuitous chance and by *genesis*" (i.e., the position of the stars at the time of one's birth; 8.2.2). He is sure of this, both because of what has happened in his own life and because he has studied astrology. Nicetas, who has specialized in the study of Epicurus (just as Aquila has specialized in the skeptic Pyrrhon, and Clement in Plato and Aristotle), replies in a long discourse with a philosophical coloring, in which he infers the rule of the divine providence in the life of the individual from the fact of a planned creation (8.9–34; there is no direct parallel in H).

The debate is continued on the following day in the house of a rich, hospitable citizen of the town. The old man gives a brief and accurate summary of the arguments presented by Nicetas on the previous day but declares himself unconvinced. Aquila now takes the floor. His task is more difficult because he must discuss the destructive powers that are at work in the creation. Free will and the consequence of sin are a part of the solution (8.51); besides this, everything that is good has a negative counterpart. For example, the divine providence is counteracted by magical arts (8.53). The old man speaks once again of fate, and here Aquila says that Clement, as the specialist in *scientiam mathesis*, is the one best suited to reply (8.57.5). Before this, however, Peter closes the day's discussions with a magisterial affirmation: The ultimate answer to every question can be given only by the true prophet, not by philosophy. These words make a lasting impression on the old man (9.2).

Dispute about Astrology

Bibliography: T. Hegedus, *Early Christianity and Ancient Astrology* (Patristic Studies 6). New York: 2007. esp. 261–77 (on Bardaisan), 319–27 (on the Pseudo-Clementines). – **B. Rehm**, "Bardesanes in den Pseudo-clementinen." *Phil.* 93 (1938): 218–47. – **H. J. Schoeps**, "Astrologisches im pseudoklementinischen Roman." Pages 107–16 in idem, *Studien zur unbekannten Religions- und Geistesgeschichte* (Veröffentlichungen der Gesellschaft für Geistesgeschichte 3). Göttingen: 1963.

On the following day, Clement has the opportunity to hold a long discourse. If astrological predictions prove true in individual instances, it is only because demons are at work, seeking to create an illusion of science (9.12). Through baptism, one can escape from their influence and from fate, and the fear of God keeps the destructive lust in check (9.15). The old man replies by adducing specific constellations of the stars (Mars with Mercury, or Venus in the center of the heavens) that certainly produce murderers and adulterous women (9.17).

In his reply, Clement quotes, at 9.19–29, a lengthy section from a work attributed to Bardaisan (*Liber legum regionum* 25–47), in which the Syrian philosopher argues in favor of the free will against the determinism of astrology, although he concedes that astrology does possess a relative value. The fact that exotic peoples have a variety of customs argues against a unitary determination by one particular constellation. Ultimately, all that the old man can do is to appeal to his own life story. His wife's horoscope predicted that she would run away with a slave, and this did in fact happen, as his brother confirmed (9.32f.).

This misunderstanding can now be cleared up, and there is no longer anything to prevent the reunion of the sons with their father. Peter once again gives a remarkable summary of the family novel, accurate in its details; and now the summary is complete for the first time (9.35f.). As an example of the text of PsClem, I quote this long section in full:

> **35.1** And when he [Peter] had said this, he turned to the crowds, and thus began: "This person whom you see, O men, in this poor garb, is a citizen of the city of Rome, descended of the stock of Caesar himself. **2** His name is Faustinianus. He obtained as his wife a woman of the highest rank, Matthidia by name. By her he had three sons, two of whom were twins; and the one who was the younger, whose name was Clement, is this man!" **3** When he said this, he pointed to me with his finger. "And his twin sons are these men, Nicetas and Aquila, the one of whom was formerly called Faustinus and the other Faustus." **4** But as soon as Peter pronounced our names, all the old man's limbs were weakened, and he fell down in a swoon. **5** But we his sons rushed to him, and embraced and kissed him, fearing that we might not be able to recall his spirit. And while these things were going on, the people were confounded with very wonder.
>
> **36.1** But Peter ordered us to arise from embracing our father, lest we should kill him; and he himself, laying hold of his hand, and lifting him up as from a deep sleep, and gradually reviving him, began to set forth to him the whole transactions as they had really happened: **2** how his brother had fallen in love with Matthidia, and how she, being very modest, had been unwilling to inform her husband of his brother's lawless love, lest she should stir up hostility between the brothers, and bring disgrace upon the family; and how she had wisely pretended a dream, by which she was ordered to depart from the city with her twin sons, leaving the younger one with his father; **3** and how on their voyage they had suffered shipwreck through the violence of a storm; and how, when they were cast upon an island called Antaradus, Matthidia was thrown by a wave upon a rock, **4** but her twin children were seized by pirates and carried to Caesarea, and there sold to a pious woman, who treated them as sons, and brought them up, and caused them to be educated as

gentlemen; and how the pirates had changed their names, and called the one Nicetas and the other Aquila; 5 and how afterwards, through common studies and acquaintanceship, they had adhered to Simon; and how they had turned away from him when they saw him to be a magician and a deceiver, and had come to Zacchaeus; and how subsequently they had been associated with himself; 6 and how Clement also, setting out from the city for the sake of learning the truth, had, through his acquaintance with Barnabas, come to Caesarea, and had become known to him [Peter], and had adhered to him, and how he had been taught by him the faith of his religion; 7 and also how he had found and recognized his mother begging at Antaradus, and how the whole island rejoiced at his recognition of her; and also concerning her sojourn with her most chaste hostess, and the cure that he had wrought upon her, and concerning the liberality of Clement to those who had been kind to his mother; 8 and how afterwards, when Nicetas and Aquila asked who the strange woman was, and had heard the whole story from Clement, they cried out that they were her twin sons Faustinus and Faustus; and how they had unfolded the whole history of what had befallen them; 9 and how afterwards, by the persuasion of Peter himself, they were presented to their mother with caution, lest she should be cut off by the sudden joy.

This wonderful story so moves the hearers that all begin to weep (as do the implicit readers; 9.37.1). To crown everything, a demon who has used the daughter of the house as his instrument since she was seven years old, so that she had to be bound with chains and shut up in a closet, flees (9.38). Here too, the happiness of a family is restored.

A Harmonious End to the Story

On the next morning, Peter proposes that the father be given a year to ponder his own decision with regard to the Christian faith. When Nicetas asks anxiously what would happen to his father in the afterlife if he were to die before the end of the year, Peter replies that this may be safely left to the judgment of God, who can save Faustinianus even if he is not baptized (10.1f.). Various subjects are now discussed in the family circle: the origin of evil; astrology and the freedom of the will; "the histories of the gods, which are usually declaimed in the theaters" (10.15.2), including Jupiter's amorous adventures; (Orphic) cosmology and mythology; the cult of heroes; allegorical interpretations; and the fine arts.

Peter, as spiritual father, reacts by exhorting his hearers to listen to the teaching of the true prophet and to repent in time (10.43–51). It is only at 10.52 in R that we meet Apion, Annubion, Athenodorus (10.55.5), and—once again—Simon. (Rufinus translated this closing passage from a version of H that was more complete than the version we know and added it to R.) The transformation of Faustinianus into the form of Simon and Peter's clever exploitation of this metamorphosis occur as in H, but this time we also learn that the father regains his own form (R 10.67) and receives baptism in Antioch on a day of the Lord (10.72).

3. The Underlying Text (G)

Bibliography: W. **Heintze**, *Der Klemensroman und seine griechischen Quellen* (TU 40.2). Leipzig: 1914. – B. **Pouderon**, "Origène, le pseudo-Clément et la structure des Periodoi Petrou." *Apocrypha* 12 (2001): 29–51. – J. **Rius-Camps**, "Pseudoclementinas." – C. **Schmidt**, *Studien.* 240–313. – G. **Strecker**, *Judenchristentum.* 35–96. – M. **Vielberg**, *Klemens.* – J. **Wehnert**, "Abriss der Entstehungsgeschichte des pseudoklementinischen Romans." *Apocrypha* 3 (1992): 211–35.

If we keep to the basic principles that (a) common passages in H and R are derived from G; (b) R has left the narrative sequence intact (thus Vielberg; a different view is taken by Wehnert and Pouderon); and (c) in terms of contents, H often preserves the older form (thus also Rius-Camps), it ought to be possible to reconstruct G in its basic outlines and occasionally even in its wording. The text is structured by means of information about place and time, especially the rhythm of the day ("on the next morning," "on the following day"; on the motif of the "early morning," cf. Vielberg 35: "Getting up early symbolizes waking up in time from the lethargy of every-day life"). A number of larger blocks can be distinguished:

1. Clement's self-presentation and his search, his journey from Rome to Caesarea, his reception by Peter, and his initial instruction

2. The debate with Simon, which takes place in Caesarea and lasts for three days, with a fourth day that is used for evaluation; and a stay of three months in that city

3. The missionary preaching in Tripolis, which once again lasts for three days; with three further months there, ending with Clement's baptism
4. The onward journey to Laodicea, with a detour to Arados, where the mother is rediscovered, followed by the recognition of the brothers and the baptism of the mother
5. The encounter with the old man, detailed discussions with him that last for several days, his identification as the father, and his baptism

The problems begin as soon as we turn to the material preserved only in R or in H. Some scholars declare that one particular section belongs to the oldest stock of PsClem and is even earlier than G, while other scholars declare that exactly the same passage goes back only to the redaction of R or of H or to even later revisions.

Let me give some examples of the passages in question. Most scholars (though not all) agree that the three introductory documents that we discussed above as the "prooemium" to PsClem belong to G. They turn PsClem into a "more than oversized epistolary communication to James, the chief bishop in Jerusalem" (Wehnert, 226). There seems to be an emerging consensus that the long flashback in R 1.27–71 comes from an old source that has been integrated into G (and is then omitted by H). The fact that the debate about mythology from R 10.31–41 is conducted in H 4–6 not with the father, but with Apion, could be interpreted as the simple transposition of a motif; but the trick played on Apion in H 4–5—a literary *pièce de résistance* in PsClem—remains a puzzle, especially when this lengthy passage is supposed to come from an earlier work of Jewish apologetics (cf. the "document from a Jewish disputation" in Heintze 50). This makes the question of sources even more complicated. If the scene was created only by H (thus Strecker; Pouderon takes a different view, attributing it to G), then its redactor had at least as much literary skill as the author of G. Here, scholarship still faces formidable tasks.

C. Evaluation

Bibliography: K. Cooper, "Matthidia's Wish: Division, Reunion, and the Early Christian Family in the Pseudo-Clementine Recognitions." Pages 243–64 in *Narrativity in Biblical and Related Texts* (BETL 149). Edited by G. J. Brooke and J.-D. Kaestli. Louvain: 2000. – **H. J. W.**

Drijvers, "Adam and the True Prophet in the Pseudo-Clementines." Chap. 14 in idem, *History and Religion in Late Antique Syria*. Aldershot: 1994. – **F. S. Jones**, "Eros and Astrology in the Περίοδοι Πέτρου: The Sense of the Pseudo-Clementine Novel." *Apocrypha* 12 (2001): 53–78. – **S. Légasse**, *L'antipaulinisme sectaire au temps des Pères de l'Église* (CRB 47). Paris: 2000. – **G. Lüdemann**, *Paulus, der Heidenapostel II: Antipaulinismus im frühen Christentum* (FRLANT 130). Göttingen: 1983. 228–57.

If they are known at all in the theological world, the Pseudo-Clementines are known—or more accurately, they enjoy a bad reputation—because of their anti-Pauline stance, in connection with which they are regarded as witnesses to a Jewish Christianity that (it is believed) has otherwise disappeared without trace. It is indeed true that this work criticizes Paul, but that is certainly not the main concern of our two surviving versions, and it is questionable whether this was the main concern at any stage of the work. The criticism can be seen most clearly when Paul appears as the persecutor of the Christians; likewise, the critique of the reception of revelation in visions is directed against him. The criticism would assume more comprehensive dimensions only if we could safely identify Simon Magus with Paul throughout the work, but this is scarcely possible. He can be interpreted as a cipher for Paul in some scenes, but certainly not in every passage.

The most explosive theological position that Simon maintains, the distinction between a "foreign," highest God and two other gods who function as creator and law-giver, points in a different direction. Here, we can glimpse behind Simon the outlines of the figure and the teaching of Marcion as well as elements from the gnostic systems in general. The salvaging of Adam's honor, as the first embodiment of the true prophet, points in the same direction (cf. Drijvers). In other words, this portrait is directed against Marcion, whose teachings found a wide reception in Syria, and against gnosis. Accordingly, although some gnostic elements were in fact adopted in the struggle against gnosis, especially the doctrine of the syzygies, it is better not to classify PsClem as "gnostic."

Taken together with the defense of the Old Testament, which is firmly upheld (though at the price of the theory of the false pericopes), it indicates a Jewish and Jewish-Christian background. The Jewish-Christian patrimony can be seen at other points too.

There is a decisive affirmation of the "monarchy" of God, and this has consequences for the Christology, which remains adoptionist. The basic title given to Jesus is "true prophet." The few statements about his preexistence are extremely unclear; "Son of God" is far from meaning "true God." Further indications are the leading role played by James, Peter's stance of faithfulness to the Law, the appeal to "Hebrew" customs, and the refusal to eat together with unbaptized persons. However, the possibility and, indeed, the urgency of the mission to the Gentiles are not called into question.

This too is the *locus* of the attitude to sexuality and marriage, which recalls the Pastoral Letters in many ways and is clearly different from the attitude of the apocryphal Acts of the Apostles. The renunciation of marital intercourse is never even considered, and celibacy is only the exception. Young people should marry, as should older persons. On the other hand, the behavior of a widow who does not remarry is praised highly (cf. the anonymous woman who befriends Matthidia on Arados). One particular form of marital chastity is, however, demanded: the limitation of intercourse to those times allowed by the Law; and PsClem insists that procreation must be the goal of intercourse.

This does not have a positive effect on the position of women in the communities. The woman is the less valuable part of a couple. There are no women among the disciples of Peter nor among the ecclesiastical office-bearers whom he appoints. Peter's wife "appears in the text only when a female guest of the entourage is in need of a respectable chaperone" (Cooper, 244).

Clearly, PsClem accords a high value to the Christian family. In the ideal case, which is attained by Clement's family at the close of the narrative, the physical and the spiritual family—the secular household and the household of God—coincide. In the structure of the narrative, this is also the reason why the recognitions begin so late, in the twelfth book in H and the seventh book in R. First, at least Clement must be baptized before he can draw his relatives after him. This results in an appeal to the reader to do everything in his or her power to ensure that all the members of one's own family become and remain Christians.

One reason for this may be that the clash with the pagan world is obviously far from finished in the eyes of the authors and revisers of PsClem. On the contrary, it occurs every day anew. In the text, this victorious encounter takes place by means of the numerous disputations about mythological and philosophical themes, as well as through the discrediting of pagan worship as magic and as the service of demons.

A key role here is played by astrology, which had become in late antiquity a power that determined people's lives. It is not attacked head-on, as are other aspects of the pagan milieu, perhaps because there were also Christians who continued to lend the astrologers a sympathetic ear. But PsClem shows how one can escape from the fate decreed by the stars and employ one's own free will against their power: through repentance, faith, and baptism (cf. Jones). On this point, it is appropriate to quote Theodotus, who begins his well-known definition of the gnosis that sets people free with the following words: "Until baptism, they say, fate (*heimarmenē*) holds sway. After baptism, the astrologers are no longer right" (Clement of Alexandria, *Exc.*, 78.1). And perhaps the title that this narrative has, for example, in Epiphanius, *Periodoi Petrou*, refers not only to the "wanderings" of Peter but also to the "orbits" of the stars, to whose hegemony Peter puts an end—especially since, as Jones notes (78), the noun *periodos* is employed in H 6.10.1 for the orbit of the sun around the earth.

The great popularity of this work in the West, as seen in the large number of Latin manuscripts, had unexpected consequences. The name of Doctor Faust in the popular book that prompted Goethe's great drama comes from PsClem. Traits of the father and of Simon Magus found their way into the eponymous hero of Goethe's work, and Simon also inspired the figure of Mephistopheles (cf. Cullmann, *Problème*, 166–68). Only a very few non-biblical texts were honored in such a fashion.

Chapter 8

Later Acts of Apostles

Bibliography: R. A. Lipsius, *Die apokryphen Apostelgeschichten*, Vol. 2: 2.
– **T. Schermann**, *Propheten- und Apostellegenden, nebst Jüngerkatalogen des Dositheus und verwandter Texte* (TU 31.3). Leipzig: 1907. – **F. Haase**, *Apostel und Evangelisten in den orientalischen Überlieferungen* (NTAbh 9.1–3). Münster: 1922. – **A. de Santos Otero**, NTApo 6th ed. II: 381–438. – **J. K. Elliott**, *Apocryphal NT*. 512–33.

We have already mentioned some of the later apocryphal Acts of Apostles when speaking of the subsequent influence of the five ancient Acts. For example, the Acts of Titus were presented briefly after the discussion of the Acts of Paul, and the Acts of Nereus and Achilleus were presented in connection with the Acts of Peter (cf. the Index). From the fourth and fifth centuries onward, in the West and especially in the East, the relevant material becomes more and more copious and crosses the always fluid border into pure legend and hagiography. Some of these texts still slumber undisturbed in manuscripts; those that have been edited can be found in the massive tomes of the *Acta Sanctorum*, which are published by the Bollandists in Brussels.

The Acts of Philip (ActPhil) occupy a prominent place in this group, not least thanks to fortunate textual discoveries and to an excellent new edition with a comprehensive commentary, and this is why we shall look at this work in greater detail. Otherwise, we are content with some "snapshots" that seek to give at least an impression of the contents of this wide literary field. Food for thought is also provided by the fact that although 120 years have passed since the publication of Richard Adalbert Lipsius' work, it remains by far the most extensive presentation of this field.

A. The Acts of Philip

Editions: M. Bonnet, AAAp II: 2. 1–90. – **F. Bovon, B. Bouvier, and F. Amsler**, *Acta Philippi*, Vol. 1: *Textus* (CChrSA 11). Turnhout: 1999.

Translations: M. Erbetta, *Gli apocrifi*, Vol. 2. 451–90. – **F. Amsler, F. Bovon, and B. Bouvier**, *Actes de l'Apôtre Philippe* (Apocryphes 8). Turnhout: 1996. – Idem, Pages 1179–1320 in *Écrits apocryphes chrétiens*, Vol. 1. Edited by F. Bovon and P. Geoltrain.

Bibliography: F. Amsler, *Acta Philippi*, Vol. 2: *Commentarius* (CChrSA 12). Turnhout: 1999. – **F. Bovon**, "Les Actes de Philippe." *ANRW* II: 25.6 (1988): 4431–4527. – Idem, "Women Priestesses in the Apocryphal Acts of Philip." Pages 109–21 in *Walk in the Ways of Wisdom* (Festschrift for E. Schüssler Fiorenza). London: 2003. – **R. A. Lipsius**, *Die apokryphen Apostelgeschichten*, Vol. 2: 2, 1–53. – **A. de Santos Otero**, NTApo 6th ed. II: 424–42. – **C. R. Matthews**, *Philip: Apostle and Evangelist. Configurations of a Tradition* (NovTSupl 105). Leiden: 2002. 156–215.

1. Context

Philip is not one of the best known of the twelve apostles, and a confusion arose at an early date between this Philip and the evangelist Philip, one of the group of seven recorded in Acts 6:5 (unless, as Matthews has recently suggested, these are in fact one and the same person). Among the sources of Eusebius, Clement of Alexandria relates that the apostle Philip took care to arrange good marriages for his four daughters (who according to Acts 21:8f. were the daughters of the evangelist Philip); this is an argument against the encratites (cf. *Hist. eccl.* 3.30.1). Polycrates of Ephesus localizes Philip's final activity and his tomb in Hierapolis (*Hist. eccl.* 3.31.3). Papias claims to have heard with his own ears marvelous stories from the daughters of the apostle Philip in Hierapolis (*Hist. eccl.* 3.39.9). We must therefore bear the city of Hierapolis in mind.

The "Gelasian Decree" (ca. 500 CE) classifies "Acts under the name of Philip" as apocryphal. For a long time, it was believed that only a few fragments of these Acts had survived, with the exception of the Martyrdom, which could be used in the liturgy on feasts of the saint. This situation was remedied by two manuscripts in particular. The first is *Vaticanus graecus 824*, which contains ActPhil 1–9 and the Martyrdom with a longer introduction; Bonnet's edition, which long remained standard, was based on this manuscript. It was only in 1974 that François Bovon discovered *Xenophontos 32* in a monastery on Mount Athos and photographed it. Its great importance is due to two factors: first, that only this manuscript contains ActPhil 11–15 (which were completely unknown hitherto) with two small gaps, followed by a shorter Martyrdom; and secondly, that it offers a parallel text to ActPhil 1 and 3–7 in *Vaticanus graecus 824*. Usually, the text in *Xenophontos 32* is more detailed, but in this case the rule that the shorter reading is more original cannot be applied as if it were an absolute axiom; it suffices here to recall the epitome of ActAndr by Gregory of Tours. There is, unfortunately, one serious gap. Up to three quires have fallen out of the codex in the middle, so that ActPhil 10 is missing (see below). However, thanks to the combination of these two textual witnesses with some other fragments, we now possess an almost complete version of ActPhil—something that was not available for many centuries.

The textual criticism leads almost automatically to literary criticism (on what follows, cf. especially Amsler). From ActPhil 8 to the end of the work, there is a self-contained narrative line focused on Hierapolis (as in the second half of ActThom). ActPhil 3–7 are a more loosely connected group of stories. It is easy to imagine them being told about Philip, the evangelist whom later tradition raised to the apostolic dignity. When the traditional material was reshaped to form one long narrative, ActPhil 1 was included because of its general tendency, which agrees with ActPhil 8–15; the editor did not iron out all the inconsistencies in the logic of the narrative or in the localization of events. ActPhil 2 is in a special category thanks to its manuscript attestation: It is transmitted on its own in several manuscripts and is missing in Xenophontos 32. Its narrative depends heavily on ActPhil 6, and its contents are emphatically orthodox. It may have been the last element to be included in the work.

For reasons that will become clearer later on, this final redaction probably took place shortly before 400 CE in Phygria, and perhaps in Hierapolis itself.

2. Contents

Act 1: To Hell and Back

Bibliography: R. Slater, "An Inquiry into the Relationship between Community and Text: The Apocryphal Acts of Philip 1 and the Encratites of Asia Minor." Pages 281–306 in *The Apocryphal Acts*. Edited by F. Bovon et al.

On his journey from Galilee (cf. Matt 28:16), Philip encounters a Gentile widow who laments the death of her only son (cf. Luke 7:11-17). She caricatures the rites that she once practiced in the cult of her gods and the false information given by the soothsayers. She praises the ideal of a pure (i.e., sexually continent) life, with bread and water as nourishment instead of meat and wine. In a free variation on the Word of God, the apostle praises all those who are subjected to lying discourses (cf. Matt 5:11) and raises her son from the dead. The young man relates (only in *Xenophontos 32*) how the archangel Michael led him through the underworld, where he saw the dreadful torments inflicted on all those who had attacked in word and deed the office-bearers of the church, men who lived in celibacy, and virgins. The implicit criticism is addressed to those who represent other tendencies in the church. Both mother and son convert to the Christian faith and become adherents of Philip.

Act 2: Philip in Athens

The second Act brings the apostle to Athens (cf. perhaps John 12:20f. and the description of the evangelist Philip as a "Hellenist" in Acts 6:1-5). Three hundred philosophers, who are always keen to hear something new (cf. Acts 17:21), gather around him, but his message disturbs them. They write a letter to the high priest Ananias in Jerusalem, telling him of Philip's miracles. Ananias comes to Athens with an entourage of five hundred persons and gives his own hostile version of the events concerning Jesus and his disciples. He and the five hundred are stricken with blindness. Jesus descends from heaven in radiant splendor so that all the idols burst apart and all the demons flee. When he ascends again to heaven, the earth is split open, and Ananias sinks gradually down into it (cf. Num 16:30-34). Finally, since he absolutely refuses to believe in

Jesus Christ, he goes down into hell, while simultaneously a dead man returns to life. Ananias' companions have their sight restored.

Philip remains in Athens for two years and builds up the local church. He then departs for Parthia (originally, this may have read "Samaria" or "Syria").

Act 3: Apparitions of the Lord

In a city of Parthia, Philip meets Peter and John (cf. Acts 8:14-25), who inform him—in an intertextual allusion to the figures and the apocryphal Acts of these apostles!—about the whereabouts of Andrew, Thomas, and Matthew. Philip is confirmed in his ministry by his two fellow apostles and by a voice from heaven. On his journey, in answer to a lengthy prayer, there appear to him a huge tree and a great eagle with wide outspread wings, recalling the cross. Jesus speaks to him from the eagle's mouth and promises that he will always be with him in the Spirit. Philip boards a ship, which at once runs into a storm and is attacked by swarms of locusts. Around midnight, a luminous cross becomes visible, and the fish and monsters of the deep sing hymns to it in their own language. This is the occasion for a lengthy prayer of thanksgiving, with a rhythmical structure, by the apostle. The journey continues without any further disturbances.

Act 4: A Female Disciple

In Azotus (cf. Acts 8:40), the apostle's exorcisms and healings provoke the usual mixed reaction: While some hold him to be a man of God, especially since he wears a kind of monastic garment of the uttermost simplicity, others do not hesitate to call him a magician. Women from the highest circles in society find him interesting. Jesus appears in the form of a beautiful child and shows him where he can find lodgings for the night. Philip heals the daughter of the house from an eye disease. She puts on men's clothing and follows him. It may be merely a coincidence, but her name is Charitine—one of the names traditionally given to the four daughters of the evangelist Philip (cf. Acts 21:8f.). ActPhil never mentions these daughters in order to safeguard the strictly ascetic profile of the apostle.

Act 5: The Conversion of a Family

In the next city, Nicatera (perhaps Caesarea by the sea?), the people do not want to welcome Philip and his companions because they have already heard that he demands that married couples separate and live in purity. Only one rich Jewish citizen named Ireus is drawn to Philip and his teaching. This time, the drama is played out under a reversal of the usual constellation: Ireus himself is willing to live in sexual continence and to renounce his possessions, but his wife, Nercella, refuses to accept this idea. Philip demonstrates his ability to read thoughts and to hear conversations at which he himself is not present. Thus he converts the entire household, step by step, to his own rigorist vision of the Christian life. Finally, even Nercella and her exceptionally pretty daughter Artemilla are converted. They discover him transfigured in a form of light, which he lays aside as soon as he notices the shocked reactions of the new converts (this is the beginning of a series of striking points of contact with ActPet 21–29). A meal of bread and vegetables is held, in which everyone shares—except Philip, who remains fasting. (Even if the meal contained a sacramental component, the completely dematerialized spiritual communion would be enough for him.)

Act 6: Exegesis of Scripture and Miracles as Proof

These events stir up the Jewish inhabitants of the city, who want to have Philip scourged. He threatens to strike them with blindness. One of their leading men, Aristarchus, pulls Philip's beard; his hand withers, he becomes deaf, and he loses the sight in his right eye. Philip charges Ireus to heal Aristarchus by making the sign of the cross on his head. Aristarchus then opens the disputation about Jesus, the crucified God, with a list of rather abstruse quotations from Scripture that are intended to demonstrate the absurdity of the Christian truths of salvation; but Philip smiles because he knows that he has the better arguments. Philip adduces Isaiah 42:1 and 53:7f. (cf. Acts 8:32f.), but it is only a miracle that decides the matter. The dead son of a rich couple is borne past on a bier by twelve slaves, who are to be burned together with the corpse. Aristarchus tries his luck, but it is Philip who restores the boy to life. After demanding that the slaves be set free, he takes the hand of the boy and begins to pray. The boy starts to breathe, opens his eyes, speaks, and walks around. Three thousand souls are added to the number of the believers, and after this victory Philip can end his five-day fast—although, of course, only with bread and vegetables (and water).

Act 7: A Church Is Built

Ireus and Nereus, the father of the boy who has just been raised to life from the dead, compete with each other to see who will be allowed to build a hall on his land for the assembly (§2: *sunagôgê*) of the believers, who have now become so numerous. When it is completed, the building meets with the apostle's approval and provides a fitting scene for his words of farewell.

Act 8: A New Beginning

For §1–15 of this Act, we follow the only textual witness, a manuscript from Athens; we return to *Vaticanus Graecus 824* only for §§16–21. Act 8 goes back into the past, since it begins with the division of the missionary territories among the apostles after Easter. Philip is very unhappy when Greece is assigned to him, and his sister Marianne (behind whom Mary Magdalene lies concealed) intervenes. The Lord observes that Philip is too impulsive and therefore ordains that Marianne and Bartholomew are to accompany him. Marianne must dress as a man. This is not only in keeping with her personality; there is a deeper reason. The Lord sends this apostolic trio into a city full of snakes, where the inhabitants worship the mother of all snakes. He links this to a customary exegesis of Genesis 3 that is hostile to women: It was only via Eve, the woman, that the snake found a way of attacking the man. Philip is moved once more to tears by his fear that, in the last analysis, he will be repaying evil with evil, but the Lord delivers him from his fear by the even more detailed exhortations, consolations, and promises with which he sends the group on their way. In the subtitles in the manuscripts, the "city of snakes" is usually identified as Hierapolis, the city in Asia Minor where the tradition (probably correctly) locates the activity of Philip.

The journey begins in §16. In the wilderness, a huge leopard runs up to the apostolic trio, prostrates itself at their feet, and speaks with a human voice. It confesses that on the previous night, it had carried off a young goat from a flock. The goat began to weep like a little child and counseled the leopard to desist from its wild behavior, especially in view of the fact that the messengers of God were drawing near. The young goat is healed of the wound caused by the leopard's bite. The leopard loses its wildness and becomes a vegetarian. The leopard and the goat raise their front paws and pray to God. From then on, they accompany the group. This is the realization of the vision of eschatological peace among the animals (Isa 11:6-9), with a transparent message about the taming of human wildness and bestiality; and as we shall see, it also involves a polemic against pagan cults.

Act 9: The Fight with the Dragon

The ninth Act is short; it may have been abbreviated in *Vaticanus graecus 824*, our only witness to this part of the text. The apostolic "quintet" is confronted by an immense, dark dragon that is followed by numerous snakes and their brood. After a prayer for divine help, Philip, Marianne, and Bartholomew sprinkle (blessed?) water in the air from a cup that they carry with them. A fiery bolt of lightning blinds the dragons and snakes and dries them up. It also destroys all the serpents' eggs in their hidden nests.

Act 10: A Baptism of a Particular Kind?

Act 10 no longer survives in any manuscript. The editors suggest that the leopard and the young goat were baptized at this point in the story. *Xenophontos 32* resumes only in the middle of the eleventh Act.

Act 11: The Demons and the Church Building

Preparations are made for the reception of the Eucharist, which, however, is celebrated only after a demonic intermezzo. The earth quakes, and fifty demons who dwell there show themselves in the form of snakes. Their leader too appears as a huge black dragon. They helped Solomon during the construction of the Temple and propose to build a church within six days, provided that the apostle will then allow them to move to another place where they will not be endangered by his presence. The demons then assume their true form as spirits of the air, and the church is built.

A few days later, three thousand men, besides women and children, assemble for worship. The prayer of praise which the apostle intones is inspired by the hymnic texts in ActJoh 94–96.

Act 12: The Partial Metamorphosis of the Leopard and the Goat

The leopard and the goat weep bitterly, and Philip asks why this is. The leopard holds an eloquent discourse in which it laments that although the two animals were considered worthy to receive the apparitions of the Lord, they remain excluded from the reception of Holy Communion—through which they hope that their animal nature will be transformed into human nature. Philip is sympathetic. He sprinkles them with water and gives them the sacramental bread. The effect seems to be that the two animals feel like human beings. From then on, they speak only in human language and walk upright on their back legs; they do not, however, lose their animal forms.

Act 13: The Arrival in Hierapolis

The group draws near to Hierapolis, the city of snakes. The access roads are patrolled by seven men who bear snakes on their shoulders, which they unleash on strangers: True worshipers of the snakes remain unharmed, while critics and enemies are bitten and cannot get any closer to the city. The snakes prostrate themselves before the apostolic trio and their tame animals and bite their own tongues. Two dragons guard the main city gate, but a ray from Philip's eyes disposes of them.

In the city, the travelers immediately find an abandoned doctor's practice, or pharmacy, where they can establish their own multidimensional praxis of healing. Philip asks what has happened to the medicine chest that Jesus gave them in Galilee (see above on ActPet 12). The day closes with a long prayer of thanksgiving.

Act 14: The Healing of Stachys

The first to visit the apostolic trio is Stachys, a man from the neighboring house who has been blind for forty years. He had been the high priest in the cult of the mother of the snakes, and because he believed that the liquid from the snakes' eggs had healing power, he had bathed his eyes in it. This only made things worse (and the message is that the cult of false gods makes their worshipers blind). He had found some relief in the dew that his wife gathered for him in the woods high on the mountains, but she was killed by a monster. In the past three nights, he had had the same dream: A young man appeared in three forms (*prosôpa*, the technical term in reflections on the Trinity): as a young man bearing on his shoulder a jar of water with which he baptized many of the inhabitants; as an old man; and as a young woman with a burning torch which she shone into his eyes. This may remind us of the apostolic trio, but a trinitarian interpretation is more likely. The woman (via Sophia) represents the Holy Spirit. The threefold dream alludes to rites of incubation, which are known from the cult of Asclepius and which were practiced in this city too.

In order to heal Stachys, Philip takes spittle from Marianne's mouth with his finger and anoints the sick eyes. The details are not completely clear at this point because a page has been torn out of the codex by a reader who was enraged by the robustness and the direct physical contact of this technique. But there is no question about the success of the healing because Stachys holds a great feast where immense quantities of meat are served and rivers of wine flow. Philip finds this unacceptable, and he criticizes it in the following Act.

Act 15: The Tyrant and his Wife

The proconsul, with the eloquent name Tyrannognophos ("somber tyrant"), has a Syrian wife named Nicanora, who later converses with Marianne in Hebrew. Because she is a foreigner, she was bitten by the snakes and still suffers from the after-effects. She has an edifying experience in the house of Stachys, who is destined to be the future bishop of the city: Philip exhorts his hearers to renounce such festivities and to lead a continent and ascetic life. He plants his traveler's staff in the courtyard; at once a laurel tree grows out of it (the laurel is associated with Apollo, the god of oracles). Corn, wine (?), and olive oil are distributed to the poor from three vessels, but these vessels never become empty. Out of fear of her husband, Nicanora returns to her house; she does not seek a personal contact with the apostolic trio. Her husband promptly warns her not to have any contact with the foreigners. Later allusions suggest that the missing page (see above) related how the Lord heard Nicanora's prayer by night and appeared to her.

The Martyrdom: Philip's Impatience

As in many other cases, the Martyrdom was extracted from the narrative for liturgical purposes and transmitted in numerous manuscripts. It exists in three recensions, with new introductory summaries that vary in the amount of the narrative they cover and in the details they present. Here, we continue to give preference to *Xenophontos 32*.

Despite her husband's prohibition, Nicanora speaks with Marianne and attempts to persuade her husband to adopt a chaste and sober life; but the tyrant ill-treats her and has the apostolic trio arrested and dragged to the temple. The apostles are stripped naked so that their bodies can be searched to see if they are concealing magical devices. Philip's ankles and heels are pierced, and he is hanged head-downward on a tree outside the temple, while Bartholomew is nailed to the wall of the temple, facing him. The stripping of Marianne is meant to be a high point, but her body is transformed into a glass vessel full of light and fire. Philip asks whether he ought not to have fire rain down from heaven; at once, John appears on the scene—he too had once expressed the same wish (cf. Luke 9:54). John preaches to the people and attempts to convert them, but in vain. The only result is that he puts himself at risk, and now Philip can no longer hold back: With curses in Hebrew, he makes the earth open up and swallow everyone apart from the apostolic group and the Christians.

This leads to a harsh rebuke from the Lord. Philip will have to spend forty days outside paradise because of this action. Only Philip will end his life here; a different fate is reserved for Bartholomew, Marianne, and John. A cross of light, which the Lord sketches in the air, reaches down into the depths of the underworld and can be used as a ladder so that everyone re-emerges, with the exceptions of the tyrant, the priests of the snakes, and the mother of the snakes. Philip utters some profound reflections on the way in which he dies, and here the wording of *Vaticanus graecus 808* may be preferable: "I bear the form of the first man, who was brought upon earth head downwards" (§140), and "Unless you make that which is above to be beneath and the right to be the left, you cannot enter the kingdom of heaven" (cf. EvThom 22). He orders that after his death, a church is to be built on this spot and that the leopard and the goat are to be allowed to live there; Nicanora is to care for them.

3. Evaluation

Bibliography: F. Amsler, "Les Actes de Philippe. Aperçu d'une com-
pétition religieuse en Phrygie." Pages 125–40 in *Le mystère apocryphe*.
Edited by J.-D. Kaestli and D. Marguerat. – **F. Bovon**, "Facing the
Scriptures: Mimesis and Intertextuality in the Acts of Philip." Pages
138–53 in *Mimesis and Intertextuality in Antiquity and Christianity* (Studies
in Antiquity and Christianity). Edited by D. R. MacDonald. Harrisburg,
Pa.: 2001. – **E. Peterson**, "Die Häretiker der Philippus-Akten." *ZNW* 31
(1932): 97–111.

The intertextual relationships between ActPhil and the Bible and
the ancient apocryphal Acts are much more numerous than the
few allusions mentioned above (cf. Bovon). Here, however, we
content ourselves with following two other traces that help us to
locate the text within the church and in the history of religion.

The encratite orientation of ActPhil is obvious, but (according
to Amsler) it is expressed with varying degrees of intensity in the
principal sections 3–7 and 8–15 (with the Martyrdom). The asceticism is particularly severe in ActPhil 3–7, where the obsession
with sexuality is extended to include clothing, food, possessions,
and societal structures. On the basis of Luke 14:33, scholars have
coined the term *Apotactics* for this group, which they locate in the
fourth century in Asia Minor, and more precisely in Phrygia,
where the Montanist movement began. A provincial synod at
Gangra in Paphlagonia ca. 355 (or 342?) condemned radical ascetics "who reject on principle such things as marriage and sexual
intercourse, throw off familial ties and obligations, separate from
the community and from married clergy and hold their own acts
of worship, wear special clothing, lay down their own regulations
for fasting, and forbid the eating of meat" (G. Schöllgen, *LTK* 3rd
ed. 4 [1995], 289; cf. Peterson). The author of ActPhil would not
agree with this condemnation; on the contrary, this text reads like
a list of all those things that he would insistently recommend. It is
highly probable that we hear in ActPhil the voice of this group,
which was marginalized by the church and fought to survive.

In classical antiquity, the people of Phrygia had the reputation
of preferring archaic and wild forms of religious praxis; this is the
second front on which ActPhil fights, with the help of mockery,
parody, persiflage, and demonization. Predatory big cats were
associated in literature and iconography with Cybele, the Great

Mother, and the young goat was associated with her companion Attis; all Christians regarded idolatry as the worship of demons. In their own tradition, snakes and dragons carried very negative overtones. Besides this, they were brought to Asia Minor by Apollo, and although he was a competitor to Cybele, the Christians saw the two deities as equally evil. In the city of Hierapolis, with its impressive location, there were warm, chalky springs; a cave containing lethal gasses; a temple of Apollo; and a healing cult that included incubation, that is, a preparatory sleep in the sanctuary.

We can see how each of these items is attacked individually in ActPhil. The mother of the snakes is Cybele, who perishes. Her favorite cat and her pet animal convert to Christianity. Apollo, with his snakes and dragons, loses his power. The case of Stachys shows what pagan incubation leads to. The apostle reopens the abandoned doctor's practice in Hierapolis, and it is the apostle who brings effective healing.

There is probably a good confirmation of this hypothesis outside the text (although the results of excavations are not entirely certain). Around 400, a grandiose *martyrion* of Philip existed just outside the city of Hierapolis, built in the form of an octagon with a cross inside it. The quadrilateral was surrounded by small rooms where the pilgrims who sought help could sleep and practice incubation (cf. the illustration in F. Amsler, *Commentarius*, 545).

B. Other Highlights

1. The Acts of Bartholomew

Bibliography: **M. Bonnet**, AAAp II: 1. 128–50. – **L. Leloir**, *Écrits apocryphes*, Vol. 2. 479–524. – **M. B. Riddle**, ANF 8 (1886; Repr. 1995): 553–57. – **R. A. Lipsius**, *Die apokryphen Apostelgeschichten*, Vol. 2: 2. 54–108. – **A. de Santos Otero**, NTApo 6th ed. II: 406–8. – **J. K. Elliott**, *Apocryphal NT.* 518–20.

In a Coptic tradition (which borrows from ActThom), Bartholomew works primarily in Parthia and Egypt. The Latin *passio* of the apostle (with a secondary translation into Greek) corresponds to the eighth book in Pseudo-Abdias (Ps.-Abd.). Here, the apostle fights against idols and demons in India and converts the royal family. The text offers a personal description: "He has curly black hair, white skin, large eyes . . . his beard long and griz-zled . . . he wears a white *colobium* with a purple stripe" (2; this may be a sign of royal birth). In formal terms, though not in its sub-stance, this recalls the description of Paul in ActPaul. The breadth of variation in the legendary elaboration can be seen in the accounts of Bartholomew's death: "The gnostic legend of Philip has him *crucified*, the Coptic narrative has him *put in a sack* full of sand and then sunk in the sea, the local Armenian saga has him *beaten with clubs*, a fourth tradition (probably originating in Persia) has him *flayed*, and finally a fifth tradition has him *beheaded*" (Lipsius 101; emphasis in original).

2. The Acts of Matthew

Bibliography: **M. Bonnet**, AAAp II: 1. 217–66. – **M. B. Riddle**, ANF 8 (1886; Repr. 1995). 528–34. – **R. A. Lipsius**, *Die apokryphen Apostelgeschichten*, Vol. 2: 2. 109–41. – **A. de Santos Otero**, NTApo 6th ed. II: 414–17. – **J. K. Elliott**, *Apocryphal NT*. 520–23.

The Greek and Latin text printed by Bonnet has nothing in com-mon with the seventh book of Ps.-Abd., which is devoted to Matthew, but it has parallels to the "Acts of Andrew and Matthias in the City of the Cannibals" (cf. chap. 4 above). It has a strongly visionary character. It begins with an apparition of Jesus to the apostles in the form of a child. Matthew does not recognize him but thinks that he is one of the children who were murdered by Herod in Bethlehem and who now spend their time singing psalms in paradise; Matthew is the only evangelist who relates this cruel deed in his gospel (Matt 2:16-18). The apostle's martyrdom takes a long time. His hands and feet are nailed to the earth. First, paper soaked in oil, asphalt, and tar are poured over him (§18), then glowing coals (§20); but the fire cannot do him any harm. He breathes his last of his own free will, with a Hebrew prayer on his lips.

3. The Acts of James the Great

Bibliography: **M. Geerard**, *Clavis*. 166f. – **L. Leloir**, *Écrits apocryphes*, Vol. 2. 267–88. – **R. A. Lipsius**, *Die apokryphen Apostelgeschichten*, Vol. 2: 2. 201–28. – **A. de Santos Otero**, NTApo 6th ed. II: 432–35.

The older formation of legends has much to say about John but largely ignores James the son of Zebedee, perhaps because of his early death (Acts 12:2; this is cautiously elaborated by Clement of Alexandria or Eusebius, *Hist. eccl.* 2.9.2f.). Nevertheless, the little that was known of him was expanded (it suffices here to read the fourth book of the collection by Ps.-Abd.) and transformed into a success story that ultimately provided the basis of the local Spanish tradition and the cult of the apostle in Santiago de Compostela.

4. The Acts of James the Lesser

Bibliography: M. Geerard, *Clavis*. 168–70. – **R. A. Lipsius**, *Die apokryphen Apostelgeschichten*, Vol. 2: 2. 229–57. – **W. Pratscher**, *Der Herrenbruder Jakobus und die Jakobustradition* (FRLANT 139). Göttingen: 1987.

Since the time of Jerome, James the son of Alphaeus (Mark 3:18) has been identified with the James called "the Lesser" or "the Younger" at Mark 15:40; but this on its own would not be as problematic as the other continuous confusion between this apostle and James the brother of the Lord (cf. Mark 6:3) which makes it difficult, or perhaps indeed impossible, to distinguish any clear lines of tradition. Nevertheless, we can identify the basis of almost all the later elaborations in Hegesippus' account of the person and the death of the brother of the Lord, surnamed "the Just," which Eusebius quotes (*Hist. eccl.* 2.23.4–18). The description of James (23.5f.; translated by Lawlor and Oulton) is remarkable:

> Now he was holy from his mother's womb, drank no wine nor strong drink, nor ate anything in which was life; no razor came upon his head, he anointed himself not with oil, and used no bath. To him alone it was permitted to enter the holy place; for he wore nothing woolen, but linen garments. And alone he entered into the sanctuary, and was found on his knees asking forgiveness on behalf of the people, so that his knees became hard like a camel's. . . .

His enemies throw him down from the pinnacle of the temple, where he stood speaking to the people, and then stone him. When even this does not kill him, "[o]ne of them, a fuller, took the club with which he beat out the clothes, and brought it down on the just one's head. Thus he was martyred" (23.18). Eusebius then cites the account by Flavius Josephus (*Ant.* 20.20), who mentions the death by stoning but not the pinnacle of the temple and the fuller's club.

5. The Acts of Matthias

Bibliography: M. Geerard, *Clavis.* 168–70. – **R. A. Lipsius**, *Die apokryphen Apostelgeschichten*, Vol. 2: 2. 258–69. – **R. M. Kloos**, ed. *Lambertus de Legia: De vita, translatione, inventione ac miraculis sancti Matthiae apostoli libri quinque* (TThSt 8). Trier: 1958.

Except where he was confused with Matthew, there was no independent formation of tradition about Matthias, the apostle who replaced Judas Iscariot, with one notable exception. In Trier (my own hometown in Germany), we have not only the tomb of the apostle in the church of a Benedictine abbey which bears his name, but also an appropriate legend. Lipsius judges it to be "probably [sic] without doubt . . . the most recent" of all the apocryphal Acts (264), since it goes back no further than the eleventh or twelfth century; as an example, this too is very instructive.

6. The Acts of Simon and Jude

Bibliography: M. Geerard, *Clavis.* 173–76. – **R. A. Lipsius**, *Die apokryphen Apostelgeschichten*, Vol. 2: 2. 142–78. – **A. de Santos Otero**, NTApo 6th ed. II. 435–37f.

Simon the Cananaean (Mark 3:18 par.) was often confused in the East with Simon, the son of Cleopas (cf. John 19:25) and successor to James as bishop of Jerusalem (Eusebius, *Hist. eccl.* 3.32.1f.). In the West, he was united to Jude (Thaddeus) to form a pair. Correspondingly, Eastern texts locate his activity in Jerusalem and Samaria, while Western texts locate it in Persia and Babylon. In the Coptic legend, his encounter with a virgin named Theonoë, who is modeled on the biblical Judith, also brings him to Egypt. The Latin version of the Acts of Simon and Jude in the sixth book of Ps.-Abdias is particularly important because it is here that the fiction which is meant to authenticate the entire collection is presented (see below).

7. The Acts of Barnabas

Bibliography: M. Bonnet, AAAp II: 2. 292–302. – **M. B. Riddle**, ANF 8 (1886; Repr. 1995). 493–96. – **B. Kollmann**, *Joseph Barnabas. Leben und Wirkungsgeschichte* (SBS 175). Stuttgart: 1998. (With a German translation). – **R. A. Lipsius**, *Die apokryphen Apostelgeschichten*, Vol. 2: 2. 270–320. – **A. de Santos Otero**, NTApo 6th ed. II: 421–43.

The church in Cyprus and the church in Milan both appealed to the Acts of Barnabas in the fifth and sixth centuries in the course of their conflicts with Antioch and with Rome concerning jurisdiction. (We recall that in the Pseudo-Clementine *Recognitions*, Barnabas appears in Rome at a very early date; in the *Homilies*, he appears in Alexandria.) The Greek text published by Bonnet, which claims to be the work of Mark (a nephew of Barnabas, according to Colossians 4:10), describes his second visit to Cyprus, his native island (Acts 4:36), and his martyrdom there. The anonymous author found his model in the canonical Acts of the Apostles, especially in Acts 13:4-13.

The fact that Barnabas conducted missionary work together with Paul is one reason why the title of "apostle" can be ascribed to him in a similar manner, although he was not a member of the group of the twelve (cf. also 1 Cor 9:5). This was probably an additional motive for the production of Acts under the name of Barnabas. We conclude this section with other examples that show this could also happen in the case of evangelists and of the pupils of the "genuine" apostles, as well as of the men and women who accompanied them. (For Stephen, cf. F. Bovon, "The Dossier of Stephen, the First Martyr," in *HTR* 96 [2003]: 279–315.)

8. The Acts of Mark

Bibliography: M. Geerard, *Clavis*. 173–76. – **R. A. Lipsius**, *Die apokryphen Apostelgeschichten*, Vol. 2: 2. 321–53. – **A. de Santos Otero**, NTApo 6th ed. II: 417–21. – **F. Halkin**, "Actes inédites de saint Marc." *AnBoll* 87 (1969): 434–71. – **G. Lusini**, "Les Actes de Marc en éthiopien: remarques philologiques et histoire de la tradition." *Apocrypha* 11 (2000): 123–34.

The New Testament provides a considerable amount of information about the figure of Mark, quite apart from the existence of the gospel that bears his name. We meet him as the companion of Paul, of Barnabas (cf. also Acts 15:39), and possibly also of Peter in Rome (1 Pet 5:13). These data were not forgotten, but the Acts of Mark, the origins of which may go back to the fourth century, follow a different track. Their point of departure is the information preserved by Eusebius (*Hist. eccl.* 2.16.1) that Mark "journeyed to Egypt and was the first to preach [there] the gospel, which also he had written; and that he was the first to form churches at Alexandria itself." This brief note is expanded by means of Mark's struggles against Sarapis and his worshipers and by the tortures that he endures. For example, he is dragged on a rope through the streets of the city. Mark is regarded here as the first bishop of Alexandria, and the bishops who succeed him (and whose names Eusebius transmits) are all selected from among his pupils.

9. The Acts of Luke

Bibliography: M. Geerard, *Clavis*. 182. – **R. A. Lipsius**, *Die apokryphen Apostelgeschichten*, Vol. 2: 2. 354–71. – **A. de Santos Otero**, NTApo 6th ed. II: 423f.

"Acts of Luke" in the strict sense of the term seem not to exist, and the Western tradition knew little of his martyrdom. The dominant view was, rather, that he had died a natural death at an advanced age. The legend of Luke as the first to paint an icon of Mary goes back to other sources, not to Acts. It is only in the Eastern tradition that we find some accounts of the martyrdom of Luke, which localize his death in Rome under Nero. This is an obvious borrowing from the martyrdoms of Peter and Paul, and probably also from the Acts of Pilate (which were integrated into the Gospel of Nicodemus, where they can be read).

10. The Acts of Timothy

Bibliography: M. Geerard, *Clavis*. 182. – **R. A. Lipsius**, *Die apokryphen Apostelgeschichten*, Vol. 2: 2. 372–400.

The *passio* of Timothy was written in the late fourth or fifth century. Its starting point is the Pastoral Letters, and it links the figure of Paul's pupil to Ephesus and the apostle John. The author, who has reliable local knowledge, shows Timothy in full action at a pagan feast known as *katagôgia* (roughly, "the bringing down") held in January. He attempts to put an end to the wild and violent goings-on but himself falls victim to the orgies.

Latin textual witnesses identify the author as Polycrates, who was bishop of Ephesus ca. 190 CE. Photius, the learned patriarch of Constantinople whom we have mentioned in the introduction to the present book, gives an account of the contents of the Acts of Timothy in his *Library* (Codex 254).

11. The Acts of Thaddeus

Bibliography: R. A. Lipsius, AAAp I. 273–78. – **M. B. Riddle**, ANF 8 (1886; Repr. 1975): 558f. – **R. A. Lipsius**, *Die apokryphen Apostelgeschichten*, Vol. 2: 2. 178–200. – **A. de Santos Otero**, NTApo 6th ed. II. 436–37. – **V. Calzolari**, "Réécriture des textes apocryphes en arménien: l'exemple de la légende de l'apostolat de Thaddée en Arménie." *Apocrypha* 8 (1997): 97–100. – **A. Palmer**, "Les Actes de Thaddée." *Apocrypha* 13 (2002): 63–84.

(Jude) Thaddeus appears not only in tandem with Simon (the Cananaean; see above), but also as a soloist. A Coptic (Arabic, Ethiopic) legend simply transposes to him the *Acta Petri et Andreae*, a continuation of the "Acts of Andrew and Matthias in the City of the Cannibals." The Greek text in Lipsius is based on the legend of Abgar and sees Thaddeus as the apostle of Edessa. This brings us back to Eusebius (cf. especially *Hist. eccl.* 1.13.1–22, which reproduces the letter which King Abgar sent to Jesus and the letter which Jesus sent in reply). The Acts of Thaddeus go beyond Eusebius by speaking in §3 (like the Syriac *Doctrina Addai*) of the miraculous picture of Christ, not painted by human hands and possessing powers of healing, which arrived in Edessa. This not only reflects the Byzantine iconoclast controversy but also refers to a specific point in history: a picture of this kind was shown to the public when Edessa was besieged by the Persians in 544. This can be taken as an indicator of the date of composition of these Acts.

12. The Acts of Xanthippe and Polyxena

Bibliography: M. R. James, *Apocrypha anecdota*, Vol. 1 (TS 2.3). Cambridge: 1893. 43–85. (Greek text.) – **W. A. Craigie**, ANCL 25 (Additional Vol., 1896) and ANF 9 (1896) or 10 (1896; Repr. 1980) 203–17. (English translation, quoted in this chapter.) – **E. Junod**, "Vie et conduite des saintes femmes Xanthippe, Polyxène et Rébecca (BHG 1877)." Pages 83–106 in *Oecumenica et Patristica* (Festschrift for W. Schneemelcher). Stuttgart: 1989. (With bibliography.) – **S. L. Davies**, *The Revolt of the Widows*. Esp. 64–69.

We have already met a Xanthippe in ActPet 34f., the wife of Albinus in Rome. Under the influence of the apostle's preaching, she refused to have intercourse with her husband. She is the protagonist in the first half (§§1–21) of the Acts that James edited from an eleventh-century manuscript, which present a real potpourri of names. She is married to Probus, the Roman governor of Spain. Paul comes to Spain, and the result is the drama in married life with which we are familiar by now; Christ appears both as a radiant young man and in the form of Paul; dreams hint at future complications, and Xanthippe has many opportunities to speak prayers and monologues. As an example, I quote an epiphany scene (§15):

> And while she was still speaking thus, there appeared a cross on the eastern wall, and straightway there entered through it a beautiful youth, having round about him trembling rays, and under him an extended light, on which he also walked. And as he entered within, all the foundations of that house shook and sounded with a great trembling. Xanthippe seeing him cried out and fell to the ground as if dead; but he being pitiful and kind, changing immediately into the shape of Paul, raised her up, saying, "Arise, Xanthippe, and fear not, for the servants of God are thus glorified."

Xanthippe has a younger sister named Polyxena, who takes center stage in §§22–42. An admirer carries her off by force and sets sail. On their journey, they meet Peter, who is traveling to Rome in order to combat Simon. When they land in Greece, the apostle Philip is there, and Andrew comes soon afterward. Polyxena flees and meets a lioness, which does her no harm and addresses Andrew in a human voice (in §30). Polyxena wins the friendship of the Jewish slave Rebecca. She puts on men's clothes and is informed about Thecla by a friendly young man (§36). The young man's father, who is the city prefect, has the two young women thrown to the beasts in the arena, but a wild lioness (apparently *not* the same animal as earlier in the story) merely licks Polyxena's feet. Finally, Onesimus appears on the scene. He wants to visit Paul in Spain and takes the whole group with him.

James' dating of this text to the mid-third century owes much to his delight at discovering these Acts; but it is untenable on linguistic grounds. (Davies is completely wrong to date it to 160–225 CE). The fifth or sixth century is more likely (cf. Junod, who also gives a list of the Greek words and forms that are attested only at a late date). This, however, does not mean that scholars have been right to ignore the Acts of Xanthippe and Polyxena to such an extent.

C. The Collection of Abdias

Bibliography: K. F. Borberg, *Bibliothek der Neu-Testamentlichen Apokryphen*, Vol. 1: *Die apokryphischen Evangelien und Apostelgeschichten*. Stuttgart: 1841. 391–721. – **J. P. Migne**, *Dictionnaire des Apocryphes*, Vol. 1. Paris: 1856. – **M. Erbetta**, *Apocrifi*, Vol. 2. – **L. Moraldi**, *Apocrifi*, Vol. 2. 517–682. – **R. A. Lipsius**, *Die apokryphen Apostelgeschichten*, Vol. 1. 117–78. – **J. K. Elliott**, *Apocryphal NT*. 525–31. – **K. Zelzer and P. L. Schmidt**, *Acta Apostolorum apocrypha*. 402–4.

We have referred on several occasions to Abdias and to the collection of *Virtutes apostolorum* that is transmitted in Latin under his name. In most of the manuscripts, it consists of eleven books; in the (inadequate) editions, there are ten books. It takes up older and more recent traditions, and it found a very wide readership in the mediaeval West. The only complete and continuous modern translation of this work is by Moraldi (Erbetta scatters the individual sections throughout his entire text, as does Migne; and both Migne and Borberg are antiquated). There is no modern edition, although some individual parts have been published separately (e.g., the *Passio* of Bartholomew in Bonnet and the *Virtutes Johannis* in Junod and Kaestli, ActJoh).

The pseudepigraphical author, Abdias, is presented as bishop of Babylon and one who has been taught directly by the apostles (cf. the conclusion of the *Passio* of Simon and Jude, 6.20: "In the city of Babylon, the apostles ordained a bishop named Abdias, who had come with them from Judea. He himself had seen the Lord with his own eyes, and the city was filled with churches"); he is sometimes said to have been one of the seventy disciples in Luke 10:1. As an eyewitness and hearer at first hand, he wrote down his knowledge in a Hebrew text that was then translated into Greek (by Craton, who is mentioned in the same chapter) and Latin (by "Africanus, an historian"). In fact, however, the collection was probably made only in the sixth century and was in Latin from the outset. Let me give only one example, an excerpt from a lengthy discourse by Simon Magus in the part devoted to Peter. This passage shows how older material was taken up and reused (1.9):

> I am the first glory, and I am always this glory, without beginning. After I entered the womb of Rachel, I was born of her as a human being, in order that I may be visible to human beings. I flew through the air and entered the fire. . . . I have made pillars move, I have given life to that which was lifeless, and turned stones into bread. I flew down swiftly from a mountain, and borne by the hands of the angels, I descended to the earth. I can make myself invisible to those who want to seize me; and again, when I want to be seen, I can stand there openly. When I want to fly, I cleave mountains and penetrate rocks as if they were clay. When I hurl myself down from a high mountain, I am as it were carried on hands and then set down unharmed. If I am bound, I free myself . . . if I am shut up in a prison, I make the locks open of their own accord. . . . I wish to have new trees grow up, and to have bushes spring up all at once. I change my face, so that people do not know me. . . . I will fly through the air in flight and show a great quantity of gold. I will appoint kings and have myself adored like the Lord. . . . Whatever I wish, that I will also accomplish. For I have already done many such things as evidence.

Obviously, however, Peter knows how to reply to this.

We give here an overview of the titles of the ten books (in the most common division, which, as mentioned above, does not correspond to the arrangement in the manuscripts):

1. Peter
2. Paul
3. Andrew
4. James the Great
5. John, apostle and evangelist
6. The brothers James the Lesser, Simon, and Jude (Thaddeus)

7. Matthew, apostle and evangelist
8. Bartholomew (associated with India)
9. Thomas (also associated with India)
10. Philip

Paul is included in the group of apostles, as is James the brother of the Lord (thanks to a complicated genealogical construction). Judas Iscariot is missing, because Ps.-Abd. concentrates entirely on the activities of the apostles after Easter; but he also passes over Matthias, perhaps because of the frequent confusion with Matthew, which we have already mentioned. The apostle Philip is given daughters who, strictly speaking, belong to the evangelist of the same name.

Although this influential compilation has limited value as a source, a new edition of the text with a translation into a modern language and explanatory notes is one of the many *desiderata* in this field of research, since, as Borberg remarked more than 160 years ago, "This is why we can explain—but not accept—the fact that scholars have paid so little attention to it hitherto" (405).

A Look Back and a Look Ahead

At the End of a Journey

Bibliography: A. Cameron, *Christianity and the Rhetoric of the Empire: The Development of Christian Discourse* (Sather Classical Lectures 55). Berkeley: 1991. 89–119. – **H. Rhee,** *Early Christian Fiction.*

Wanderings and journeys are a motif which the apocryphal Acts, in varying degrees of intensity, share with the novels of classical antiquity. We now look back on the path we have taken through these texts—a path which itself has something of the character of a colorful and occasionally adventurous journey through regions seldom visited by travelers.

It is surprising that these texts should be so relatively unknown, since the reader will find them both informative and entertaining. Apuleius begins his *Metamorphoses* with the words, *Lector intende: laetaberis!*—"Reader, pay attention! You are going to have fun!" (1.1.4); but this does not prevent him from integrating the philosophical fable of Amor and Psyche into his narrative, nor from adding the conclusion to book 11 with its exalted religious fervor (although the latter may also be meant ironically).

One cannot simply apply to the apocryphal Acts of the Apostles the slogan "The medium is the message." But there can be no doubt that the medium chosen by the authors, with the motifs that it borrows from proven and popular narrative patterns, is meant to help ensure that the theological message reaches its intended audience safely.

This, however, does not mean that the apocryphal Acts were written only as popular literature for the entertainment of an undemanding Christian readership. Most of their authors must have had a considerable level of education and knew how to give their narratives a hidden dimension, which was meant to be perceived by their implicit and ideal readers—and, where possible, by their actual readers as well. These were, in more senses than one, "Stories People Want" (to use Cameron's phrase), and this is why they made such an important contribution to the emergence of a Christian rhetorical and literary culture in late antiquity. The principal factor that distinguishes them from the novelistic literature is their specific form of a "happy ending," which does not consist in the marriage of the two main characters but in the martyrdom (or at least the death) of the hero, who thus returns to his heavenly homeland and is united to the exalted Lord. This element is inspired by the Gospels rather than by Luke's Acts of the Apostles, which was later to become canonical.

The Martyrdoms of the apostles were transmitted independently and provide a link to another genre of early Christian literature, the Acts of the Martyrs. Astonishingly, scholars tend largely to work on these two bodies of texts in mutual isolation, without exploiting these links to help explain the texts they are studying (but cf. now perhaps Rhee).

We have also seen that it can be dangerous to treat the apocryphal Acts only as a unified group. Each work has its own individual profile, even where they touch on themes that are common to almost all the representatives of this genre.

The Question of Gnosis

Bibliography: U. U. Kaiser, "Neuere Gnosisforschung." *VF* 48 (2003): fasc. 2, 44–64. – **K. L. King**, *What is Gnosticism?* Cambridge, Mass.: 2003. – **C. Markschies**, *Die Gnosis.* Munich: 2001. – **M. A. Williams**, *Rethinking Gnosticism.*

Let us begin with a central issue. The principle stated in the previous paragraph also applies to the slogan "gnosis." Our first step must be to admit that the church fathers created here a collective concept by subsuming a plurality of partly divergent tendencies and developments under the heading of "gnosis" and that this concept is proving more and more problematical today (cf. Williams); but if we do nevertheless apply such a concept, which modern scholarship has refined somewhat, to the apocryphal Acts, we at once notice considerable differences. The most unambiguously—indeed, aggressively—gnostic text is the revision of the story of Jesus' passion in ActJoh 94–102. The integration of this passage into ActJoh gives a new signal about how the work as a whole is to be read, so that the polymorphy of the Lord in the framing chapters now takes on an unmistakably docetic aspect. We have observed a certain closeness to gnosis in ActAndr and ActThom (including the Song of the Pearl), but it must be conceded here that a somewhat watered-down Middle Platonism could form a common background to these two ancient Acts; in the case of ActThom, this Middle Platonism was mediated by Syrian theology (Tatian). In ActPet12, elements of the gnostic systems are given a new configuration, which ultimately points the reader back from the highest heaven to the earth and insists on the obligation of serving the sick and the poor. In the last analysis, PsClem is waging polemic against the heads of the gnostic schools, who are represented by the figure of Simon Magus, but the author has borrowed from his adversaries elements of the doctrine of syzygies and of the repeated appearances of the true prophet. The question of gnosis does not really appear in ActPet, and ActPaul is unambiguously anti-gnostic, as we see with particular clarity in the exchange of letters between Paul and Corinth. In the later Acts, this problem often seems to have lost its contemporary relevance; at any rate, it has left scarcely any discernible echoes here.

Marriage, Celibacy, and the Renunciation of Marriage

Bibliography: P. Brown, *The Body and Society: Men, Women, and Sexual Renunciation in Early Christianity.* New York: 1988. – S. Elm, *Virgins of God.* – J. A. Francis, *Subversive Virtue.* – K. L. Gaca, *The Making of Fornication.* – A. S. Jacobs, "A Family Affair."

Another central thematic complex is the debate concerning sexuality, marriage, celibacy, and the renunciation of marriage. (The last term can also be understood as the refusal of sexual intercourse in marriages that continued to exist or as the formal dissolution of these marriages.) The authors can presume that their readers know that disordered sexuality outside marriage and adultery are considered to be vices in the mainstream Jewish and Christian tradition; this is seldom stated explicitly, because the authors' intentions go further than this. Let us begin with the two most widely divergent positions found in our texts. At one radical extreme, we have the "Apotactics" in Asia Minor from chapters 3–7 of the later Acts of Philip, where the fundamental opposition to marriage and sexual intercourse is only one aspect of an asceticism that rejects the world and which implies a critique of society. This affects questions of clothing, food (vegetarianism), and possessions; and the institution of slavery is rejected. At the other extreme, we find PsClem, which is more conciliatory on this point. This text not only permits marriage, it actually enjoins marriage, although we should not overlook the restriction of intercourse to the periods allowed by the Law and the insistence that the only acceptable purpose is the procreation of children (here, one should compare what Gaca, 247–72, writes about Clement of Alexandria, who is often supposed to have taken a conciliatory stance on this issue).

The other apocryphal Acts occupy various places on this spectrum. The ideal picture of the ascetic life, embodied by the apostle, is nowhere called into question. Existing marriages are, at best, tolerated in view of the necessity of procreating children, although it is only PsClem that explicitly mentions this factor. The real goals envisaged by the text are celibacy, virginity, and widowhood. Most of our texts agree on this; the question is to what extent they take the next step and propagate a clear encratism, namely the prohibition of marriage and the demand that those already married cease having intercourse. It is here that the debates among scholars begin. How are we to understand the undeniable rhetoric of the "stories of purity"? This problem must not be underestimated. Do the authors merely intend to present a heroic ideal picture with an appeal to the audience to do at least what they can? Or is the audience meant to understand the story literally and to put it into practice? The latter seems to me to be the case, at least in ActAndr and ActThom, but ActJoh, ActPaul, and ActPet can probably be read in a more open sense.

The last word has still to be said on the question of the sources of this early Christian hostility to sexuality. One can, of course, refer to ascetic tendencies even in the pagan world at that period (cf. Francis), but these did not attain anything like the same intensity; the same is true of the marginal groups in Judaism (the Essenes and Philo's Therapeutae) who are often mentioned in this context. Something more was needed, namely the radical impulses that were contained in the earliest Christian message or that could be deduced (rightly or wrongly) from it. For example, the exegesis of 1 Corinthians 7 played a significant role here. Kathy Gaca also mentions the notions of purity in the Septuagint, which led to the elevation of sexual contact with nonbelievers into a central issue of the confession of faith.

The apocryphal Acts also show that mechanisms of suppression have their price. Often enough, that which is suppressed makes its presence felt in a way that cannot be misunderstood—whether as "Platonic" love (e.g., between Andrew and Maximilla, who take on the roles of a new Adam and Eve) or in the form of perversion (as in the attempted necrophilia in ActJoh, which is the tip of an iceberg). More than once, the nakedness of women (Thecla in ActPaul, Marianne in ActPhil, the prostitute in the "Acts of Peter and Andrew," and so forth) entails a dangerous playing with fire. Our texts have more in common with the eroticism of the classical novels than one might at first suppose.

The Encounter with Pagan Culture

The Christian literature of the first three centuries could not rely for support on the structures of a Christian society. It established itself in the framework of the culture of the imperial period, which had a predominantly pagan character. Thanks not least to the theater and to literature, the forms of non-Jewish and non-Christian religiosity had become the common property of all educated persons and left a deep imprint upon daily life. Magic and astrology accompanied this culture like an ever-present shadow.

As we would expect, this constellation has left its traces in our texts as well. The controversy finds its most acute form in PsClem, where there are detailed descriptions of pagan myths and rites and their allegorical interpretation, as well as a critique from the biblical perspective—but despite this, the entire company sets off (like package tourists in the twenty-first century) to go sightseeing on the island of Arados, where there is a notable temple and a statue by Pheidias. The destruction of the pure belief in astrology is one of the main themes in PsClem, indeed perhaps the principal theme. Other narratives are less subtle. John brings the temple of Artemis in Ephesus crashing to the ground. Paul does the same to a temple of Apollo in Sidon, but he also discusses "idols" and the "table of the demons." Through her miracles, Thecla drives away Athene, Aphrodite, the hero Sarpedon, and even Zeus himself. In ActPet, a demon who is expelled smashes a statue of the emperor (which, however, is then repaired). Even Philip in the late Acts destroys a pagan cultic center, including its personnel, and transforms the site into a center of Christian healing.

We must investigate in each instance how far traditional standard motifs of the Jewish and Christian polemic against idols dominate the narrative and how much must be read against the background of contemporary historical experiences. Often enough, both elements will be present: The situation in the story is elaborated using the means offered by the tradition. This aspect of the apocryphal Acts deserves more attention than it has received up to now.

The Miracles

Bibliography: **P. J. Achtemeier**, "Jesus and the Disciples as Miracle Workers." – **F. Bovon**, "Miracles, magie et guérison." – **C. R. Matthews**, "Articulate Animals." – **G. Pupon**, "L'accusation de magie." – **A. Reimer**, *Miracle-Workers and Magicians in the Acts of the Apostles and Philostratus' Life of Apollonius of Tyana* (JSNT.S 235). Sheffield: 2002.

There is no shortage of miracles in the apocryphal Acts, and some of them belong in this context. Miracles have an evidential function, guaranteeing the quality and superiority of one's message. The delicate question of the relationship between the performance of miracles and magic is personalized and acted out with the help of the antithesis between Simon Magus and Simon Peter. Despite the massiveness of many miracles, one should not overlook the symbolic dimension that they often have in the narrative. This is particularly clear in the raisings of the dead, where the return to life on earth functions as an anticipation of the raising of the soul, its turning to the faith, and its reception into the heavenly homeland.

Many have found the miracles involving animals ridiculous, even where their charm is irresistible; but they too have this orientation to the symbolic dimension. The wild lion embodies the unfettered power of the instincts of human nature; the obedient bugs are pseudonyms for "girls"; the dried fish that swims may be an allusion to the term "fisher of men" and to the fish as symbol of Christ; most wild asses live in sexual continence, even if not on a wholly voluntary basis; and so on.

The fact that miracles, especially raisings of the dead, can be delegated to persons who are not themselves apostles is a clear sign that we are now de facto in a post-apostolic age. Christian men and women must attempt to do what the apostles, who are long dead, can no longer do.

The Role of Women

Bibliography: L. C. Boughton, "From Pious Legend to Feminist Fantasy: Distinguishing Hagiographical License from Apostolic Practice in the Acts of Paul/Acts of Thecla." *JR* 71 (1991): 362–84. – **V. Burrus**, *Chastity as Autonomy*. – **M.-A. Calvet-Sébasti**, "Femmes du roman pseudo-clémentin." Pages 285–97 in *Les personnages du roman grec* (Collection de la Maison de l'Orient Méditerranéen 29). Edited by B. Pouderon. Lyons: 2001. – **S. L. Davies**, *The Revolt of the Widows*. – **P. W. Dunn**, "Women's Liberation, the Acts of Paul, and Other Apocryphal Acts of the Apostles: A Review of Some Recent Interpreters." *Apocrypha* 4 (1993): 245–61. – **J.-D. Kaestli**, "Fiction littéraire et réalité sociale: que peut-on savoir de la place des femmes dans le milieu de production des Actes apocryphes des Apôtres?" *Apocrypha* 1 (1990): 279–302.

Women are at least as numerous as men among the "cast" who appear in the narratives of the apocryphal Acts; in fact, they are probably more numerous. We encounter them in a great variety of roles and social classes: the consort of a king—or at least of a governor—just as much as the servant maid and slave woman; the virgin just as much as the prostitute; the widow and the daughter; young and old; healthy and ill (or even possessed by a demon); the woman willing to live in chastity and the woman intent upon fornication or even incest. In exceptional cases, a woman's name is found in the title of the story.

Let me anticipate my conclusions here and affirm that this phenomenon per se is ambivalent. It cannot simply be regarded as historical information about the real position held by women in the circles who wrote and read this literature. In an initial phase, scholars maintained that these narratives were collected and handed on among groups of women; that women wrote the texts that we have; and that the world of the texts reflects the experience of groups of women who had developed their own forms of life in common. In the meantime, these points are evaluated much more cautiously and circumspectly, and here too, each individual case requires a differentiated verdict. PsClem (to take one example) speaks more positively about marriage than any of the other ancient Acts but tells us nothing about an active role played by women in the communities, for example, as preachers of the Word or administrators of sacraments. Their status remains that of a (mere) married woman.

This observation may, however, also point in another direction. It is possible that in a society with patriarchal structures, the renunciation of married life with its obligations, including that of motherhood, was experienced precisely by women as a liberation and as a step toward greater autonomy. The objection that the price paid was very high—going as far as taking on the external appearance of a man (cf. Thecla and Marianne) —is not necessarily insuperable, for this all depends on how the basic situation of women was experienced and what alternatives existed. The Acts of Paul may have been toned down, and Thecla's conduct made not entirely clear in this text, but it is clear that her figure inspired other women, as we see from Tertullian's arguments against those women who follow Thecla's example and want to teach, preach, and baptize. It is in this milieu that we are most likely to find indications of a differentiated perception of gender roles.

The "Afterlife" of the Apocryphal Acts

Bibliography: D. R. Cartlidge and J. K. Elliott, *Art and the Christian Apocrypha*. London: 2001. – **D. R. Cartlidge**, "Evangelist Leaves Wife, Clings to Christ: An Illustration in the Admont 'Anselm' and Its Relevance to a Reconstruction of the Acts of John." *Semeia* 80 (1997): 277–90. – **R. Debray**, *The New Testament Through 100 Masterpieces of Art*. London: 2004. – **C. Nauerth and R. Warns**, *Thekla—ihre Bilder in der frühchristlichen Kunst*. Wiesbaden: 1981. – **R. Warns**, "Weitere Darstellungen der heiligen Thekla." Pages 75–131 in *Studien zur spätantiken und frühchristlichen Kunst und Kultur des Orients*, Vol. 2. Edited by G. Koch. Wiesbaden: 1986.

A visitor to the cathedral of Tarragona in Spain today can admire two cycles of illustrations of the Acts of Thecla: a more recent cycle on the altarpiece of the high altar and an older cycle on the front of the altar *versus populum*, which faces the nave of the church, where the apostle Paul bears the traits of Christ (or vice versa). In the Brancacci Chapel in Santa Maria del Carmine in Florence, there is a painting by Filippino Lippi (ca. 1457–1504) which depicts Peter and Simon Magus together in the presence of Emperor Nero (cf. Debray, 206f.). Illustrations in manuscripts in the abbey of Admont and in St. Petersburg describe a scene that can only be inferred from ActJoh but that perhaps formed the beginning of this work, namely the apostle's failed attempt to become engaged to be married (cf. Cartlidge). A manuscript in Trinity College depicts the entire life story of the apostle in a cycle of numerous pictures based, in many cases, on Pseudo-Prochorus and the apocrypha (cf. Cartlidge and Elliott, 190–205). A fifteenth-century Martyrdom of Andrew already employs the well-known cross of Saint Andrew (218). Pious eyes may at first be offended by a twentieth-century painting, Anita Ekberg as Saint Thecla by Warrington Colescott (162), but this may catch something of the sexual energy which merely slumbers under the surface of the text.

This is only a rapid and accidental survey of the history of art in search of our ancient narratives, which were thrust aside by the mainstream church. It would be well worth investigating all the elements that entered iconography and hagiography from these sources, but this cannot be done within the limits of the present book—not least because reliable preliminary research has been done only in specific areas such as Thecla (cf. Nauerth and Warns). My intention here has been to let the texts themselves speak, as far as possible, with the exhortation: *Lector intende*, "Reader, pay attention!" Whether a *laetaberis*, "You are going to have fun!," follows will depend not least on the reader's taste, but these texts are certainly both interesting and instructive. And we do not have such a great quantity of Christian texts from the second and third centuries that we can afford to ignore even a small portion of this literature.

Appendix

Back Matter from the German Edition

Readers have high expectations of "Apocryphal Acts of the Apostles" that are not satisfied by the better-known Acts of the Apostles by Luke.

Do we at last find the whole truth here—if not about Jesus of Nazareth (see the "Apocryphal Gospels"), then at least about all his apostles? Do they reveal, in the form of exciting narratives, things that the church hushed up and suppressed?

What do the Acts of John, of Paul, of Peter, or of Andrew tell us? And what about the Acts of Thecla?

Hans-Josef Klauck's book is a compact, serious, and extremely competent overview of the great wealth of extra-canonical traditions and of their significance for the church.

This presentation of the present state of research is unique, since no monograph on this subject has appeared for many years.

Hans-Josef Klauck was born in 1946. He was professor in Bonn (1981–1982), in Würzburg (1982–1997), and in Munich (1997–2001). In July 2001, he became Professor of New Testament and Early Christian Literature at the Divinity School of the University of Chicago, and in 2006 he was inaugurated as Naomi Shenstone Donnelley Professor at the same institution. From 1999 to 2005, he was also Honorary Professor in the Faculty of Protestant Theology at the University of Pretoria in South Africa and lectured there several times.

Index of Selected Texts

NAG HAMMADI TEXTS AND GNOSIS

GREEK AND ROMAN AUTHORS

Index of Subjects and Names

Index of Authors